SURVIVING THE ZOMBIE APOCALYPSE™

SURVIVING THE ZOMBIE APOCALYPSE

SAFER COMPUTING TIPS FOR SMALL BUSINESS MANAGERS & EVERYDAY PEOPLE ™

MAX NOMAD

Bohemian Griot PUBLISHING ™

www.bgpublishing.com

For more information please visit: www.bgpublishing.com

Graphic Design (Book Cover, Illustrations and Layout)
by Max Nomad

Index by John Cullenton, Able Indexers and Typesetters

"Reaching Zombie" (image repeated on computer screens on front cover)
provided by Izzy Gramp, www.shrubber.com.au

ISBN: 978-0-9715442-9-1 (Print)
ISBN: 978-0-9715442-8-4 (EPUB)
LCCN: 2013957049

Printed in the United States of America.

First printing . Fall, 2014

This book is dedicated to anyone that ever lost
something special to criminals and zombies—
and wants to make sure it doesn't happen again.

Table of Contents

The Dangers of Dead Computers

Corporate Zombies: Living, Dead and Unemployed

Remote Access to your Small Business Network

The Cloud: Sanctuary or Sacrificial Altar?

Disaster Recovery for Home and Office

Dirty Secrets about your Computer

General Defense Tactics Against Zombies

Foreword

by Keith Basil

It was around 1991 that I had settled into college life as a Computer Science major in the southeastern Virginia area. As a brash hacker new to the 757 area code, my first order of business was to find out "who was who" in the local underground. After a few months of surveying the local network, one name kept coming up—"Max Nomad." Messages like "Max Nomad is the guy you want to get in touch with," "Max Nomad has that type of information" and "Max Nomad was here a few days ago" were replaying on the top underground systems at the time. "Max Nomad" was larger than life, apparently. I finally met Max Nomad... and as fate would have it, we were on the same campus.

And so our crazy journey began.

Max and I were two of the co-founders of the Internet Service Provider mentioned in this book. With the new venture, all underground activities were put away and becoming "Mad Hackers Bent on Corporate Plunder" was our new mission. We opened up shop Friday, June 10, 1994 in the World Trade Center in downtown Norfolk, Virginia.

So imagine if you will, taking a short break from the insanity of running a startup. Sitting on the couch in our reception area and looking across the posh lobby at the signage of a fellow commercial tenant, a few questions came to mind. Why do I know that name? Why is this familiar? And then, it hit me. I recognized the company name not for the services they provided but for what type of system they ran. Years earlier, I had hacked into their system, stayed around a few days, noted the system users and left without a trace. Can you imagine my surprise when the system administrator came over to chat about our new startup and our cool black NeXT computers? She introduced herself as 'Pat'. With a smirk I replied "Yes, I know"—luckily she didn't catch the inference. We chatted about each other's systems for a while—hackers, in the truest sense of the word, one to another. All was well and after she left Max and I had yet another story for the archives.

Why is this story relevant? Two reasons: That moment in the reception area, talking to Pat marked a transitional period for us. It represented a move from offense to defense. Just like Pat, we were now responsible for running production systems critical to the success of the business. It's a direct point of reflection and relevance for this book because here in your hands is a work written by someone who has seen and been on both sides of the fence.

You will not find a better perspective.

"As society becomes more technologically complex, the bugs, loopholes, and defaults will exist and the underground will thrive. Whether the masses choose to acknowledge this or not, we are a subculture of and to ourselves, much like the Grateful Dead followers. Some will move on, die off, or fade away, and others will stream in to fill the empty spaces."

Addressing the computer underground, Max wrote those words over two decades ago for a popular hacker magazine. That passage still holds true today—the empty spaces will always be filled. The nefarious nature of the threats and bad actors have continued to evolve... and Max has as well. The work presented in this book will educate, entertain and most important help keep you, your information and your computers a bit safer.

Keith Basil is a serial entrepreneur, inventor and technology executive, with over 20 years of experience related to Internet services, startups, funding, security, and cloud architecture. Most recently as a Red Hat executive, he is focused on OpenStack product management, development and strategy with emphasis on elastic cloud management and security. He has also worked with members of the OpenStack community to co-author the first edition of the OpenStack Security Guide. His past experience includes managing two startups (where he raised several rounds of capital), and working as a senior consultant at Cisco Systems where he holds two patents in the areas of unified messaging and application development. He has also been an expert witness and member of the legal defense teams of Amazon and Ebay.

Keith can be reached through his personal website www.noslzzp.com .

Disclaimer

This book is presented solely for educational and entertainment purposes. It is not intended as a substitute for computer manuals, the advice of IT professionals, or professional IT services. While best efforts have been used to verify the accuracy of all information presented in this book, the author and publisher make no representations or warranties of any kind and assume no liabilities of any kind with respect to the accuracy or completeness of the contents and specifically disclaim any implied warranties of merchantability or fitness of use for a particular purpose. Neither the author nor the publisher shall be held liable or responsible to any person or entity with respect to any loss or incidental or consequential damages caused, or alleged to have been caused, directly or indirectly, by the information or programs contained herein. No warranty may be created or extended by sales representatives or written sales materials. Every company is different and the advice and strategies contained herein may not be suitable for your situation. You should seek the services of a competent IT professional before beginning any major security improvements to your home or office network.

Unless stated otherwise, the events and scenarios described in the author's personal anecdotes are based on real events. Names (and some descriptions) have been changed or omitted to maintain client anonymity. In some cases the genders, ethnicity, or professions have been changed or omitted unless they are pertinent to the story.

Real world zombie outbreaks are so similar to zombie computer outbreaks that it only made sense to use the hordes of walking dead as an allegory for the destructive power of these menaces. Real world zombie outbreaks described in this book are all based on rare recorded materials that have since been confiscated by Men in Black. The intention of this book was not to document the events of those zombie outbreaks, the people that survived them, containment methods, survival techniques or the conspiracies that covered up these incidences.

With any book that mixes computers, Information Security, the Internet and zombies, there is one underlying irony that should be kept in mind: Information has a mortality rate. Different types of information become obsolete at different speeds. Some topics are nearly timeless while others change faster than the price of gasoline. Although the author plans to do everything within his power to make sure this book is as current as possible as each edition goes to print, when it comes to Information Security, updates happen every day... sometimes hourly. Don't depend solely on this (or any) book—be sure to do some research on your own.

No humans—living, dead, or undead—were harmed during the writing of this book.

Apocalyptic Assumptions

This book was written for anyone of age (it would get a PG-13 rating in the theaters) and makes the following six assumptions:

1. You can read at an 8th grade level.
2. You own or manage at least one computer running a reasonably current version Microsoft Windows, Mac OS X, or some flavor of *nix.
3. You are computer literate enough to turn on the machine and use a keyboard and mouse.
4. You know how to use Email and get around the Web using any standard web browser (Internet Explorer, Mozilla Firefox, Safari, Chrome, or Opera).
5. You have a need to protect information on your computer(s) from prying eyes.
6. You have a healthy fear of Zombies and you're not afraid to dispatch them.

If you meet any two of these assumptions, you've picked up the right book.

About this Book

Every book starts with the kernel of something: an idea, a truth, or a question. Mine started with the kernels of mistakes, disasters and mayhem. That's at the core of most of my typical client experiences. Can't get your iPod to connect? Call the kid next door. Have you experienced a major computer crash or your network is out of control? I'm your man. I help residential and commercial clients, city to city and sometimes even state to state. Some would call me a Hired Gun Geek but I'm somewhere between an IT Road Warrior and a Digital Consigliere. Only after months of writing did I realize a big part of this book concept started out as a series of conversations with a fellow IT Road Warrior that was a little before her time. Her name was Libby.

Usually when Libby was on the phone there were three things happening: it was midday, the highway was roaring by in the background, and she was on a mission. She had received a call from a panicked soul at one of her offices. Their world was about to end due to some computer crash that couldn't be fixed from remote, and less than 24 hours later she was speeding to the rescue. During these conversations she would go over the particulars of the problem as I searched for clues; together we worked out possible solutions. Even while sorting out tech headaches there was always an air of lighthearted fun involved. Often the calls started and ended as fast as the speed limits she was breaking.

As the IT coordinator for their organization, Libby and half-an-assistant maintained computers in a few dozen satellite offices located throughout Virginia. Although her degree was probably in Business, everything she knew about IT she learned on the job. Somewhere in her early 50s, the technology was changing faster than she cared to keep up with. The stuff she didn't know she was smart enough to know how to ask the right people and use their answers to help put all the pieces together. I was honored to be one of those people she kept on speed dial. And unlike many supervisors and managers, when a problem arose and her assistant was on location somewhere, she had no problem driving up to five hours to go fix a problem.

For several years I was one of Libby's proverbial aces in the hole. Occasionally she hired me to fix problems in local offices when her team was too swamped. Those were among my earliest experiences with SOHOs. Short for "Small Office/Home Office", SOHO refers to any business environment with roughly 10 to 15 employees or less. They depend on their computer networks just as much as big corporate offices except they don't have the number of employees to warrant having a full-time System/Network Administrator in-house. And, like most small businesses, they can't afford a dedicated IT person on the payroll, either. This lack of professional IT support makes SOHOs the perfect targets for cybercriminals… and their zombie attacks.

Yes, I said zombies.

In tech circles, a zombie refers to a computer that has been infected with malicious code (i,e, - malware) that allows a cybercriminal to take control of it without the owner's knowledge. These zombie computers are secretly made part of a Botnet—a digital army of infected machines, usually spread out across the Internet. Under the control of a Botmaster, these Botnets are used to commit all sorts of cybercrimes, everything from sending spam emails to extortion to large-scale cyber attacks.

SURVIVING THE ZOMBIE APOCALYPSE (StZA) wasn't born out of a paranoid fear of the Zombie Apocalypse. As an IT professional dealing with Information Security, battling zombies of all kinds has become a constant part of what I do—and not all of them are digital. Most computer users are happily unaware of how often they are a click away from being hacked or ripped off by countless unseen entities. The trend is only going to get worse before it gets better.

Think about it. Money has become a digital commodity for most of us. Thanks to the plastic, we can go for days without spending a dime of hard currency. With a computer, tablet, or smart phone we can do all of our banking, bill paying, or shopping from just about anywhere. It only made sense that this paradigm shift would affect the way theft is committed, too. Anyone old enough to remember the emergence of the Internet can recall a time where if a thief wanted to steal $1 million in $20 dollar bills he needed a plan, the strength to run with a 100 pounds in a duffle bag, and a machine gun. The transfer velocity was only as fast as the heist and the getaway car. Today, a savvy cybercriminal can steal that million with a laptop, a little hit-or-miss action, and some lines of information that would fit on one side of an index card—with a transfer velocity of light speed.

Case in point: In February of 2013, an Associated Press report circled the planet about 18 people in Jersey City—all raided by the FBI as part of a credit card ring. With both interstate and international reach, this crew scammed credit rating agencies and used thousands of false identities and fake businesses to steal around $200 million dollars in cash and merchandise. According to a statement made by U.S. attorney Paul Fishman, the ring had been in operation since 2007 with funds being transferred to Canada, China, India, Japan, Pakistan, Romania and the

UAE. No guns, drugs or bad stock tips involved. Even the Feds had to admit that it was mainly the crew's own greed and arrogance that led to their downfall.

In another story from early spring 2013, researchers at the Russia-based security firm Group-IB have discovered yet another malware also hailing from Mother Russia. This one targets Windows-based Point-of-Sale (PoS) cash registers and stand-alone ATM machines.

Known simply as "Dump Memory Grabber" (DMG), this malware is not the first of its kind. Like its predecessors, it collects credit card data and sends it back to a remote C&C server like a typical zombie. The scary part is that it grabs all the data stored on the physical card and whatever the cardholder presses on the keypad. Since no one expects a cash register or ATM machine to be infected with malware, people always consider the units themselves to be safe. A single infected machine can grab hundreds, if not thousands, of credit and debit cards per day. This would continue indefinitely until an IT professional either runs detection software to destroy the DMG contagion or removes the compromised unit for recycling.

> "...a zombie refers to a computer that has been infected with malicious code that allows a cybercriminal to take control of it without the owner's knowledge."

And almost as if there's a competition rumbling somewhere in the underground, vSkimmer is yet another threat to PoS systems has risen up from the depths. Security experts at McAfee considered it the next generation version of Dexter, the malware that stole about 80,000 credit cards from Subway restaurants in 2012. This is more of a credit card theft tool that is for sale in Black Market cybercriminal websites in the Deep Web. Different than PoS malware like DMG, this tool is designed for inside jobs. And unlike most malware that phone home to a remote

Botnet with unusual data transmissions, this one collects data and lies in wait, making it virtually undetectable. Once the cybercriminal plugs in a specific USB device, vSkimmer dumps the stolen data to the device and waits for more. As of this writing, the infection rate of both malwares is still on the rise.

Stories like this are slowly starting to make their way into the mainstream news every day. Each score is becoming more spectacular than the last, only a hint as to what is still happening undetected by the Feds. Cybercriminals will be the Meyer Lanskys of the 21st century—and if we're not careful, our computers will be the armies that help them rise to power.

Although this book comes from an IT security perspective, it's far from being a manual. Most IT professionals would find this book as redundant as teaching a baker how to make bread. My goal is to make basic Information Security accessible to small business managers and everyday people by teaching how it works, simple ways to protect data, and how to recover quickly from the digital catastrophes that can (and will) occur. It's a compilation of tips, advice and cautionary tales from scenarios I've experienced with past clients and zombie battles. Within these pages are the kinds of practices that people should know... without having to learn them the hard way.

About the Author

Max Nomad is an IT consultant, graphic designer and creative entrepreneur. His international roster of past clients includes the U.S. Department of Veteran's Affairs, STIHL, ESPN's production facilities (Washington DC), Sumitomo Drive Technologies, the City of Norfolk (VA), and the Northern Territory Government of Australia (Racing, Gaming and Licensing Commission).

As a co-founder of one of southeastern Virginia's first Internet Service Provider / Web Development companies, Max's early involvement with cutting-edge Internet technology exposed him to a myriad of companies, ranging from ostrich farmers to Fortune 500 corporations. This unique blend of client experiences and training, coupled with his lifelong love for IT Security research, gave him the ability to gain an intimate understanding of virtually any small business, determine their needs and help them implement best practices with their networks.

Max graduated from Norfolk State University with a BFA in Graphic Design, dual emphasis on Computer Science and a minor in Writing. He is also a member of the Information Systems Security Association (ISSA).

Author's Statement

"I have to clear."
 - Morgan Jones, *THE WALKING DEAD (Season 3, Episode 12)*

Like with any good apocalyptic story about the living dead, my first encounter with a zombie started with a horrifying shock: a phone call alerting me that my business website was down. The caller was the regional Marketing Director with an international manufacturing company. I was attempting to win their business and my proposal was one of the few still in the running. With my website offline I lost some credability; I didn't have an immediate answer for when it would be back online so he could view the samples. The next morning I was notified that the contract was awarded to someone else.

Embarrassed and beyond angry, I called my web hosting service provider intending to raise hell about the outage. The tech support person immediately stopped my tirade with more bad news—less than 24 hours earlier something attacked my website, trashed it and "turned it into a spammer zombie".

"Zombie?" I screamed. "What the hell?"

I was devastated by what I found: most of the core website pages and files were trashed beyond repair. Whatever ravaged the site completely flooded the database with tons of stolen porn and junk mail templates. Even worse, more than a dozen of my articles, essays and blog entries were only saved the website—and it had been almost a year since I'd made a backup. After spending a day searching through the remains, I conceded that most of those writings were lost forever.

That was 2007. Although it only took a few days to set up my new website, the loss of my old one still makes me angry to this day. Computer security had been in interest of mine since my early teens—more than half of my life. The pain and embarrassment of losing my website to a zombie attack made me swear that I'd never let it happen again. I spent the next several years studying various forms of malware, Botnets, and all things connected to the cybercriminal underworld. As crazy as it sounds, this helped me develop an intuitive talent for finding and destroying malware and rescuing data. Then again, when it comes to Information Technology insanity is part of the game.

Yes, as in mental illness. Crazy.

Whether it's Bill Gates, John McAfee or the local help-desk tech, the lunacy can't be avoided. The computer users we help are constantly finding new ways to jam square pegs into round holes and we have to clean up the mess. We battle organized cybercrime rings that often arm themselves with Botnets with as much distributed computing power as the entire U.S.S.R. had during the Cold War—and most of the time they're in another country and out of reach of local law enforcement. Keeping up with the ever-expanding IT knowledge base is like being stuck taking college senior courses, regardless of the fact that the textbooks constantly change and no one ever graduates. Most of what we learn has a shelf-life of about four years. The industry is a fast moving target comprised of moving targets. Information Security is an arms race; we have to be passionate about what we do to be good at it. Protecting our clients from the threats in cyberspace requires the kind of crazy that only comes from loving our profession. It's from that same crazy that I bring you this book. Hopefully you'll find these pages educational, enlightening and enjoyable.

About the use of "Pathogens", "Contagions" and "Contaminants"

Throughout this book the words "pathogens", "contagions", and "contaminants" will be used interchangeably as a catch-all term for computer viruses, worms, backdoors, Trojan horses, spyware, malware, adware, ransomware, malvertisements, rootkits, and other malicious programs.

In the biological world, a pathogen refers to what causes a disease. A contagion refers to what spreads a disease by direct or indirect contact. And a contaminant refers to foreign matter, poison or toxins in the body.

In cyberspace, these are all effectively one in the same. They are all considered malware. Since anti-virus and anti-malware programs commonly exist as separate packages in the marketplace, I needed a different catch-all to avoid confusion about the meanings. Besides, when it comes to zombie outbreaks, pathogens, contagions and contaminants are the only terms authorized by the Centers for Disease Control and Zombie Computer Dispatch Commission.

About the use of the term 'anti-virus software'

At times I'll use "anti-virus software" as a catch-all term for any combination of software programs used to scan for and remove computer viruses, worms, backdoors, Trojan horses, spyware, malware, adware, ransomware, malvertisements, rootkits, and other malicious programs. Although most contagion cleaning software is generally touted as anti-virus, anti-spyware/malware, or rootkit removal, most non-techs tend to use the term virus to identify any infection. Since you're reading this, I must also take the opportunity to say **"Anti-virus software is <u>not</u> enough!"**

About "Identity Theft" and "Identity Fraud"

Throughout this book, the term "Identity Theft" will be used as a catch-all for both "Identity Theft" and "Identity Fraud". Of the two terms, Identity Theft is what happens first. This is when a criminal has compiled a profile of someone's personal information without their knowledge for the purpose of committing fraud as that person. Usually this is sensitive information like a full name, birth date, Social Security Number, one or more home addresses, bank account numbers, PINs, credit/debit card numbers, driver's license numbers and/or etc. The more sophisticated the criminal intent, the more details that are collected in relation to a victim's identity. Sometimes this can even include arcane facts such as the names of the victim's parents, mother's maiden name, children's names, past employers and etc. Ultimately this information profile becomes a digital clone of the victim—and the victim is completely unaware that it exists.

Identity Fraud happens when the stolen identity is actually used in the commission of a crime. This can be anything from using stolen identities to apply for lines of credit, using stolen credit card numbers to buy goods and services, and all the way over to living under the stolen identity. Although most victims aren't held liable for the crimes committed with their stolen identity, it can take months or even years to get it all sorted out.

NOTE: There are other forms of Identity Fraud (e.g. - creating false identities for fraudulent purposes) but since they don't involve Identity Theft or malicious computer hacking, they have been largely omitted from this book.

About the use of "Piracy", "Cracking", "Ripping" and "Warez"

For the sake of this subject, the terms "Digital Piracy" and "Piracy" will be used synonymously as a catch-all for the distribution of illegal copies of software, movies/TV shows, music, ebooks and [scanned] printed books.

And contrary to popular street use, "crack" has nothing to do with crack cocaine. In the computer underground, crack (a small program) or cracking (the process) refers to removing all copy protections from copyrighted media to make it so that it can be easily copied and distributed.

To "rip" (or ripping) is similar to cracking except it refers to taking content from DVDs, Blu-Rays and music CDs and making it distributable. Often this also means making that content playable in various devices, too (e.g. - a movie released on Blu-Ray converted for play on an iPod, a CD audio book converted for play on an Android cell phone, etc.).

"Warez" is pirate slang that is a play on words for "tradable goods" and "software". Generally it refers to any copyrighted material (especially software) that has been cracked and made available for trade or free download.

In cyberspace, if you are on a website that is providing copyrighted materials for free then more than likely it either comes with a crack or it has already been cracked. This is important to note because infecting pirated materials is fast becoming a common method of distributing malware to infect vulnerable computers.

About the use of 'Safer' Computing?

I use the term "Safer" because words like 'safe' and 'safety' tend to give people the incorrect notion that what they're learning will make them impervious to damage—a mode of thinking that fosters a carelessness that leads to accidents. People learn Safe Driving practices in Driver's Ed yet there are more than 6 million car accidents in the U.S. each year (National Highway Traffic Safety Administration). A gun with a safety is no more or less dangerous than a gun without one. The only safe sex that is 100% safe is abstinence.

Using a computer these days has become much like driving a car. If your vehicle is parked with the engine turned off, you've got almost no chance of getting into an automobile accident. The minute you get on the road, your chances of getting into an accident dramatically increase. While it's true that there are many things we do to reduce our risks on the road, even the safest driver will experience a car accident within their lifetime. It's a statistical destiny.

As soon as you've turned on your computer and visited a website, you've effectively put your car in drive and hit the road. Unlike real world traffic, cyberspace is crawling with hostile entities. Sooner or later your computer will get infected with some kind of contaminant. The contagion will come from either (1) something you click on, (2) a page you look at, or (3) through a zombie attack from somewhere else on the Internet. Statistically speaking, it will happen, just like with car accidents. The key is to mitigate your risks through safer computing.

About the ACME Corporation

In different examples throughout this book you will see mention of the ACME (or Acme) Corporation. Some people like to think the acronym stands for "A Company that Makes Everything". According to Dictionary. com, Acme refers to "the highest point; summit; peak".

Many of my commercial anecdotes will often involve two different companies—my client and another company I'm dealing with on their behalf. Both will remain unnamed in order to protect the innocent. To keep explanations simple I'll refer to the other company as ACME [whatever they do], such as "Acme Internet" or "Acme Manufacturing".

By using Acme as a generic name I am in no way referring to any companies out there who happen to use ACME or Acme in their name. The biggest reason I had to stick with using this fictitious name because I'm a huge fan of the Chuck Jones Looney Tunes cartoons.

About the Zombie Apocalypse

"The normal question, the first question is always, are these cannibals? No, they are not cannibals. Cannibalism in the true sense of the word implies an intra-species activity. These creatures cannot be considered human. They prey on humans. They do not prey on each other—that's the difference. They attack and they feed only on warm human flesh. Intelligence? Seemingly little or no reasoning power, but basic skills remain and more remembered behaviors from normal life. There are reports of these creatures using tools. But even these actions are the most primitive—the use of external articles as bludgeons and so forth. I might point out to you that even animals will adopt the basic use of tools in this manner. These creatures are nothing but pure, motorized instinct. Their only drive is for food, the food that sustains them. We must not be lulled by the concept that these are our family members or our friends. They are not. They will not respond to such emotions. They must be destroyed on sight!"

- Dr. Millard Rausch, DAWN OF THE DEAD (1978)

Question: Can the Zombie Apocalypse really happen?
Answer: Yes, it sure can. Outbreaks affect countless victims around the world every day.

In most modern zombie outbreak tales, the survivors find themselves in the middle of a catastrophic event; a Zombie Apocalypse. Usually of unpredictable origin, the zombies have risen up out of nowhere and begun a relentless assault to feed on everyday people.

We are them, and they are us.

Sometimes these outbreaks happen when a business is about to go bankrupt or layoffs are imminent. Sometimes they happen when civil unrest overrules law and order, like with the revolutions in various developing countries. And, still, sometimes the outbreaks are just too weird for fiction. In almost every case, the victims that aren't slaughtered (or eaten) usually end up infected by the plague and become zombies themselves. This exponential outbreak leads to the widespread collapse of civilization within the affected perimeter. During this indefinite period of time, the uninfected survivors find themselves living in a hostile new era.

In computer security jargon, a zombie is a computer that has been infected by malware that has given a cybercriminal complete control of it from somewhere else in cyberspace. These zombies are corralled into a Botnet, an army of thousands of infected machines spread out all over the Internet, under the control of one person or entity, referred to as a Botmaster. The computers in the Botnet are sent commands to perform malicious (and illegal) tasks, including attacking other susceptible computers and turning them into zombies, too. Every day, millions of people are under attack by zombies—and millions more are blissfully unaware of the dangers they narrowly avoided. Aside from possibly noticing some performance anomalies, most people are clueless that their computer has been turned zombie… until it's too late.

Unlike the typical Post-Apocalyptic outbreak scenario, most of us aren't under siege from hordes of vicious crazies in the streets—at least not yet. Instead of creeping corpses that see joggers and children as fast food, most of the time we're up against zombies controlled by unseen cybercriminals that want to feed on our identities. Sometimes they are impersonating people we know and love. At the very least they just want to steal our address books and email accounts to spam millions of people. Mostly they want to rob us of our money or use our identities to commit other crimes. Either way, damage is done. And for each form of malware that becomes outdated and rendered inert, dozens of new ones are unleashed into cyberspace. Such cyberthreats were the basis for this book.

At first glance it might seem like I've watched way too many zombie movies. And as a fan of the genre, I'd have to agree; even the corniest zombie flicks will hold my attention at least once. There are many parallels between dangers in cyberspace and the mayhem in those Zombie Apocalypse movies. Whether we're talking about the walking dead or that computer on your desk, zombies are relentless in their pursuit of human prey. During an outbreak, the spread of their infection is exponential and uncontrollable, making zombies the perfect allegory to help people understand the dangers our identities face in cyberspace.

About Baron Samedi

In the interest of my mission to battle zombies living, dead, and digital, allow me to introduce you to The Baron.

Baron Samedi is a Haitian Voodoo spirit that spends most of his time at the crossroads between the worlds of the living and the dead. Somewhere between a deity and a human, when the Baron is seen he often has the face of a skull, wears a black tuxedo, black top hat, black sunglasses, and a walking staff. Those who have met him (and remained in the world of the living) say he has the grandeur of a Shakespearean actor mixed with the personality of Richard Pryor in his prime—a wild party animal, known for drinking, smoking, an outrageously crude sense of humor and constantly trying to hook up with [mortal] women. Along with the Baron's duties over death, life and sexuality, he is also known for making sure that the departed aren't brought back to life as zombies (a punishment worse than death).

Because the Baron prevents the creation of zombies, I like to think of him as the closest thing to a patron saint of Safer Computing. That's why I've included him in this book. To highlight key tips and advice in this book, look for the sections called "**Baron Samedi says**".

The Tao of Information

Information is like water. It's a big part of our world that we all need to survive. When we need it to be around forever it's prone to disappear. When we need it to be temporary it can become as persistent as unpaid traffic tickets. And when it gets into the wrong place at the wrong time, it can wreak havoc on our lives, or at least make an incredible mess. This is the Tao of Information, especially in the form of computer data.

Data is merely a digital representation of reality. And unless you live completely off the grid or never had a job beyond running a lemonade stand, there is all kinds of data floating around in cyberspace about your personal and professional reality. It's unavoidable. Whether it's a printed receipt for last month's car payment or a Social Security Number, day to day life requires us to retain some of that data for a certain amount of time. We often disregard the fact that proper data disposal is just as important as how we maintain it. Keeping data around longer than its usefulness poses a risk—particularly if it falls into the wrong hands.

So what does this have to do with zombies? Everything. Zombies feed on living people. And cybercriminals create viral contagions to infect our computers, turning them into digital zombies to feed on our data—pieces of our lives—and consume as much as possible. The data they capture is used to steal from us, steal from other people, steal our reputations to do dirt, secretly use our computers for mayhem, or all of the above.

The reasons usually include one or more of the following:

- ▶ Financial gain,
- ▶ Acquisition of power,
- ▶ To cause enough damage to an opponent with the goal of putting an end to a conflict, or
- ▶ Vandalism and destruction for no reason.

…and unfortunately people like you and I are stuck in the middle as potential casualties.

Among Information Security professionals, the Tao of Information revolves around maintaining a balance between:

- **Confidentiality**—making sure that information is disclosed only to those who are supposed to see it.
- **Integrity**—making sure that information is consistently kept accurate
- **Availability**—making sure that information is available when it is needed.

(The fact that it spells out CIA is purely coincidence)

And in terns of every day purposes, Information Security means having a practical understanding (and application) of three basic principles:

- **Data Retention**—how to keep useful information for a long as you need it,
- **Data Protection**—keeping your information safe from harm and unauthorized access,
- **Data Destruction**—how to permanently get rid of sensitive information.

Lifecycle of Data (Your Information)

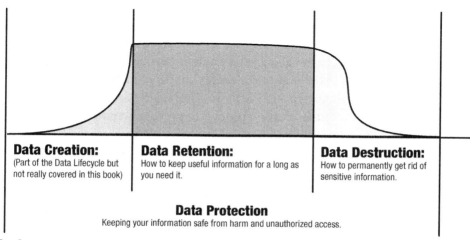

Data Creation:
(Part of the Data Lifecycle but not really covered in this book)

Data Retention:
How to keep useful information for a long as you need it.

Data Destruction:
How to permanently get rid of sensitive information.

Data Protection
Keeping your information safe from harm and unauthorized access.

Beginning　　　　　　　　　　　　　　　　　　　　　　　　**End**

At the core of the Tao of Information is Authentication—proof of identity, the process of verifying that the right person is granted legitimate access to something. Authentication has three factors:

- ► **Knowledge**—something you know, like a password, your ATM PIN number, or the answer to a secret question.
- ► **Ownership**—something you possess, like a key, credit card or ID badge.
- ► **Inherence**—something you are (or something you do), like your signature, fingerprint or DNA.

Each factor has many options. All the factors can be implemented individually or in combinations. A good example of this happens every time you come home.

- ► **One-Factor Authentication** would be the use of a house key (something you possess) to enter through the front door. This also means anyone with a key can enter the house.
- ► **Two-Factor Authentication** would be the use of a house key (something you possess) and then once inside immediately entering a code (something you know) to disarm an alarm system.
- ► **Three-Factor Authentication** would be the use of a house key (something you possess), disarming the alarm system (something you know), and then another resident already inside recognizes you as being a tenant (something you are).

As you can see, the more factors involved in the authentication process, the lower the chances of an unauthorized person successfully gaining access to the home. The same thing applies with our computers and websites in cyberspace. The more sensitive the data, the more factors involved in the authentication process to prevent unauthorized access.

…and as it all relates to the Tao of Information, the trick is to seamlessly put all of these concepts and principles into practice. This is often easier said than done.

The Reality Behind Zombies—It Can Happen to You

If you're a hypochondriac or just plain creeped out by anything dealing with deadly microbes, you'll probably want to skip this chapter.

Still here? Cool.

Zombie outbreaks are real. They're already a part of nature.

According to the University of Edinburgh's Centre for Infectious Diseases, as of this writing there are a little over 1400 known human pathogens, about 38 of which have emerged in humans within the past 25 years. That's roughly two or three new pathogens discovered every two years, typically introduced into humans through contact with infected animals or contaminated food/water.

Among the most common sources of diseases are parasites. And among those are the kinds of parasites that infect their victims and turn them into zombie-style slaves. Although this might sound like something from a bad comic book, parasites that cause behavioral changes in their infected hosts have existed in nature for millions of years.

Our first example lives in the rainforests of Thailand, a species of carpenter ant that lives in the trees. The Ophiocordyceps unilateralis fungus, in order to spread its spores, actually infects these ants and takes control of them. After being infected, the ant will climb down the tree and fasten itself to a certain spot on a leaf. Once there, the ant is killed by the fungus and a few days later spores come growing out of its head. Myrmecologists have even nicknamed them zombie ants.

Another ant zombie master is the Dicrocoelium dendriticum, a flatworm better known as the Lancet Liver Fluke. Snails eat cow feces that are loaded with young flukes. The worms end up in the snail's slime trail. Ants love to eat the slime and once inside their newly found hosts, the flukes embed themselves in the ant brains. At certain times of day when cows are out grazing, the flukes force the ants to position themselves on vegetation. The cows unknowingly eat the infected ants along with the vegetation and once inside the flukes bust out of their ant hosts. They burrow out of the stomach, making their way to the liver where they grow into adulthood eating liver tissue. Eventually the mature worms lay eggs and the newborn worms pass from the cow in its feces. Snails come along, eat the feces with the young flatworms and the cycle begins again. All mammals are susceptible to these worms… including humans.

One last example of parasitic mind control (and my personal favorite) is the Toxoplasmosa gondii. Also known as T. gondii, this microscopic menace spends the first half of its life dedicated to the murder of its host—birds or rodents (commonly rats). And as one of the many bizarre ironies of nature, it can only breed inside of cats. In order to get from the rat to the cat, it alters the rat's brain. An infected rat is reprogrammed with a fatal attraction to the scent of cats. Eventually the rat gets itself eaten by a cat. Once inside its feline host, the parasite happily grows into adulthood and multiplies. The baby parasites venture out into the world by way of the cat's excrement where they become part of the soil, water or plants that eventually gets eaten by rats. The circle of life continues.

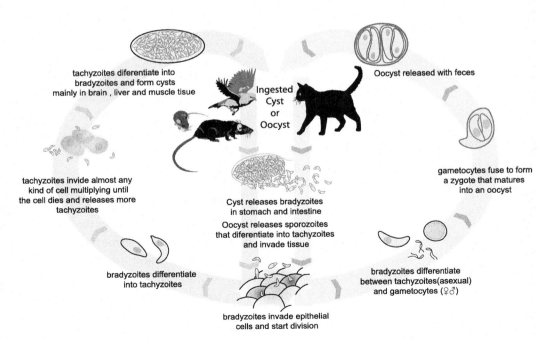

Lifecycle of Toxoplasmosa Gondii. Source: Mariana Ruiz Villarreal / Wikipedia

Of all the zombie outbreaks in the animal kingdom, the T. gondii parasite has especially gruesome possibilities. Rat neurons are similar to human neurons. Even more frightening, at least 22% of the U.S. human population is infected with toxoplasmosis. Fortunately, the rat reprogramming trick doesn't work on the human brain. As of this writing, the parasite's effects are still inconclusive. All it would take is for a more evolved strain of T. gondii to get loose in the human population, one that affects us the same way it does rats. Faced with a threat like that we could find ourselves in a world where infected people are normal and then suddenly become irrational, losing all instinct for self-preservation. The effective outbreak would be a mix of bizarre suicides and homicides similar to events in films like THE HAPPENING (2008) and THE CRAZIES (2010).

Aside from the parasitic freaks of nature, another infectious example is Creutzfeldt-Jakob disease (Mad Cow disease in humans). Symptoms include all the classic zombie traits: a degenerating brain that leads to a lack of coordination with a messed up walk, twitchy muscles, impaired speech and jerky movements. And if this wasn't sick enough, people can contract this by eating tainted human flesh. Add hallucinations and total dementia and if there's an outbreak you'll have unchecked mayhem in the streets.

Beyond all the natural possibilities there is still the threat of a Biopocalypse—a widespread epidemic ushered in by the sociopathic side of science. One false move while weaponizing some pathogens and the juice is loose. If this, or any other mind-altering pathogen, mutated to a point where it damages the brain and removes the serotonin without killing the victim, outbreak survivors could be faced with a biological nightmare that reduces its victims to psychotic savages as seen in films such as 28 DAYS LATER (2004) and QUARANTINE (2008).

It should be kept in mind that viruses are natural genetic engineers. Not only are they are able to transfer genetic material between cells but between different animals, regardless of species. This fact, along with all those pathogens and their devastating possibilities, brings up two haunting possibilities:

1. All it takes is an instance where someone or something introduces genetic material into humans that sets off an evolutionary spark. or
2. One instance where someone introduces a cure where the negative side effects become bigger than the original problem.

With the second possibility, an almost legendary example of this involves the Indian Mongoose. Back in the 1800s, rats and snakes posed a big problem to sugarcane farmers throughout the Caribbean. Since the mongoose was known to feed on these vermin in its native environment, someone got the bright idea to introduce them to the farms as a biological solution to control the rodents and reptiles. These fast-breeding carnivorous critters not only served their purpose, they went on to spread and get a stranglehold anywhere they were introduced. This resulted in the extinction of certain species of birds, reptiles and amphibians. Farms became cafeterias to this menace because they also fed on chickens, smaller livestock and occasionally crops. Even worse for the human population, the mongoose also carried rabies. To this day, anywhere the varmint was introduced to the land it presents a general public health threat and has done millions of dollars in damage.

The same threats apply to our computers and Internet-accessible devices. Unlike with the potential hazards of biological warfare, there is the new frontier of cyberwarfare. Out of the 196 countries on the planet, more than 100 have the ability to do battle in cyberspace—and more than a third of those have active military units devoted to state-sponsored hacking. All it takes is for one to launch a viral form of cyberattack that gets out of control or the source code falls into the hands of some tech-savvy lunatic. On a much smaller scale this happens all the time, particularly with poorly-written programs that cause memory leaks or buffer overflows, glitches that can cause system failures that can cause computers and network to crash. The idea that any platform can be considered immune from the dangers addressed in this book is a fallacy. PC, Mac, or *nix, those days are gone. It's not a matter of "if" but "when".

Within the pages of this book, the Zombie Apocalypse has multiple meanings. On the surface it's an allegory for all the unseen dangers that constantly threaten our computers, networks and businesses. It also refers to any widespread catastrophe or state-sponsored cyberwarfare. This book is a pastiche of zombie lore, advice and lessons learned from the kind of digital anarchy that cybercriminals, major corporations, and government agencies would prefer not to have shared with the general public.

ZOMBIE FACTOIDS

Based on reports on file with the Zombie Dispatch Commission (ZDC), there are a wide variety of zombies still roaming the planet, both on land and in cyberspace.

Shortwave Radio Terms for Zombies (in no particular order): Zed, Walking Dead, Corpses, Cadavers, Muertos, Berserkers, Ghouls, Skunks, Skunkers, Slouches, Stenches, Stinkers, Stumblers, Clutchers, Grippers, Rippers, Bones, Groaners, Biters, Grungies, Ramblers, Chompers, Lurches, Walkers, Mutants, Zudes, and Bob Dole.

WHITE ZOMBIE (1932)

Godfathers,
Zombie Masters and Magic:
The World of Cybercrime

The Sprinters
(l. Homo Sapiens Animata Mortuus Snyder):

These fiends were brought to 21st century awareness through films like DAWN OF THE DEAD (2004), 28 DAYS LATER (2002), and the TV mini-series DEAD SET (2008). As a mutant variation of the modern zombies, Sprinters are generally identical in appearance and intelligence. The trademark difference is that they are more ferocious. They snarl and move as if hopped up on cocaine, crystal meth, and jet fuel, giving them the ability to run farther and faster than they ever could before reanimation. They don't get winded because they don't breathe. When a Sprinter spots prey and begins to pursue, others nearby will race toward the same target. As grunts and hungry snarls from the mob increase, so do their numbers. In an urban setting, an unlucky person may get spotted by a single Sprinter and within a minute find himself scrambling to outrun a zombie marathon.

Among the living, this best describes the average Internet user in their teens and twenties, mostly because they'll click from link to link with reckless abandon until they get what they want.

Basic Internet and Computing Terms used in this Book (a must read)

In the IT world, most inventions and innovations have suave engineering-style names—except the malicious stuff. Everything in cyberspace that is questionable or destructive sounds like it was labeled by Willy Wonka: Fraggle, Man in the Middle, ZEuS, and Spam to name a few. This is because every time a new contagion, problem, attack method or type of cybercrime is discovered, there isn't a name for it. Some of it is even beyond easy description. There isn't a New Jargon committee, either. Computer geeks have a penchant for double-entendres, pop culture references, weird humor and junk food, hence the reason a Cookie is a Cookie, Spam is Spam, and a Trojan is a Trojan. Once the jargon catches on that's it… another kooky label for the books.

Many of the dangers of cyberspace are carried out by tiny hidden programs that perform functions that cannot be seen. Like the flu, they are constantly morphing and even though we can't see the infection by the time we spot the symptoms we're usually going to catch hell trying to get rid of it. To make all of this madness easier to grasp, it was necessary to provide some basic terms. Instead of listing them in alphabetical order I've presented them in an order where each definition lays a conceptual foundation that makes it easier to better understand the definitions that follow. And while hardcore literalists and computer nerds may balk at the oversimplifications I've made with some of these definitions, my intent was to convey the overall concept—not draft an IT dictionary.

SOHO

SOHO is an acronym for "Small Office / Home Office", referring to any small business or office environment that has 10 to 15 employees or less. This trend flourished in the 21st century to include satellite offices for larger corporations and telecommuters. The business models behind most SOHOs depend on their computers and network infrastructure just as much as their larger corporate competitors—sometimes more.

Hardware

In regards to your computer, if you can physically touch it, consider it hardware. Everything from the mouse and keyboard to the circuit boards inside the machine. For the sake of keeping things simple, every hardware component that is part of your computer requires a piece of software (called a 'driver') to make it work.

Software

Also referred to a "computer program" or "code", software is a set of instructions that tells a computer what to do, how to do it, and when. Some software is meant solely for the computer to use to control the functions of its hardware components, such as your monitor or network card. Other software is more complex and meant for people to use for productivity or entertainment, such as Microsoft Word, QuickBooks, and iTunes.

Operating System

An operating system (OS), also called "system software", is a collection of programs and hardware drivers that control every part of your computer. Seconds after you press the power button on your computer it loads up these system programs, most of which continue to run behind the scenes until you turn the computer off. Microsoft Windows, Mac OS X and Linux are three of the most common operating systems available today on desktops and laptops. The OS also manages the space where all the programs and your information are stored.

Storage (Desktop and Laptop)

Inside every computer, storage refers to the place where the operating system, all the software and your information is stored. Most desktop and laptop computers still use hard drives, sometimes referred to as a "hard disk drive", "hard disk" or an HDD. And while storage come in different sizes, types and configurations, for the sake of this book we'll be working under the assumption that you're using the typical personal computer with at least one hard drive inside.

Encryption

Encryption is the process of transforming digital information so that it is unreadable to everyone except its intended recipient(s). This is done using mathematical algorithms, often incorporating some kind of pass key or pass-phrase, and the transformation happens in such a way that end users only see the plaintext (readable) information. A common example of this is when you go to a website with a URL that starts with "https". When you see https, it means that all the information sent back and forth between your computer and that website has been encrypted, preventing hackers and other prying eyes from intercepting the connection and stealing your information. Due to the increased security concerns, it is becoming more common for data to be stored or transmitted in an encrypted fashion.

Plaintext

In contrast to encryption, digital information that is readable by anyone is considered plaintext. It is also called Cleartext, as in meaning "in the clear, not obfuscated". The drawback to plaintext is that anyone who has the ability to intercept it can read it, like the fact that a postcard can be read by any number of people between the sender and the receiver. Cybercriminals love data that is transmitted or stored in plaintext because there are hacking tools that can filter through it to search for things like passwords, credit card numbers, and other sensitive information—anything that can be stolen or exploited.

Internet Service Provider

An Internet Service Provider (ISP) is a company that provides Internet access to residential and commercial subscribers. For most home and SOHO environments, traditionally the options are dial-up, Cable, DSL and Wireless (Mobile Broadband, not to be confused with Wi-Fi). Some of the national providers include AT&T, Comcast, Time-Warner, Verizon, Cox, Earthlink, and Sprint. NOTE: For those readers who may not be aware, there is no single corporate entity that owns the Internet.

Web Browser

The web browser on your computer is a program that is used to visit websites on the Internet. A more accurate way to think of a web browser is to compare it to a television. While there are different brands of televisions on the market (e.g. - Sony, Samsung, Panasonic, etc.) and each model has slightly different features, all televisions essentially provide the same TV viewing experience. As of this writing, the major web browsers that are available include:

- ▶ Internet Explorer (standard with Microsoft Windows, no longer available for Mac OS X)
- ▶ Safari (standard with Mac OS X but also available for PC and Linux)
- ▶ Mozilla Firefox (very popular alternative, available for PC, Mac OS X and Linux)
- ▶ Google Chrome
- ▶ Opera
- ▶ Epic

People often see the standard browser on their computer (e.g. - 'Internet Explorer' on a typical PC or 'Safari' on a typical Mac) and get the wrong impression that it is the only way "to get to the Internet". Just like you can have a television in each room around your home, you can have several different web browsers installed on your computer. Some websites may require certain browsers for the best user experience (e.g. - many online banking websites are specifically designed for use with Internet Explorer or Safari).

Firewall

A firewall is set up as a gatekeeper that controls the incoming and outgoing traffic between the Internet and your internal network. Its purpose is to keep your internal network safe by blocking unauthorized requests that can be potentially used to harm your computer(s) or steal data. Firewalls can be software (e.g. - ZoneAlarm, Comodo, Hands Off!, etc.) or hardware-based (e.g. - Cisco, Netgear, a dedicated computer running firewall software, and etc.). And while some PC users may confidently declare that [Microsoft] Windows comes with a built-in firewall, this is not something to brag about. Compared to a stand-alone firewall, the typical Windows firewall is about as dependable as birth control at a frat party. Most modern hubs and routers also have firewalls built-in.

Bug

A software bug is a programming error; a tiny flaw in the design. And while it seems innocent enough because most bugs will simply cause a program to crash, an advanced programmer can sometimes make the crash produce unforeseen results. Most major computer or network threats can often be traced back to someone finding and exploiting a software bug. Computer viruses and worms are often created to exploit bugs. Under the right circumstances, a bug can be used to cause the computer to grant an unauthorized person rights to take advantage of a system in ways it wasn't originally intended to be used. A real world example of a bug is an IRS tax loophole, such as the ones reportedly exploited by multi-billionaire Warren Buffett's accountants that enabled him to pay his 2011 taxes at a lower rate than his secretary. And just like the IRS seems to be forever trying to close its loopholes, Microsoft, Apple, and other software companies are constantly working to patch up their bugs. When these vulnerabilities are discovered, it's often a race against time to fix them before cybercriminals can write a small program to exploit the flaw as part of some kind of attack.

Software Updates

A software update is a small program that makes improvements to a larger program and, more importantly, fixes bugs that were recently discovered. With any kind of newly released software, sooner or later there will be updates, usually downloaded from the software developer's website. Although software engineers do their best to debug their program before releasing it to the public, there will always be bugs. The more complex the software, the more updates it will probably require over its lifetime. Operating systems need updates often, particularly to patch up any newly found security holes that can be exploited to attack your computer. Software updates are part of your computer's first line of defense against cyber attacks as well as a natural part of its recovery and healing process.

Cybercrime

Cybercrime refers to any criminal offense where computers, networks (such as the Internet), or smart devices (cell phones, tablets, etc.) are used during the commission of the crime. They generally fit into one or more of the following categories: 1) the computer is the target of the crime, such as hacking (cracking), writing malware and viruses, vandalism, etc. 2) the computer is a tool used to commit the crime, such as theft, extortion, fraud, forgery, stalking/cyber-bullying and etc. 3) the computer is incidental to the commission of the crime, such as with corporate espionage where someone uses a computer to send stolen information to a buyer, or a murderer uses a computer to research the best way to kill their victim. Most cybercrimes addressed in this book will fit in categories #1 and #2.

Anonymous Internet Banking

Anonymous Internet banking is general term referring to a secure means of conducting online banking in such a way that goods and services can be bought and sold in complete anonymity. The bank issues currency in the form of electronic tokens, those tokens can be given to someone, and then they can be redeemed at the bank and converted into some other form of local currency. Implementations such as *Bitcoin* and *Perfect Money* are among the favorite decentralized, nonpolitical digital currencies. Although this book doesn't address the world of Anonymous Internet banking, its existence had to be noted because the cybercriminal underground economy is based on these systems and uses them to conduct business and launder money.

Viruses, Worms, Backdoors and Trojans

Originally, a computer virus was a small program that spread between computers by hiding itself within a file. A worm was a program that replicates itself and spreads from computer to computer without injecting itself into anything else on the system. A Backdoor opens up a hidden portal on a computer that can allow anyone who finds it a way to gain unauthorized access that computer. A Trojan horse looks like a legitimate file but when a user clicks on it, a secret payload is unleashed, usually designed to do anything from steal information (like passwords or credit card info) or turn a computer into a zombie.

Over time, malicious code programmers began to combine traits and features from all of the above in order to create powerful contagions that were more resistant to anti-virus programs. For everyday practical purposes, Viruses, Worms, Backdoors and Trojan Horses might as well be treated as different parts of the same elephant.

When it comes to Viruses, Trojans, and Worms, one of the best ways to put their functional similarities and differences into perspective is to compare them to the card games Texas Hold'em, Seven Card Stud, and 5-Card Draw. Even though all three games use a standard 52-card deck, each deals out the cards to the players in a different fashion. Each game requires its players to use a different set of strategies and tactics to win. And while the games may all look different to the casual onlooker, all three share the same winning hands, hence the reason they're all considered Poker.

Malware

Short for "malicious software" and a reference for "malicious code", malware is a catch-all term for any kind of unwanted programs that were installed on your computer without your proper consent. Examples of malware include viruses, Trojans, worms, rootkits, ransomware, spyware, crimeware, scareware and any other kind of malicious code that hasn't been given a name yet.

Ransomware

Ransomware, also referred to as a cryptotrojan, cryptovirus, or cryptoworm, is a form of malware that was written by cybercriminals specifically for extortion—hijacking control of your computer in exchange for you to pay for its release. Many forms of ransomware tend to just block you from being able to use your computer until you pay them. A variant of this, often referred to as Scareware, forces its victims to "buy" their product (e.g. - fake anti-virus programs). Regardless of the type, some of the more sophisticated versions will actually hide your data making you believe it has been deleted or, even worse, make it unreadable to you without an encryption key.

Rootkit

A rootkit is a program that penetrates a computer, hooks into it at the operating system level, and hides itself (and its payload) in folders, files, system processes, and other components, making them more difficult to detect. That payload may be a worm, virus, Trojan, spyware, or other type of malware. If a computer virus was an F-22 fighter jet, a rootkit would be the stealth technology that makes it nearly invisible to most forms of modern radar.

Spyware

Sometimes referred to as Privacy-Invasive software, there are two main types:

The first type is a covert program that usually gets installed on a computer in connection with a free software application. With this type, there is almost always a secret function, such as tracking a user's online activities for marketing purposes, making changes to system settings (like changing a user's homepage or default search engine), or secretly connecting to some website to display pop-up ads. Adware often falls into this category.

The second type, also known as Crimeware, is a covert program that gets installed on the computer specifically to either monitor a user's behavior or send a user to a cybercriminal's website without that user's control or permission. Common examples include a keystroke logger, used to secretly record everything a person types (including passwords, backspaced characters, etc.), browser redirects, and password snatchers.

Cookies

There's a common perception that a cookie is spyware. This is only partially correct. The cookie itself is not a program, nor can it directly do any damage to a computer like all the other malicious things discussed in this section. Simply put, a cookie is a tiny bit of data in a text file, stored there by a website and eventually sent back to that website by your web browser. Regardless of whether you use Internet Explorer, Safari, Mozilla Firefox or Chrome to browse the web, a cookie is the equivalent of a Post-It note for your web browser.

When the web was originally created, it was meant solely as a way to share information on pages that weren't meant to have the limitations of a printed page. Web pages back then passed almost no information between each other. The problem was that in order for web developers to be able to make cool applications, the websites had to be able to remember and exchange information.

Cookies were meant to allow websites to remember a little bit about what a user did in order to give some continuity to the user experience. It's like the difference between buying food from a vending machine compared to talking with a human server at a restaurant. This is how websites like Amazon.com can remember what products you've selected while you continue to browse other product pages. Without cookies, websites that provide services like online shopping or online banking would be impossible.

Even though cookies cannot carry contagions or install malware, they are sometimes used by third party companies to spy on users, particularly by tracking a person's web browsing habits over a long period of time. This is why many anti-spyware programs sniff out cookies along with other forms of malware.

Zero Day Exploit

Zero Day Exploit, also known as a *Zero Day Attack, Zero Day, 0day* or *Oh-Day* refers to any form of malicious cyberattack or system/network vulnerability that was previously unknown to security experts or the public. The most dangerous viruses have been known to use multiple zero day exploits in their attacks. Although the average person doesn't see or hear the term too often, I'm including it because when you do see it, consider it the equivalent of hearing the Emergency Alert System alert buzz across your television: "This is not a test. There has been an outbreak in your city with symptoms similar to the Ebola virus. Please stay indoors and take the following precautions..."

Contrary to how the name sounds, a zero day exploit may have been out in the wild for days, months and even in some cases a few years. Zero Day means that it was just discovered and little or nothing is known about it. Network security professionals treat Zero Day attacks with high priority with because (1) the methods are often more sophisticated than most currently out there, (2) no one knows how severe and widespread the damage may be, and (3) no one can say how long it will take to come up with a defense.

Zombies and Botnets

A zombie refers to a computer that has been infected with virus-like malware that allows a cybercriminal to take control of it without the owner's knowledge. Like their walking dead counterparts, zombies will also infect any other vulnerable computers it can sink its teeth into. Well-constructed zombies are usually a hybrid of functional traits found in rootkits, viruses, worms, Trojans, spyware and other forms of malware.

Zombie computers operate much like locusts in that they attack using a decentralized sort of fearless collective intelligence. Once they receive instructions from their command center, they go into action infecting other vulnerable computers in range, forcing them to participate in achieving the swarm's objectives. The swarm is commonly referred to as a Botnet.

Short for "roBOT" and "NETwork", a Botnet is an army of zombie computers. Like a human army, it can range in numbers from a squad to legions. To put the scope of such an outbreak into perspective, in recent years notorious Botnets like Conficker and Storm were estimated to be comprised of over 10 million zombified computers—about the size of the entire population of Haiti. And unlike with living (and undead) military forces, these zombies can be spread out all over the world and still be part of a Botnet.

The Botmaster (the person that controls the Botnet) only needs an Internet-ready device to send commands to the command-and-control center which then forwards the instructions to the zombies throughout the Botnet. These digital militias are used for stealing email accounts to send spam emails (e.g.—Gmail, Yahoo, AOL, etc.), stealing financial data (e.g.—credit card numbers, bank/stock trading accounts, etc.), personal information (e.g.—names, SSNs, addresses, etc.) and usernames/passwords to popular accounts (e.g.—Facebook, various Instant Messengers, etc.). At the high end these attacks cover everything from cyber-extortion to large-scale cybercrime attacks against major corporate and government networks. For this reason, it's not uncommon for cunning Botmasters to stay mobile and host their control centers on web servers and networks in countries where local/state/federal law enforcement can't reach them.

More and more Botnets are being set up and controlled by transnational organized crime syndicates. As of this writing, Botnets and Botnet "kits" have started to become so prevalent in some regions within the underground economy that cybercriminals have resorted to selling them for a little as $700 dollars USD.

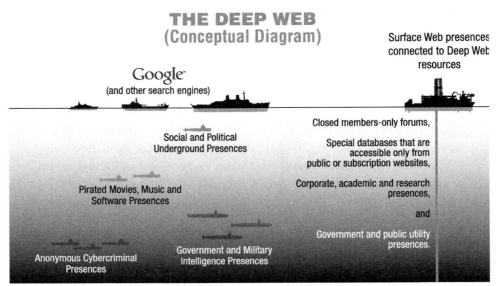

THE DEEP WEB
(Conceptual Diagram)

Surface Web presences connected to Deep Web resources

Google
(and other search engines)

Closed members-only forums,

Social and Political Underground Presences

Special databases that are accessible only from public or subscription websites,

Corporate, academic and research presences,

Pirated Movies, Music and Software Presences

and

Government and public utility presences.

Anonymous Cybercriminal Presences

Government and Military Intelligence Presences

'Presences' refers to websites and/or networks.

Deep Web

Throughout this book, on occasion you may read references to "Deep Web". Also called "The Invisible Web" and "Hidden Web", this term uses the allegory of ocean depths to explain the accessibility of different parts of the web.

There is the Surface Web: those websites that are widely advertised, open to the public and easily reached by Google or any other search engines. With the Deep Web allegory, websites like Facebook, Amazon or even the typical business website would be considered like destinations on land masses, continents and islands (not shown in the conceptual diagram).

The Deep Web, by contrast, refers to those parts of the web that are both restricted access and/or invisible to normal search engines. These places are shielded behind various barriers to prevent unauthorized access to the information and resources within. Since search engines can't reach them, these places are hidden to the rest of the world, much like the landscape at the bottom of the ocean. By many estimates, this invisible web is considered to be several hundred times larger than the overall Surface Web. This is where the term can sometimes be a bit of a misnomer.

On the more familiar side, most internal-use-only web resources for governments (especially military and intelligence agencies), schools, and businesses are considered Deep Web. This even includes websites and networks as common as your company's internal Intranet.

Many websites can also be considered both Surface Web and Deep Web. Something like an offshore oil rig, they have a website available on the surface yet they are the gateway to huge reservoirs of data and network resources that cannot be accessed any other way. A good example of this is the Library of Congress (www.loc.gov). Anyone can find the website itself through Google, making it Surface Web, but the databases connected to the LOC also make it Deep Web; the information found there can't be retrieved by any means other than using the search on the LOC website or making a trip to 101 Independence Avenue SE in Washington, DC.

On the more duplicitous extreme, Deep Web also refers to the clandestine websites and networks that exist where the people prefer to remain anonymous and secret. Finding these places can be like climbing into a submersible and diving down into the Marianas Trench, the deepest regions of Earth's oceans. And just like those murky unexplored regions are home to glowing fish, giant squid and other aquatic life that were previously unknown, the same kinds of strange surprises can be expected. Many cyberattacks originate from this space—whether they are criminal assaults or state-sponsored aggressions. Hackers of all types dwell at these depths and quietly move through these spaces like phantoms pass through walls. Most cybercriminal deals happen here, too, often between people that will never meet face to face. Pirated movies, music, software and even books can be found here, typically on websites funded by banner ads for every type of fly-by-night business and porn website imaginable. Also existing in this abyss are the websites and networks belonging to every terrorist, extremist and activist organization on the planet. Tech-savvy privacy advocates, political dissidents and journalists reporting from countries with censored Internet also use Deep Web resources to safely exchange information with the free world.

Mark

Slang for a victim of fraud, identity theft or cybercrime. Other synonyms include patsy, target, fish, sucker, trick, chump, pigeon, sap, fool, pushover, and sitting duck.

Spam

Junk email. Many spammers have resorted to paying Botmasters to allow them to send out spam through their Botnets. Spam sources are difficult to find and shut down because Botnets are comprised of zombies that are often spread out all over the world. More and more spammers have begun to use the same methods to send unsolicited advertisements through SPIT (Spam by Internet Telephone) and SPIM (Spam by Instant Messenger).

Malvertisements

As if online advertising wasn't already bad enough, malvertisements are now on the rise. Short for "malicious advertisement", malvertisements are the equivalent of watching an ad on TV that can either give you a disease, force you into making a payment on your credit card, or both.

A malvertisement is designed to infect a user's computer with some kind of malware, often turning the computer into a zombie. Among organized crime rings, malvertisements are fast becoming the computer hijacking method of choice. Infectious malvertisements are commonly exposed to users on websites through either pop-ups or legitimate advertisements.

With the pop-up ads, the culprit can deliver a malicious payload the instant the ad appears on the screen. In other instances, the malicious code will execute as soon as the user clicks on the "X" to close the pop-up window. This is happening more and more, especially with fake anti-virus programs that are hijacking people's computers, blocking them from any other activity until they either agree to pay with a credit card (which just gets sent to the cybercriminals) or they manage to go through the process of removing the malware and undoing all its damage.

With legitimate ads, the process is harder to detect but has a greater area of effect. The culprit might place any number of normal ads on a trusted website. The uninfected ads might be on display for weeks or months in order to establish a good relationship with the trusted website. Eventually the culprit will inject the malicious code into the ad, leaving it there long enough to infect as many computers as possible, and then either removing the malicious payload or dropping the ad altogether. To further complicate matters, if these ads are being run through the larger syndicated online ad services, thousands of websites can be inadvertently turned into carriers of the infection—and each of those websites is viewed by thousands of visitors a day. The websites that run third-party ads can't provide much protection for their visitors because the ads are often coming from other ad publishers.

Malvertisements are becoming so rampant that I recommend that it's better to be safe than sorry: Block all pop-ups and set your computer to only allow programs to run on your computer that either you (or a security-minded IT professional) has approved.

Phishing

Phishing emails are the 21st century version of the short con—a scam with the intent to take you for all your money and anything else that can be monetized. It could be the money in your bank account, your credit card, your entire identity, or even the photos you take.

The most common form of phishing these days comes through emails. For this chapter I'll elaborate on four types: The "Get Rich Quick", "Letter from your Bank", "Notification Letter", and "You Gotta Check This Out" letter scams. I should also note that this list is far from complete. Just like short cons have been around since the invention of money, phishing scams will continue to change with the times. I guarantee that these examples will already be outdated by the time this book is in print. As of this writing, a large percentage of phishing thefts can be traced back to either the Russian Federation or West Africa (particularly Nigeria) and they're almost always sent out through some Botnet.

The "Get Rich Quick" email is a scam that has been around forever but people still seem to fall for it. The story always changes but it's along the lines of some national stuck in some country and has millions of dollars tied up in some bureaucracy that they're willing to split with you if you put up X amount of money to help them get it out. This capitalizes on the Greed of those who will fall for it.

Another variant of the Get-Rich-Quick emails will come in the form of "Get millions of visitors to your business website" type messages (if you manage or own a business) or even "work from home" emails if the spammer got your email from one of the job search websites. In these cases, sometimes they want you to buy something; other times they want you to click on a link that will infect your computer with some kind of malware. Again, Greed is the motivator here.

Finally, there's a variant of the Get Rich emails called the "Distress message". It is the exact opposite of the others because it capitalizes on the recipient's desire to help out a friend, family member, or associate in need. The email comes from the address of someone that knows you—a friend, relative or associate; someone who is familiar enough with you that your name and email have been saved in their address book. This typically happens because a zombie has managed to crack the password to the sender's email account (usually one web-based email services such as Yahoo, Gmail, or Hotmail). Unlike the typical zombie spam, this scam does a good job of using first names from the address book in the desperate plea for help. The story is that the sender was on vacation somewhere outside the country (e.g. - Mexico, Canada, the Bahamas, etc.), they ran into some tough luck (e.g. - lost wallet or purse, got ripped off, got arrested, etc.) and they need you to help by sending a few hundred dollars to [wherever]. The letter is usually short and often very convincing. Ironically, the believable nature of this scam is also its downfall, especially for those who know that the sender likes to travel. I've known several people who received similar messages and were so unnerved by the plea that they didn't bother to hit reply. Instead, they either called the sender's cell phone or called the sender's friends and relatives to see if anyone else knew what happened. In all cases, the sender was safe at home, completely unaware of the growing concern over their "misfortune" abroad. Once made aware of the email, the sender then promptly logged into their email, changed the password, and sent a mass message to everyone apologizing for the faked email plea.

The "Letter from your Bank" scam is disguised as just that—a letter from your bank. The problem is that the scammers don't know who you bank with. As a result, they'll pick out a bank like Citibank or Bank of America and play the odds that some percentage of the recipients use one of them for their banking. They'll design a very realistic-looking letter using a high quality copy of the bank's logo with the intent tricking the recipient into providing their bank account details (or online banking login/password). Variations of this scam also include letters from the IRS where the info provided will be used by the scammer to steal the victim's tax refund. Regardless of the scam type there's always the threat of the target clicking on a link which infects their computer with some kind of malware, turning it into a zombie. Once the scammer gets what they want, it may be weeks, months or even over a year before the victims discover that they've been burned by the scam.

The "Notification Letter" scam is similar to the Letter-from-your-Bank scam in the fact that both use emails that look just like they came from the real companies. You'll receive an email notification from somewhere like a major airline regarding plane tickets you didn't buy, a shipping company like FedEx for package deliveries you weren't expecting (or didn't order), eBay confirmations for products you didn't buy, or even changes to your credit report that you didn't request. And like the bank emails, they, too, will ask you to either put in account information or provide links that will infect your computer with malware upon clicking on them.

The "You gotta check this out Letter" scam is different from the others. It almost always comes from the email address of someone you know or the friend of a friend. The email address itself is usually a freebie like a Yahoo or Hotmail account. The content of the email is often a one or two liner, basically saying something along the lines of "You gotta check this out" along with a link to a website, figuring that the recipient will click on the link because it is from a trusted source. When you receive one of these messages it usually means one of a few things has happened: (A) their computer has been turned into a zombie and they don't know it, (B) the password to one of their email accounts has been cracked and a Botnet has started using it to send out emails, (C) one of your friend's friends has a zombie computer and it just happened to choose your friend's email address to use as a fake sender, or (D) someone was naïve enough to click on the link in the email, causing A, B and/or C to occur. Regardless of the source or the message, if you suspect this might be one of those types of emails don't click on the link, delete it immediately, and notify the person who supposedly sent it or block their emails. If it was a legitimate email, that's fine, too—the sender won't have a problem sending it again.

Spear Phishing

Unlike the regular Phishing where those emails get sent out by the thousands to trap unsuspecting readers, Spear Phishing is done with a specific target in mind. If you are the target of a spear phishing campaign, generally you won't know it until its too late. Someone (or some organization) out there has an agenda where they've spent a fair amount of time doing research about who you are, who you are involved with, and what you do. They use this information to carefully craft one or more emails to send to you containing booby-trapped links and/or Trojan horse attachments. Because the sender has done extensive background research on you, these messages will often seem 100% legitimate, and anything you click on in one of those messages will unleash some kind of malware, often opening up a backdoor into your computer. The purpose of this plot could be as simple as a jealous ex-lover seeking revenge by sabotaging your computer. It could also be as nefariously large-scale as a rival corporation or [foreign?] government agency seeking to steal corporate secrets from you or your computer, or even to exploit you to get to someone else close to you.

Photo Phishing

Selling photos stolen from a computer is fast adding a whole new dimension to the earning potential of phishing scams. Since the dawn of the web, stealing images from other websites has been one of the greatest drawbacks of putting anything online. I've even seen church clergy steal images and not give it a second thought. Reports have surfaced where zombies have been set to actually seek out and steal images from infected computers (along with other sensitive data).

At first, people might ask "What would someone want with my pictures?" Well, for starters, many digital cameras (including cell phone cameras) and image processing programs store metadata inside of each image. This metadata can contain descriptive information like the owner's name, location, copyright info, people in the image, etc, and can be used to further exploit the identity of the computer owner. High quality images can be sold to stock photography sites that pay per submission. And in the wake of sexting and sexy photos, explicit photos can be sold to porn sites, used in adult advertisements, or even used as leverage to blackmail the person it was stolen from. The whole concept gets bizarre if you stop and think about it. Imagine the possibility of a zombie infecting a computer only to steal porn that was viewed on a booby-trapped free porn website full of stolen images.

Hackers and Botmasters:
the Minds behind the Zombies

One of the most dangerous things I've seen about the Internet is that our society is easily mired down in misinformation, especially when it comes to cyberthreats. We have instant access to more information than ever before but comparatively speaking, most of it is about as useful as empty calories. For example, when Hurricane Sandy slammed into the coasts of New York and New Jersey, I saw three posts with relevant info pass through my Facebook feed. There were many prayers and well wishes, too. And then there were several days worth of reposted snapshots of subway stations underwater, apocalyptic Manhattan scenes and sharks swimming through flooded New Jersey neighborhoods—all Photoshopped and incredibly fake.

People fear what they don't understand. When they lack an understanding of what they fear they also tend to make irrational decisions. We've seen it happen with everything from the Salem Witch Hunts to McCarthyism and the Red Scare. And while gripped in their fears, people often become even more vulnerable to the very thing(s) they are afraid of. This is why I had to include this section—to take the mystical veil off of cybercrime. Understanding the typical personalities in this netherworld make it easier to separate the facts from the fallacies. When in Oz, a peek behind the Wizard's curtain reveals there is often more curtain than wizardry.

The Hacker

Of all the terms in this chapter, "Hacker" is probably the most overused, misused, and misunderstood. This section is longer than the others, included mostly to provide insight into who is and isn't behind all the zombies that are attacking our computers and stealing pieces of our lives bit by bit.

Among computer users, the term "hacker" was probably coined sometime in the late 1960s. A hacker was someone who either came up with a brilliant solution to a programming problem or was able to take a piece of hardware or [computer] software and make it do something it wasn't originally designed to do.

By the late 70s and 80s, hacking had come to refer mostly to computer geeks who were interested in exploration and experimenting with more powerful computer systems. The Internet as we know it today wasn't available. Data transmission speeds were as slow as Morse code and long distance calls were very expensive. As a result, in order to connect with people and/or computers outside of their own area codes, many hackers back then also engaged in phone phreaking, a form of hacking that targeted at telephone systems to make free long distance calls. Stories about hacking into institutions like a bank were often more like hearsay myths versus reality. The concept of viruses and malware was a relatively alien concept, mostly because there was nothing to gain from writing a program to damage a system that might have taken weeks (or months) to crack into.

Profiling the average hacker isn't as easy as that of the typical Script Kiddie or other cybercriminal, primarily because these people aren't motivated by malicious intent or financial gain. The typical hacker is an introverted non-conformist with a wide variety of interests, among them an almost obsessive connection to technology. Although most hackers excel with some area of technology, they tend to also sharpen their skills in other areas that aren't high-tech. Since hackers consume information like alcoholics consume booze, they are driven to learn everything they can about anything that captures their interest. Whether they are in their early teens or in their 50s (yes, there are some hackers that age), they seem drawn to intellectual challenges, the more complex the better, and are prone to lose interest in a project once the thrill of the challenge has worn off. As a result, they may or may not focus solely on IT work. Case in point: Steve Jobs and Steve Wozniak (the founders of Apple), and Bill Gates (co-founder of Microsoft) were all hackers back in the 70s.

By the late 1990s and early 2000s, thanks to the rise of the Internet, virus coders, a proliferation of easy-to-use hacking programs, and rampant media misuse of the term Hacking, most people use the term Hacker to refer to any kind of high-tech boogie-man, source of blame, or arch-cybercriminal that uses a computer to commit cybercrimes, particularly Identity Theft… programming and networking skills are optional.

White Hat and Black Hat Hackers

Aside from lopsided media misrepresentation, the role of computer hackers in the continued development of cyberspace is crucial. Claiming anything to the contrary would be like saying that the U.S. could have become what it is today without the Manifest Destiny mindset that many settlers had adopted as they migrated west of the Mississippi river in the mid-1800s. And just like the American Frontier has often been romanticized, there are many myths surrounding computer hackers and cyberspace. The biggest misconception is that these people can be divided into two camps: White Hat and Black Hat.

White Hat hackers, also known as "Ethical Hackers", "Computer Security Experts" and "Penetration Testers", are hackers who use their skills to protect information systems and networks. Whether they are working for hire or just roaming the Internet solo, ultimately they are the equivalent of white blood cells for the Internet—identifying system or network weaknesses, notifying the owner, and fixing the problem by patching up the hole. Due to state and federal laws against computer hacking, when these hackers crack into a system without the owner's permission, it's not uncommon for them to discretely notify the owner by untraceable email, phone call, or some other method to make the owner aware of the security hole.

Black Hat hackers are often generically referred to as "Hackers" (or occasionally "Crackers") when it comes to anything related to cybercrime and malicious computer activity. Commonly they break into computer systems or networks to take advantage of them for criminal purposes (e.g. - stealing data, destruction, vandalism, etc.). Identity Theft is often lumped in with malicious hacking mostly because cybercriminals often bring in these hackers to facilitate some part of the crime. Truth is, most Identity Fraud—the brokering and use of the stolen identity information— is committed by people that have no computer hacking knowledge whatsoever.

The terms for White Hat and Black Hat hackers comes from the old B&W cowboy movies where the good guys wore white hats (e.g. - Jimmy Stewart in THE MAN WHO SHOT LIBERTY VALANCE) and the bad guys wore black hats (e.g. - Lee Marvin in the same film). Although this way of classifying hackers has gained wide popularity, it's incredibly inaccurate. There's only one old cowboy movie that epitomizes hackers in cyberspace: Sergio Leone's classic Spaghetti western THE GOOD, THE BAD, AND THE UGLY: Everyone is a flat caricature of their real-world personas. Data is money and money is in the data. Between the law and the lawless there's a seemingly endless body count—without a drop of blood. And in case anyone wants to bring up the definitive lack of indigenous peoples in Leone's vision of the West, there's no such thing as indigenous in cyberspace... everyone is a settler.

Although the skills and tools for most types of hacking are virtually identical, the hackers themselves can't be categorized in such a simple White or Black Hat fashion. Very few people are absolute Good or Evil. Ideologies overlap, moral compasses change, and the law is completely indifferent. Plenty of ethical hackers got their start as malicious hackers, regularly engaged in what is considered cybercrime even if their activities were little more than harmless pranks and unauthorized exploration. Then there are Grey Hat Hackers who are basically hackers that will publicize the security vulnerabilities they expose, often to benefit their own reputations. There are also the Hacktivists, rogue hacker activists that use their talents to combat terrorists, tyrants, corporate greed and other nefarious entities by attacking the networks used by their organizations. Some of those armchair guerilla fighters commonly resort to malicious hacking practices to achieve their goals. And lastly, there are people out there who believe that all hacking is a criminal offense, regardless of the hacker or the intent.

Instead of using "White", "Grey" and "Black" Hat, terms like "Ethical", "Opportunist", "Hacktivist", "Malicious" or "Criminal" will be used to describe the inclinations of most Hackers referenced in this book.

The Phreak

Simply put, phone phreaking (combination of the words PHone and fREAK) refers to a subculture within the Hacking community that focused primarily on telecommunications and exploiting telephone networks. Phreaking saw its heyday from the early 1970s to the 1990s, declining sharply after that with the phone companies switching over to newer equipment. These days, with many phone systems being based on technologies like VoIP, most phone phreaking practices and technologies have quietly passed into computer underground history. Those few remaining phreaking practices have generally merged into the realm of network hacking. Phreaks were included in this book because a survey of the hacker subculture is incomplete without mentioning them.

The Script Kiddie

Today, what most people picture as a stereotypical Hacker is actually what would be considered a Script Kiddie. There are scores of websites dedicated to computer hacking, many of which are frequented by IT Security experts and hackers with all kinds of intentions. Many of these sites are also the home of freely downloadable hacking and penetration testing tools, put together by Ethical Hackers and security firms. They automate many of the attack methods that hackers once had to learn on their own and perform by hand. Script Kiddies are would-be hackers who rely heavily on these programs but have little or no actual knowledge of system architectures, programming, or network security.

Contrary to the label, the typical Script Kiddie is a male between the ages of 13 and 23 and often a loner. His high school teachers will generally describe him as a bright (but lazy) academic underachiever, impulsive, and has great natural talent for computers, more so than most of his peers. For every Script Kiddie that goes on to learn the technical disciplines to become an established Ethical/Opportunist/Malicious Hacker, there are countless others who are stuck in a mode where they are more in love with the myths associated with being a Hacker. The reasons vary but, from a psychological standpoint, many seek the power and respect they believe comes with the Hacker image. It's not that they can't learn the programming and networking skills associated with Computer Security but they often lack the dedication to do so. They're the nerd equivalent of those high school garage band musicians that are more concerned with dressing and acting the part of a Rock Star instead of putting in the study and practice it takes to make great music.

Script Kiddies may luck up on hacking into something relatively useless like a Facebook or Twitter account or tricking some newbie out of their World of Warcraft password. Those few that successfully crack into a noteworthy system or network are often successful due to weak passwords or exploiting old security holes that were overlooked by an untrained (or lazy) system administrator. Script Kiddies rarely get very far with their attacks because most of their methods are overused, sloppy and about as discreet as a Superbowl half-time show. This is why many of them never achieve much beyond a few thrills and some tall tales to impress their friends. And as the cycle of life within the Hacking scene goes, once they get bored and move on, more wannabes are always trickling in to replace them.

The Crackers / Malicious Hackers

Those Script Kiddies that stick with it long enough (and are inclined criminal activity) often become what many security professionals have dubbed Black Hat hackers or Malicious hackers. Plus, most malicious hacking would be more accurately dubbed "cracking", making the culprit a "Cracker", akin to a person that can crack a combination safe or other security system.

Most IT professionals can't tell the difference between hackers and crackers... and the minute they discover someone has unauthorized access to their network, they don't have time to care. There's no way to tell a hacker from a cracker on sight; no gang signs or set colors to claim. To add to the confusion, crackers often consider themselves hackers, too. The tools and techniques are the same (except most hackers can write their own programs from scratch if necessary). The way to tell the difference between the two rests mainly in their individual behavioral traits and intentions. Hypothetically, let's say a hacker and a cracker gain secret access to a high-tech bank vault any time they want:

▶ A hacker would be more interested in spending weeks to learn the inner mechanisms of the vault, figure out how to bypass the security, and might even go so far as to create a tool for other banks to use to test the security on their own vaults. Whether or not that hacker actually used the knowledge to steal the contents of the vault would depend on his or her moral inclinations.

► A cracker would do whatever it took to break into the vault—including using any tools made by the hacker. The goal would be to steal its contents, exploit the bank for financial gain, or cause some other kind of mayhem. The quest for knowledge would be completely irrelevant unless it pertained to ways to commit the crime and elude the authorities.

The Botmaster

If you were to see the Botmaster behind a typical Botnet these days, you probably wouldn't find the stereotypical whiz kid hacker. No fresh-faced Harry Potter look-alikes. Instead, you're likely to find a man (or woman) in their 30s or 40s controlling the Botnet with a laptop, tablet or smart phone. Even more bizarre, their computing skills are mediocre at best because they often lease access to a Botnet, buy the Botnet outright, or pay a Malicious Hacker to set one up from scratch. There's a good chance the Botmaster might be connected with a low level mobster who is connected with an organized crime entity like the Russian Bratva. Or a Blue Lantern with the Wo Shing Wo, set up to earn in Tsim Sha Tsui. Maybe even an Albanian middle man living down in the Caymans. Regardless of the funding source, more and more Botmasters these days are taking their marching orders from these transnational gangs. These syndicates represent a new breed of moguls in a global underground economy that is complete with its own divisions of labor within budding service industries. Cybercrime is a license to steal from countless people, 24 hours a day from anywhere in the world... without needing a gun.

ZOMBIE TRIVIA

Q: In George A. Romero's NIGHT OF THE LIVING DEAD, what Pittsburgh television personality made a cameo appearance?

(answer on page 384)

The Magic Behind Cybercrime

Cybercriminals, as with swindlers throughout history, go to great lengths to create illusions that will capture the minds of their marks.

Sometimes these illusions employ principles like Cognitive Estrangement or Suspension of Disbelief. Often the best illusions don't stray too far from what fits into our everyday reality. Unlike common robbers or burglars, most cybercriminals depend on illusion to fool their marks into thinking their reality can be made a little better if they just make a safe choice: Open this email. Click this link. Visit this special website. Verify your name and account right here if you don't mind. And in most cases, if the illusion isn't convincing enough, the mark won't make that choice. Not making that choice means the mark hasn't set off the trap. No trap means the cybercriminal doesn't score. No score means the mark doesn't get ripped off. Most of the time, simply spotting the illusion can save you from all the misfortune that comes with identity theft and cyber fraud.

One of the most powerful examples of these types of illusions happened during the Golden Age of Radio with Orson Welles' radio dramatization of H.G. Wells' WAR OF THE WORLDS. Originally broadcast as a Halloween tribute on October 30, 1938, most of us are familiar with the legend of how a few million people freaked out because they thought the news bulletins about Martian attacks were real.

The illusion was created through a combination of a well-written script, great acting, and unproven theories about life on Mars. Tensions were also high due to current events, particularly with the Nazi war machine on the march taking over Europe. Along with that was the fact that the fictional nature of the show was only announced at the very beginning and close to the end of the hour long broadcast. Anyone that tuned in between those notices found themselves immersed in news bulletins being reported live from the battlefront—and humanity was desperately losing. People are pre-programmed to react to fear first and rational thought second. Mix all those factors together and it's no surprise so many listeners went berserk. Countless news stories and urban legends have circulated for more than half a century regarding hysterical reactions to the broadcast that night. The extent of the mayhem caused by the telecast continues to be the subject of debate.

The lessons from that evening weren't enough. In early 1949 it happened again. This time in South America and the instigators were a couple of radio producers in Quito, Ecuador. They took the Welles script, reworked it in Spanish, and once again like a flame to gunpowder, the broadcast sparked widespread panic. Every cop and fireman in the city jumped in their vehicles and rolled out of town, rushing to aid the troops on the fictitious battlefront. Armageddon was in full effect. And when it came out that it was all a radio show substantiated by a fake newspaper article, hundreds of citizens rioted against the radio station and newspaper. At least half a dozen people died. The producers ended up fleeing the country.

Fast forward to the 21st century. Even after several major wars, sweeping societal changes and more sophisticated tastes in entertainment, people haven't changed much. The mysterious black box that was once the radio has since been replaced several times over, most recently with globally-connected computers and mobile devices. A day doesn't go by that social media websites like Facebook and Twitter aren't flooded with Photoshopped images that defy logic but people believe them to be genuine. The more fake or impossible the images, the faster they seem to go viral. Along with that, people that aren't computer literate tend to treat what they see on the screen as a window into what is (or isn't) happening inside. If something is convincing, it becomes real enough to adjust someone's perception of reality. If it's not visible, it doesn't exist.

The Architects of Spam

In July of 2012, the world witnessed the fall of Grum. By all accounts of those in the know, it was a brutal battle that crossed over several countries and thousands of miles. However, the showdown wasn't covered by a single major news media outlet. There wasn't even a cell phone clip posted on YouTube. Grum had an army of over 120,000 strong—larger than the entire U.S. National Guard. And with the victory there wasn't a single body carted away. They were all zombies… and Grum was one of the world's largest Botnets.

Armies of thousands. Transnational manhunts. Server takedowns in distant countries. Anyone listening in on our webcam conversation might have thought we were discussing a Tom Clancy novel. I originally met [code name] Angela somewhere on the other side of Tor—an anonymous gateway into many parts of the Deep Web. These are the places you won't find through Google, best described as taking the Red Pill then rappelling down into the Rabbit Hole of rabbit holes. Eventually we built up enough of a rapport to finally meet via anonymous Skype webcam to conduct this interview.

When I started this book I had high hopes of interviewing a few different cybercriminal operations. Unfortunately most of my old hacker contacts from back in the 80s and 90s had either disappeared or gone legit. My current contacts had only heard of the Deep Web; none of them had any ties to active cybercriminal enterprises. Putting out feelers around the Net yielded several inquiries, mostly hustlers who thought they could con me out of some money in exchange for a bogus story. The Skype session with Angela was the result of weeks of digging. She was the only one that made the cut. As the spokeswoman for a crew of spammers, they were also the only ones that proved their credibility. They submitted a sample database of 3 million email addresses and granted me temporary access to a branch of the Botnet used to steal all those accounts.

When Angela appeared on screen she had an entirely different appearance from what I expected. Between her late 30s and 40s she had an air of a Goth girl gone Corporate—Siouxsie Sioux minus the feline makeup. Earrings and necklaces were perfect, eyebrows perfect, and every hair in place. It was as if she was an Italian runway model that had just spent hours in a makeup chair.

Behind all the pleasant small talk there was still a mild apprehension between us. One wrong move could cause the other to cut the connection and walk away from the deal. Her fee had to be paid in BTC (Bitcoins), an untraceable digital currency commonly used in Deep Web. In exchange, she had to provide solid insider-style information I could use. For both of us it was an all-or-nothing kind of proposition. Every minute that passed came with its own leap of faith.

By proper definition, their company is an opt-in email marketing firm. Let reality tell the tale and they are hardcore spammers; lightweight cybercriminals. I found myself fascinated by the fact that both businesses blur the lines of legality, like the difference between being pharmaceutical distributors and drug dealers. Most of it is a matter of public perception. One culture's Capitalist is another culture's Carpetbagger.

Angela avoided answering any questions about her background; she referred herself as a "college dropout that made good". She had two other business partners, both of which stayed off camera. I listened to her ramble about Anonymous' recent antics as I waited patiently to see the rest of the space behind her. I've seen a few criminal operations. Most of the time the décor isn't unlike something you'd either see in the basement of an urban tenement or hippie flophouse. To my surprise their office space looked like a typical tech company, complete with that East Village boutique ad agency feel. The partitioned open area had three slick desks, Thomasville chairs, and PC and iMac desktops. A centrally-located All-in-One printer seemed to unify their areas. There wasn't a single phone in sight. "We don't do phones here," she explained. "All our calls are Skyped through the desktops, voice and video."

This made sense. No phone companies, no phone lines to tap. From what I know about these anonymized Skype calls, tracing a single session practically required a squad of Network Engineers across a couple of continents and the NSA to crack the encryption. When I asked about the relatively empty bookcase and no filing cabinets someone off camera replied "We don't do paper, either."

"Everything stays in the cloud," Angela added. "Anything that is usually in a printed file or on an office Intranet—document management, CRM, etc—is out in the cloud". The main office and the reps all use the same cloud-based office applications, hosted on servers somewhere offshore. The Feds could kick in the door, raid the place and after going through all the computers they would have forensic evidence of three people accessing websites in other countries—and outside of their jurisdiction. Aside from that, everything else is outsourced or handled in virtual departments located in different cities, compartmentalized so well that only the three in that office know everything that is going on. The only reason they had a physical office was to have a comfortable place to work away from home. And with this setup, plausible deniability hadn't been this brilliant since the Bush Administration condoned waterboarding terrorists.

"Time to meet the Hollywood Squares," Angela said as she turned her webcam toward one of the monitors on her desk. A grid of nine webcam windows occupied the screen; she had instructed her staff ahead of time to wear something to protect their identities. As she moved the pointer over each face an introduction and explanation followed.

Within the first few windows were an Aztec Sun Mask, two French Mardi Gras facemasks, and a Chinese Opera mask. Introduced as the call center sales reps, all three women pleasantly waved at the same time. One of the Mardi Gras women excused herself as she took an incoming call. "These aren't your average GED dropouts, either," Angela bragged. "They provide top sales and support, and we've got English, Spanish and Korean covered. Miss Shanxi has been taking a course in Mandarin Chinese to help expand our potential client base."

And she was right. Each rep was a stay-at-home mother with a degree in either business or marketing, among the millennials that graduated in time to find a stagnant job market. They organized their shifts among themselves, ultimately providing 24-hour coverage. Whoever was on duty logged into the company's virtual phone system and click a switch so all incoming calls were routed to her computer. Something about their accents and room décors hinted they were probably living somewhere in the Midwest. Although their actual salaries were never discussed, one of the ladies thanked Angela again for the raise and bonuses. Apparently they exceeded their sales goals last quarter.

The next interview was Marc, their senior Graphic Designer. Wearing a pair of Steampunk sunglasses over a Ronald Reagan mask, he was superimposed on a background that made it look like he was Skyping from somewhere in the clouds. I never learned his nationality but his cocky demeanor reminded me of some West German hackers that used to frequent the underground QSD chat rooms. He and his team were responsible for putting together spam emails and setting up the booby-trapped websites used to infect unwary visitors. The key to his success was an uncanny eye for detail.

More often than not they steal stock photography, logos and designs from other websites, chop them up, and use them in their own ad designs. With mention of names like Olena and Agarkar(?), my guess is that most of the designers were based in places like Eastern Europe and India, roughly half a day ahead of the United States east coast.

"The Count", alias Jean-Paul, wore the Phantom of the Opera half-mask and sounded like a Slavic Leprechaun thanks to a voice modulator on his mic. When I asked about his background he had somewhat proudly stated that he was formerly employed at one of the Big Five [Arthur Andersen LLP?] and lost his job due to the collapse of his company in connection to a major corporate scandal [Enron?]. "He's a comptroller with super powers," Angela interjected; the camera swayed a little as they both chuckled at an inside joke.

Managing money for a cybercriminal operation requires creative accounting with a very broad set of international connections. Money laundering in the 21st century evolved into a totally new discipline thanks to Al Qaeda and 9/11. Where it was once as simple as using Paypal and anonymous money orders through Western Union, the fees have gotten too high and it's become way too easy to end up on a Homeland Security list. And while some digital currencies like Bitcoin have become a popular way for cybercriminals to move (and pay) cash between countries, part of the problem is that it fluctuates in value based on supply and demand and other price points. In order to avoiding the risk of losing money in a flux, any payments in Bitcoins need to be traded on a trusted Bitcoin exchange (e.g. - Mt. Gox) and quickly converted to an established currency like the U.S. dollar, Euro, or Yen. And because of the amounts involved, often the cash needs to be spread out between online escrow services and Hawalas (underground banking sources commonly found in the Middle East and South Asia). These shadow banking systems are where Jean-Paul takes advantage of moving currencies through developing economies, mostly to stay off the radar of anti-money laundering laws and some Financial Intelligence Unit. There were also plenty of transactions through various legitimate ecommerce websites, particularly with a constant stream of startup LLC ventures (referred to as "burn firms") that mysteriously popped up and fell apart with great speed. The International Monetary Fund estimates that between 2% and 5% of the world's gross domestic product is made up of laundered money—a factor that might explain why so many countries are curiously far behind the curve in stemming the tide of cybercrime. It is almost reminiscent of the side effects of the cocaine crime wave of Miami in the 1980s: undocumented billions in annual profits that boosted the economies where the money was spent, all while quietly leaving behind a wake of countless victims and a staggering body count. Something about Jean-Paul smacked of a man who was connected with a larger criminal enterprise, maybe Bratva. On several occasions I dropped hints and inquiries about such involvement… and each time he whimsically elaborated on an answer to a question I didn't ask.

My last interview was with Rubik, their IT guru. Wearing a Guy Fawkes "Anonymous" mask, he spoke a Pidgin English, possibly native Hawaiian. She referred to him as their Webmaster, a title that turned out to be a misnomer since their company doesn't possess (or manage) any of their own web servers. Aside from the few virtual hosting spaces they rent, most of the hosting spaces these spammers used belong to companies running legitimate websites. Each of those websites had been hacked and secretly turned into a Command-and-Control center (C&C), operating from within the owner's website without their knowledge. Stored on the C&Cs are hidden folders with functional scripts, booby-trapped web pages, and malware installers that are used to infect computers, turning them into zombies awaiting secret commands from a C&C. Together, the C&Cs work as a swarm intelligence to control their distributed network of over 10,000 zombie computers—collectively known as a Botnet. Anyone in the office can send an instruction to the C&Cs using a web app affectionately referred to as "The Remote". Clicked commands get sent to the C&Cs, relayed throughout the Botnet and performed by the zombie computers. In this case, the Botnet is primarily used to manage and send out millions of pieces of junk emails on demand. At this point, I was so impressed with this team that I went ahead and started the Bitcoin payment process.

NOTE: The following diagram is an relational overview of this spamming company and their third-party vendors.

1. ACME company decides they wish to promote their products through a "mass email campaign" so they seek out a company that provides such services.
2. Angela's company agrees to take on the campaign.
3. Angela's team routinely outsources to vendors for services that are unethical or illegal in the United States (e.g. - purchasing email databases, buying access to pre-built Botnets of infected computers, leasing hosting space in countries with lax cyberlaws, etc.)
4. Angela's team of virtual subcontractors design the spam email and website associated with the campaign. While this is happening, daily operations include business administration, customer support, and marketing along with managing other spam campaigns.
5. Angela's Botmaster sends commands to their Botnet to launch the spam campaign. The number of active zombie computers in the Botnet Army determines how many emails get sent out per hour.
6. Emails arrive at their destinations.
7. The recipient (anyone that gets email) opens the message and decides to buy. Clicking on the link takes the recipient to a website to make the actual purchase. That website contains malware that infects the recipient's computer and secretly add it to the Botnet army. After the credit card payment is processed, sometimes the Personal Identifiable Information (name, address, credit card info, etc.) gets sold or traded to brokers to be resold again at a later date.

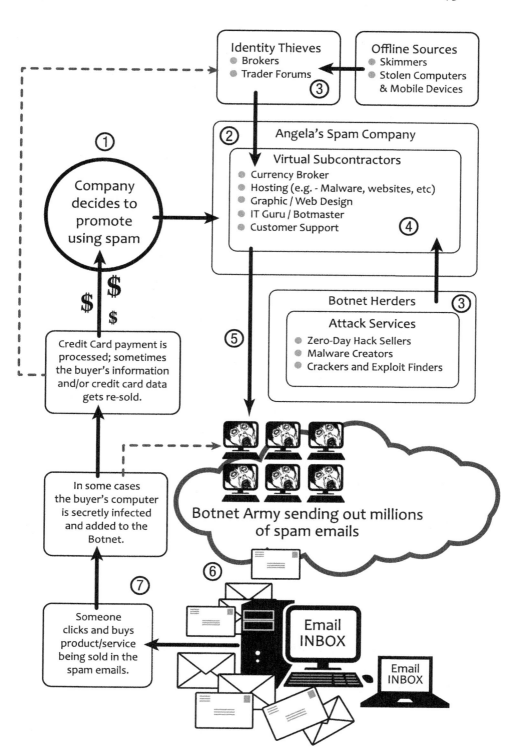

Botnets have a life of their own in cyberspace, similar to livestock on a farm. If a Botnet isn't well maintained it will eventually die off. Most zombie-infected web servers, home computers and/or devices are trying to phone home, sending out suspicious traffic across the network, similar to how we often hear a swarm of bees before we see them. Some IT person or tech support calls attention to the zombie activity and then starts the process of removing the malware or fixing the security holes, ultimately removing that machine from the hive mind of the Botnet. Due to these factors, a big part of Rubik's job is to replace those lost servers, computers and devices with newly infected ones. Sometimes he cruises underground marketplace websites and chatrooms for lists of freshly hacked servers to buy or trade. Other times he'll find a hosting company in countries like Moldova or the Philippines, anywhere that has solid connectivity and out of immediate reach of U.S. Law Enforcement or INTERPOL. These countries are often places where the middle class is almost non-existent; everyone is either very well off or rabidly poor. Automatic weapons are standard with most political campaigns. For local agents faced with such brutal challenges, combating cybercrime is about as high a priority as vandalism or jaywalking. And if the feds actually took down their entire Botnet it would only serve to be a temporary setback. Getting their operation back online would be as simple as hiring another hacker to build another Botnet or buy one pre-cultivated, similar to buying a professionally-nurtured bee hive from a Honey Farmer. Rubik's duties seemed more like a cross between high-tech beekeeping and hustling his ass off like a day trader. As strange as it may sound, Rubik doesn't see or touch any of the data that passed through the Botnets he maintained. He preferred it that way.

Angela turned the camera back on herself as she explained that they can pull up the Remote using any computer, phone or tablet. "We can select which emails go out, when they go out, how many, and what email lists are used".

One of her partners off camera mentioned that my payment had come through. She complimented me on my timing because apparently my tour was over; the rest wasn't up for disclosure. She leaned back in her chair, relaxed as if a director off camera had just said "cut". To my surprise she fiddled with her hair until it buckled completely off her scalp. The last thing I saw was a wig cap as she wished me luck on the book. A dead Skype connection bid me farewell.

As of this writing, Angela and her team didn't crack the top 10 in the world of spammers and Botnets. Some spammers claim to pull in over $1 million dollars USD per month. And with everything from weight loss products to bootleg pharmaceuticals to Get-Laid-Tonight websites, it doesn't look like they'll ever run out of clients. Even though their industry is changing (many spammers are moving toward web-spam), those numbers lead me to only one conclusion—someone is clicking on the links in those stupid junk messages.

For weeks I was unsure of whether or not I actually had enough to carve this interview into a story. That's when it hit me: Angela's company was virtually indistinguishable from any other Internet company. They have the same basic production and office requirements. Aside from the illegal Botnets their equipment was identical. They outsource to other services that trade within globally-accessible underground marketplaces. Their management structures are streamlined with all the same disciplines of any other successful business. They recruit new talent to train and place within their divisions of labor. They operate within a global underground economy that enjoys the kind of profit margins that would entice some MBA graduates to consider it as a career option. And from a criminal perspective, this is the perfect disguise, giving them the ability to hide in plain sight if necessary. Since almost all their incriminating evidence remained in the cloud, they were practically Ghosts in the Machine. As of this writing it would take a minor miracle or an Act of Congress for the Feds to catch them. They had a better chance of getting in trouble for unpaid traffic tickets.

ZOMBIE TRIVIA

Q: In SHAUN OF THE DEAD, what was Shaun's mother's name?

(answer on page 384)

The Zombie Attack Examined

According to sources like Symantec and McAfee, most businesses with dedicated network connections get hit with a little more than a dozen attacks per day. If these were real world robbery attempts, none of us would get any sleep at night. And the common misconception is that these viruses and malware are still just the vicious pranks of a bunch of anti-social whiz-kids. Those days are gone. Most malware is now the work of professional Malicious Hackers, often funded by transnational organized crime syndicates.

In years past, the average cyber attacks were perpetrated by script kiddies, would-be hackers who used readily-available hacking tools to try to crack into systems. Script kiddies were, and still are, plentiful—but beyond the use of hack tools they have little or no technical mastery over networking or operating systems. Often between 13 and 23 years old, the typical script kiddie is usually more lucky than dangerous. Their approach is to pick out a particular vulnerability, use an automated tool to scan the Internet looking for systems with that same vulnerability, and then attack those systems.

Unlike the "fame and glory" viruses and worms of attacks of those old school script kiddies, cybercriminals of today have turned malware into a service industry. These professionals have taken a far more high-powered, radically advanced approach. If the script kiddies could be compared to a neighborhood drug dealer, today's cybercriminals are connected with the top international drug cartels—literally and figuratively.

A computer that has been compromised and turned into a zombie has numerous possible functions. For the sake of simplicity, I'm lumping all of them into one beast.

Web Server—secretly set up on the owner's computer to allow:

- Spam Distribution—often used to host images and/or other files that are attached to bulk spam emails being sent out.
- Malware Distribution—hosting some malicious program or code that will be sent elsewhere on demand.
- Phishing—set up so that when victims click on a supposedly legitimate link (often a financial institution like a bank), they get directed to this fake website instead of the real one.
- Warez/Piracy Server—an online place to cache pirated goods (e.g. - software, music, video, etc.). This tactic isn't as popular as it once was due to rise in popularity of various forms of P2P file sharing.
- Illegal pornography—such as child porn and other forms of pornography where possession is a felony.

Email Attacks—

- Harvesting Email addresses from contacts and address books of infected accounts.
- Harvesting Email usernames/passwords for any standard or web-based email accounts that are accessed from that computer. This includes your home email(s), your work email (if you access it from that computer), and any freebie webmail accounts such as Yahoo, MSN, Gmail, etc.
- Any conceivable email scams (too many to list here).

Bot—

- DDoS Attack Zombie
- Fraud Zombie
- Anonymous Zombie
- Brute Force Hacking Zombie—for trying to hack passwords, various schemes that are supposed to authentic human users (e.g. - CAPTCHA, webmail frontends, etc.),

▶ Targeted Attack Zombie—for implementing code that is meant to exploit a specific system or network vulnerability.

▶ Miscellaneous—stealing information and various virtual goods that can be resold on the open market. This can be anything from corporate secrets to photos to license keys for expensive software installed on that infected computer (e.g. - Microsoft Office, Adobe Creative Suite, AutoCAD, etc.). If it can be monetized or used to exploit the computer owner in some way, it will be stolen.

▶ Stealing Account Credentials—usernames, passwords, banking info, credit/debit card info, encryption keys and every kind of authentication conceivable. Among the most unusual virtual goods I've heard of being stolen are access to certain high profile online games like Wizard of Warcraft and gambling websites.

Each zombie is recruited into a Botnet, becoming part of what is known as an APT—Advanced Persistent Threat. In contrast to the script kiddies, an APT is far more sophisticated and dangerous since the approach is based on targeting a specific system or network. Usually the target of the APT is anything that is perceived as a high-value mark. It could be a major financial institution, government agency, big corporation or even your business network. Every zombie has a built-in arsenal of weapons and methods, enabling it to exploit many loopholes—including human shortcomings—in an attempt to crack the defenses of the Botnet's target. And while attacking the main target, each zombie will also continue attacking any other vulnerable computers within reach. Each computer it infects will only add to the size of the Botnet as it contributes to the attack while also working to infect more computers.

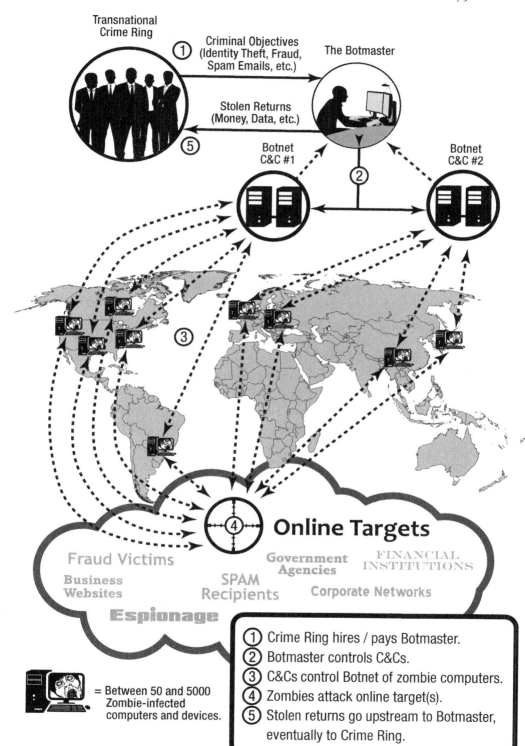

The previous illustration is a figurative description of how Botnets work. Their methods and complexity are only limited by the creativity of the cybercriminals behind them. A good way to visualize the way their threats grow can be seen in Zack Snyder's 2004 retelling of George A. Romero's DAWN OF THE DEAD: Our heroes, after a surviving the chaos of what appeared to be a Class 4 zombie outbreak, all end up together at a Milwaukee mall (still closed and locked up from the night before). The group managed to break in through a loading dock, narrowly escaping the savage clutches of a handful of vicious undead berserkers. By midday there were a few dozen zombies trying to claw their way in through the main entrance doors. After a few days, the parking lot was teaming with hundreds of zombies. Days later, the mall was surrounded by thousands. It was as if the ghouls knew to hunt for people at the mall, much the same way that grizzly bears instinctively hunt for trout in rivers and streams. All it took was a single breach—an unlocked door, weakened fence or cracked window—and the entire mall would be compromised and our heroes devoured. Game over.

Unlike typical armies (living and undead), a Botnet won't give up the assault. These types of zombies never get bored, run out of ammunition, or spot new prey. The zombies will keep at it indefinitely until the Botmaster changes the criminal directives or someone takes the Botnet out of action. Once they've cracked into a system or network, the zombies will continue to rip and tear their way through everything they are programmed to attack with light speed ferocity. The computers they infect will join in the attack. The only things they lack are the dramatic music and Arnold Schwarzenegger one-liners from The Terminator movies.

ZOMBIE TRIVIA

Q: In the 2004 remake of DAWN OF THE DEAD, what two places are key to the storyline?

(answer on page 384)

The Immunity Myth—
Why Mac has joined the PC on the Zombie Menu

Viral infections start as crimes of opportunity. If a computer is susceptible, there is an opportunity. And if that computer has one or more users, there is something on that machine that can be exploited for profit.

To make this easier to understand, let's take this into another form of crime: car theft. In 2011, according to the National Insurance Crime Bureau (NICB), with the frequency of insurance claims the Cadillac Escalade was the top stolen car. As far as raw numbers go, the top stolen car was the 1994 Honda Accord. One car has a bluebook value of between $2000 and $3000 dollars, the other goes for over $50,000. The Cadillac Escalade thefts are a no-brainer. But the reason for the old Honda thefts? Typically they have fewer built-in anti-theft devices and they are more abundant. Last but not least, there's a huge underground market among street racers; they love the engines and parts. And as strange as it may seem, most of the other vehicles at the top of the raw numbers category are all older model "everyday people" vehicles like Toyotas, Fords, Dodge, etc—mostly from the 90s with none newer than 2004. Why? Because of many of the same reasons, plus the numbers are out there. There are millions of these vehicles still on the road, far more than the elite high brow vehicles like the Escalades.

The same dynamic applies to why cybercriminals have favored PCs over Macs—the sheer number of units out there, plus the vulnerabilities in most versions of Microsoft Windows are as renowned in the underground as Bill Gates himself. Up until the later 2000s the Mac had less than 10% market share—a proverbial Cadillac Escalade among a sea of Hondas and Fords. With the increase in popularity, that is changing.

Back in 2008, security researcher Adam J. O'Donnell with the firm Sourcefire, published a widely acclaimed report that predicted that the Mac would have to have at least reached 16% market share before it became a viable target for malware coders. That time has come much sooner than expected, mostly as the result of Apple being a victim of its own success.

When Apple introduced the iPod, it revolutionized the music industry as well as media distribution on a global level. The iPhone redefined smartphones and changed the world's expectations of even the cheapest cell phones. With the iPad, Apple managed to take a previously unsuccessful product type like the tablet computer and make it sexy to the world all over again. Beyond the obvious fame and fortune, what these products did was reintroduce the world to a reinvented Apple, Inc. They were no longer just another company who sold computers and smart electronics. Instead, their mission has become to sell products that are perceived to enhance the lifestyles of their owners.

Unlike other computer and device manufacturers who more or less don't give a damn what you do with their products, Apple specifically designed its products for people incorporate into their lives. They want their consumers hooked on using an index finger to do things like capture snapshots of their lives without carrying a bulky camera, pay all their bills without a checkbook, browse a music collection of anything from John Lee Hooker to Justin Bieber, watch Netflix on-demand, or read the latest bestselling ebook. They wanted to usher in that future that once only existed in STAR TREK: THE NEXT GENERATION and futurist documentaries—and they've done a great job of it. Unfortunately, this future also gave birth to an untapped frontier of opportunities for cybercriminals: the market segment of Mac users that was previously too small to be considered profitable. Although many computer security firms predicted that this would happen, the evidence of it coming to fruition cannot be denied. For example, according to Forbes magazine as of Q3 in 2012, the value of sales of iPhones is now greater than the value of the entirety of Microsoft's sales—and there doesn't appear to be any signs of that slowing down.

Over the past decade or so, many PC users began to switch over to Mac, many of which believing the myth that Mac computers are immune to viruses. Unfortunately, that was only about as accurate as saying that women are immune to prostate cancer. Microsoft Windows-based malware is written to exploit the Windows operating system, Mac-based malware is written to exploit Mac OS X. Since Microsoft Windows PCs held the largest market share for so many years, it only made sense for cybercriminals to focus their efforts on that platform. Had Apple risen to prominence in the late 80s and Microsoft fallen into obscurity during most of the 90s, most of the malware outbreaks experienced since the year 2000 probably would have been targeted at Mac users. Instead, the opposite has been true, and as of this writing there are millions of Mac OS X computers, iPads, and iPhones out there with no anti-virus software. For cybercriminals it's like discovering a state full of exclusive gated communities where all the citizens are financially well-off and no one bothered to install home security systems.

Here's the logic behind the trend: When it comes to Apple products, few need to question why Mac owners aren't too dissimilar to zombies in their loyalty. If they have a cell phone, more often than not it is an iPhone. If they have a portable media player it is probably some version of iPod. And if they have a tablet, it is probably an iPad. No offense to my Mac friends but they love their Apple products with extreme prejudice toward everything else, often to the point that they revere them as status symbols. Because so many recent Mac converts believe their computer is immune to viruses and malware, it's pretty common to find little or no anti-virus protections on their computer or any of their smart devices. Cybercriminals are well aware of all these factors. The platform that was once only toyed with by a few misguided virus coders has now been targeted by transnational organized crime rings as a guaranteed moneymaker.

iPhone owners, like many smartphone and cell phone owners, are wide open to Cramming—a scam where the phone owners get lured into calling a number or clicking on a link that gives a third-party company permission to bill their phone for "services" they didn't ask for. These charges can continue monthly until the owner catches the scam and files a complaint. Essentially it's a way of stealing money from them without even needing a credit card number. What makes it worse is that the primary phone carriers like AT&T, Verizon and Sprint make money off the crammers, too, hence the reason this type of scam has been around since the 90s.

Another huge example of this new era was the Flashfake outbreak of 2012. Also known as Flashback, this was a breed of malware for Mac OS X that first began to flourish in late 2011. By March of 2012 it had infected around 700,000 Macs worldwide—about half the size of the active duty U.S. military. All those machines were turned to zombies and assimilated into a Botnet that did everything from send spam, generate fake search engine results, and steal data.

Between the Mac, iPhone, iPod Touch, and iPad the next threat is at the operating system level. Since the iPhone, iPod Touch and iPad are all running iOS, they are truly sibling devices. Any kind of malicious app that can successfully infect one will probably have the ability to infect the others. The idea is that if the Mac can be infected, the other Apple devices can be exploited, too. And unlike with the PC environment where there are all kinds of virus/trojan kits available from underground sources, the cybercriminals that are targeting Apple products are doing so from scratch with real organized crime funding behind them. Since Apple doesn't license their hardware and operating system to anyone else, cybercriminals only have one fort to conquer as far as writing malware specifically to get around the safeguards. For the work invested, the potential payoffs are huge.

Baron Samedi says

"This one is pretty simple—if you own any kind of computer, tablet, or smartphone, it would be wise to invest in protecting it with some anti-virus software. Eventually you'll be glad you did."

Stealing from the Matrix

Among the living dead, if there is an extreme opposite of the zombie it would be the vampire. One has virtually no sense of self-awareness; the other now has a heightened sense of self-awareness. One wanders aimlessly till it happens upon a victim; the other stalks a victim like a sniper. While zombies are at their greatest threat when in numbers, a single vampire can be far more dangerous. Zombies feed, vampires prey.

Benny was the closest thing to a vampire that most of us might meet. He's one of many. Forget about journalistic integrity—this chapter was not written as a news piece. It is a glimpse into the life of an American cybercriminal, the personal side of those mysterious incidences where "some hacker out there" stole your credit card. For the sake of balancing liabilities and authenticity, it should be noted that details in this chapter have been purposely renamed, remixed or omitted.

Sunrise brought a peaceful mood over this row of brownstones, somewhere in Brooklyn's Crown Heights. The mild autumn morning would've been perfect for sitting on the stoop enjoying a latte and reading the news—if I wasn't scrambling to scrub huge blood stains off the steps.

Among crimson-splattered pieces of a broken rum bottle I found a piece of a tooth. Drip trails and footprints faded a little ways up the sidewalk. Whatever happened on the stoop was swift and brutal, but probably not fatal. My immediate worry was that the neighbors would soon be leaving on their way to work. And while it's generally true that most New Yorkers mind their own business, when it looks like a blood sport happened on the front stoop someone was bound to ask questions. Nervous questions. And there were no good answers.

I'd be lying if I claimed to be cleaning up this mess as a kind gesture. My motives were selfish. It was only by the mercy of God that the cops hadn't already busted the party several times over the course of the night. No cops so far—and the faster I got the stoop cleaned up, the better our chances it would stay that way. None of us could afford a police visit even though the blood would have been the least of our worries. The house was full of enough criminal sin to land us all in jail for years... and I was stuck in the city for at least another day.

My associate and I had arrived a few days earlier. He was a business consultant and plaintiff in court battle suing for compensatory damages. To help win his case he hired me as an expert witness. At the time I was between IT contracts. Any incoming checks were welcomed; accepting a paid 3-day trip to The City was a no-brainer.

On the train ride up from Virginia is when the trip first started to go sideways. My associate informed me that he had cancelled our hotel reservations. To save on expenses, he arranged for us to be picked up by an old college friend and stay with him somewhere in Brooklyn. Admittedly, reservations of my own began to surface. My associate and I were acquaintances at best. I didn't feel like I knew him well enough to spend the weekend with him and his friends. I couldn't shake the nagging feeling that we'd be better off going to that hotel over in Jersey. Instead, I withheld my comments. Again, I was between IT contracts—I needed the money.

After pulling into Penn Station we were greeted by his friend, Benny. Dressed like a car salesman that had just left the lot, he also looked (and smelled) as if he stopped by a Happy Hour before coming to get us. All kinds of warnings flashed through my head. If I could have afforded it I would have gracefully declined the invitation and gone on to the hotel by myself. My associate was already pumped up, raving about Benny's famous margaritas. He had totally written off any hotel stay from his plans. Benny seemed friendly and sober enough to drive so I let go of the hotel idea, too, figuring a bit of partying over the weekend could be fun.

At the house, a haze of grilled beef, cigarette smoke and corner store incense hit us as we walked in the front door. The place was full of people milling around with either a burger or drink in hand, mostly guys still dressed in their work clothes. The few women stuck close to their men. Random music coursed through this ultimate bachelor pad; one minute the vibe was Alice in Chains or Brand New Heavies, the next it was Shakira or 50 cent. A game of doubles on the pool table was the center of attention in one room and a crowded casino-style Blackjack table in another. No matter where I looked there was a flatscreen television on a mantel, each on a different channel that no one was paying attention to. Before I had a chance to put my luggage away someone had put a beer in my hand.

Sometime after midnight the party had dwindled to the roommates and a few straglers that were in no condition to drive. While sitting around drunk and swapping wild stories from our youths, I shared a tale from my college days. Not sure which tale but I think it involved lockpicking, tapping into a phone line, and using backdoor passwords to hack into some old mainframe. Whatever the tale, it struck the right chord with this group. As the conversation progressed it was obvious they knew something about hacker scene yet most of the technical lingo didn't seem to register. Something I said convinced them that I was "in the know". That's when one of the roommates started bragging about their credit card exploits. Since it was too late to silence his roommate, Benny humbly co-signed. He was clearly the expert in this group.

Having a working knowledge of Identity Theft is almost a natural part of life for anyone that deals with computer hacking, whether they are ethical hackers (IT security professionals), Hackivists or cybercriminals. As a long time reformed hacker, some aspects of Information Security had become more important to me than others. I mentioned that I was interested in learning what I could about the latest techniques in this dark art… and as a big favor to my associate, Benny agreed to share.

Thanks to my hangover and a lack of sleep, the next morning started without mercy. Benny had to run some errands and made sure the whole house knew it. As he walked by I noticed hints of white powder on his inner nostril; his eyes were wide and engaged like an athlete at the top of his game. Just as I started to think about that hotel again he turned around and invited my associate and me to ride along with him. Somehow I could tell our cybercrime conversation was either going to continue on the road or not at all. Not that I make a habit of judging people, but old misadventures that put me around people and cocaine had taught me how to spot a cokehead—and to be wary of their unpredictability.

Some aspects of Benny's personality reminded me of a few hacker friends I grew up with. In other ways he didn't fit the bill at all. From my experiences, I learned that criminals in the computer underground generally fall into one of four main classifications:

Criminals of Opportunity: Most low-to-mid level cybercrimes are committed by people who fit into this category. You know these people because they are among your friends, relatives, neighbors and co-workers. At best, they're day-trippers that are talented with technology to some degree but crime is neither their passion nor primary source of income. On average, they're computer savvy enough to read email, use search engines like Google, and can follow instructions to install programs or play games. People who download and trade pirated media (e.g. - software, music, movies/TV, porn, ebooks, images, etc.) fall into this category—including those who commit copyright infringement by grabbing images from websites for use in their own materials. Cyberbullies and Script Kiddies also fall into this category because they use the opportunities of online anonymity to attack their targets. Opportunity can briefly turn almost anyone into a criminal because of temptation and the belief that they can take advantage of an easy situation without getting in trouble. Their perpetrators either see these crimes as minor infractions (such as driving a few miles over the speed limit) or don't consider them criminal acts at all.

Pathological Criminals: These accomplished practitioners are often gifted with their illicit specialty but socially and/or mentally unstable. Their *joie de vivre* is rooted in mayhem and money is rarely the primary motivator. Although there will always be a method to what they do, there may not be a discernable reason beyond the thrill or some extremist beliefs. Cyber-vandals and pre-2003 virus creators typically fit into this category. More often than not, subconsciously these people want the world to know they were responsible for what they've done. This mentality will cause them to keep doing what they do, raising the ante each time until they can't help but eventually get themselves caught—and prosecution isn't necessarily a deterrent for repeat offenses. Like any typical zombie on the prowl, they are wired to do what they do and there is no known cure. A quote by Alfred Pennyworth (from THE DARK KNIGHT) sums them up best: "Some men just want to watch the world burn."

Cybercriminals: Regardless of nationality, these people cover the gamut of technical prowess and earn their money through cyberspace in the global underground economy. Their demeanors range from the white-collar professional to hardcore predators. From malicious hackers to identity brokers, and even sales reps, it's not uncommon for these people to lead double lives—one in the mainstream brick-n-mortar world and the other in cyberspace. Their cybercrimes tend to be far reaching, extremely lucrative, and capable of causing life-changing damage to their victims.

Middle Men: intermediaries between the cybercriminals and the old school organized crime rings such as the Italian Mafia, the Russian Mafia, and the Yakuza. Questionable bankers and money launderers also fit into this category. Like trafficking guns and drugs, middle men allow the mobsters to separate themselves from the crimes.

Regardless of where one fits in, these people have parameters. They operate within clearly defined limits of what they will and won't do, regardless of their moral or psychological inclinations. Even dealing with the most disloyal miscreants tends to be pretty straight forward. Addicts, however, are different. They can fit into any classification but their motivations are skewed and amplified. When you deal with them you're dealing with someone whose mind is a Cerberus, a multi-headed beast—the person and his addictions—and you can't ever be sure which mentality is in control during any given situation. Where smart criminals know to lay low after a big score or a close call with the law, addicts are always living the life of a zombie between victims. And as their addictions grow, their drive to commit crimes that bring in more money grows, too. Unlike most criminals that can choose to stop or walk away from the game, retirement is rarely a voluntary act for addicts. Few legitimate sources of income can scale to support their needs. Being in business with them long-term is like driving a car to work every day and not knowing there's a bomb under the hood. Anyone that starts their morning out with a snort of cocaine is, more or less, either an addict or well on the way to becoming one. I still had to figure out how this applied to Benny.

Few cybercriminals ever set out to turn crime into a career. It always starts with a chance occurrence, sometimes as simple as a left instead of a right. Benny was no different. In a previous life he had a promising job with a shipping company with plans to marry his long-time lady love. Day after day he caught the subway into Manhattan and walked to his office at the World Trade Center—until the attacks of September 11th changed everything. He survived. But when Building 5 was demolished by falling debris his career went with it.

"After that I couldn't get a job selling popsicles," he recalled as he changed lanes without checking the rear-view mirror. "[My] unemployment ran out, then my savings. My girlfriend and I argued like crazy about money until she ran off with her supervisor. I was almost homeless when my dude put me onto selling E [Ecstasy]."

A truck horn went ignored; someone cursed somewhere. As we approached the Brooklyn Bridge his story seemed to drift as fast and aimlessly as his driving: All-night grinds of pushing pills to spoiled young socialites and clubheads at spots throughout the boroughs. "I was making good money until this girl nearly OD'ed. Her brother was one of those damn Straight Edge freaks. He kicked in my door, beat the s**t out of me and flushed all my s**t. In a way, that's how I got my start—on the hook with Little Odessa, owing for the lost package plus 15 large. Let anyone else tell it and I should be dead. Instead, they set me up earning for their crew in Belgorod."

Little Odessa wasn't a person. It's slang for Brooklyn's Brighton Beach, particularly any operator or crew connected with the Bratva; the Russian Mafia. The fall of the former Soviet Union has done for cybercrime and the criminal underworld what Steve Jobs and Apple did for reshaping the cell phone industry. They pioneered cybercriminal fraud in ways that practically redefined it as an industry.

If Identity Theft were a legal industry, Benny would be a regional wholesale supplier and owner of a holding company with diverse revenue streams. He represents a growing number of low-tech criminals engaged in Identity Theft and Fraud that the media commonly associates with Malicious Hackers—an ominous high tech reputation that Benny hadn't earned. He has no discernable talents in programming, hacking or network security whatsoever. The closest he came to being a hardcore computer nerd was male pattern baldness, a pair of horn-rimmed glasses, and being able to quote Star Trek and Monty Python. Although he never divulged exactly how much he earned, by virtue of his driving a Lexus SUV in one of the most expensive cities in the U.S., I knew it had to be over 6-figures.

Without warning my associate interrupted Benny, declaring that there had been another change in plans. "I've gotta meet someone uptown," he said, holding back a grin as he thumb-pecked something into his phone.

Benny leered into the rear-view mirror. "What's her name? And does she have any friends?"

The question went unanswered. At the stop light my associate climbed out of the SUV. "I'll catch up to you guys later," he said as he put on his tweed jacket, walking briskly toward an underground subway station. His tone was unmistakable—definitely on his way to a booty call—and I figured we probably weren't going to see him for the rest of the weekend. I couldn't help but wonder if the money was going to be worth being left to fend for myself with a bunch of strangers.

Somewhere off of Barrow we turned into an alley, slowing to a halt beside a dumpster. An Asian woman walked out with two bags in hand; one she tossed in the dumpster, the other she handed to Benny. He removed a palm-sized device and checked it, handed her a thick envelope and passed the bag to me as we drove off—it was full of cold dinner rolls. Without a word, the entire transaction took less than a minute.

That device (called a skimmer) is a pocket-sized credit card reader. Anyone with a skimmer can secretly capture the cardholder information for up to 3000 credit and debit cards. Benny targeted high-brow hotels, restaurants, bars, and country clubs around Manhattan—the kinds of establishments where cases of aged Chateau La Lagune and Dalmore Scotch are as common as Jack Daniels at TGIFriday's. Using many of his old club contacts he recruited bartenders and servers in each place. Each recruit (called a skim) was loaned a skimmer and taught how to use it. He preferred the skim to be a foreigner with average physical attributes and an expired work visa, someone dedicated to earning money while staying undetected. Fear of deportation keeps them away from the authorities. "You'd swear they were old school Mafia the way they keep quiet," he mused. "I keep a dozen skimmers in rotation. That spot we just left? It'll be next spring before I use her again."

"Let's say you're in town on business," he continued as we inched along in midday traffic. "You treat a client out to lunch, and when it's time to pay the bill you hand over your American Express. Server walks off with your card, sneaks a swipe through the skimmer to capture all the data on the magnetic strip, and then swipes the card at the cash register to pay the bill. You get your card back with the receipt, sign it, and then you and your client leave, never giving a second thought to that lunch. The skim does this for about a month until there are a few hundred cards collected in the skimmer. She calls and we meet. I get the skimmer back, check the count, and if it looks right they get the cheese."

We parked and set out on foot. Aside from the picture-perfect condos, seeing the $300 dollar cashmere scarfs and $1200 dollar purses in the boutique windows let me know we were in the heart of the West Village. Our morning run took a detour into a French bistro. Escorted through its shabby chic interior, we were seated out in their courtyard dining area. A few of the Cardigan-clad regulars glanced at me as if I had stepped out of a homeless shelter.

"These are premium cards," Benny assured me. "I pay each skim up to $10 per card for a capture of about 300 cards. Adding my markup, I can crank that up to $25 per card, selling each dump to a broker for up to $7500. They do their thing and sell that dump retail. If I collect all my skimmers I can make upwards of $60k in an afternoon—way more than I ever did selling X. No more E-tards and techno."

Among identity thieves, a dump is a compiled database of stolen information, usually credit cards. Each entry contains the owner's name, card number, CVV code, and etc. It wasn't until a few weeks after the New York trip that I got a better idea of the quality of the dumps that Benny sold. Most regular card numbers sold on the underground Deep Web forums went for cheap, less than $5 dollars a pop. He charged top dollar because he knew his cards *came with sky-high credit limits. His skims would spend weeks scoping out regulars for potential targets—business moguls, celebrities and trust fund babies—before finally skimming their card to steal their information. As far as criminal capers go, their approach was nearly perfect, marvelous in its streamlined purity.*

While Benny downloaded data from the skimmers into his laptop, I booted up my own laptop and began running some wireless network snooping software. The local digital terrain was constellation of wide open Wi-Fi spots and unprotected wireless routers all around us. It was a free oasis of relatively unrestricted Internet—a cybercriminal's dream buffet—and a law enforcement nightmare.

After compiling the database, the next step Benny mentioned was heading off to the brokers. Contrary to his turn of phrase, 'heading off to the brokers' was more of a process: visiting any one of countless online marketplaces open to selling and trading in this kind of data. They vary by language, size, ease of access, and specialty. Some are surface web sites, ranging from shady fly-by-night message forums to mega sites like China's infamous Baidu Tieba or Taobao Mall, a sort of Chinese-language hybrid of Amazon.com and eBay. Others are forums that exist somewhere in the Deep Web, only reachable through special gateway networks like Tor. And scattered throughout this criminal cosmos there were also chat networks where people communicate in real-time. In this case, Benny was doing a deal with someone on IRC.

Short for Internet Relay Chat, IRC is a chat system of hundreds of chat networks, each hosting thousands of channels (public, private and hidden chatrooms). If you can imagine a subject, someone has probably created a channel for it or you can create your own. IRC is commonly used because it is a vast, largely unregulated communication space that is great for swapping information, especially in secret. Hidden IRC channels can be changed and moved between networks with ease, making them much harder to find and generally safer for broker deals than websites. Any cybercriminal using IRC through public Wi-Fi spots will be about as difficult to track down as finding a missing tourist by first name in Southern California.

Among solo cybercriminals it's not uncommon for deals to happen between people that have never met in person, only recognizing each other by aliases, code words, specialty areas and third party payment sources. Like the drug game, the deals tend to start small and build with trust. All the players involved have accounts set up with any number of online escrow services along with other forms of decentralized electronic currency (especially Bitcoin) that can be converted into cash in their native countries. It's almost always in their best interest to do good business because the more money they make, the more money you make. Benny regularly traded and sold dumps with a broker in Bacoor, a city just south of Manila in the Philippines. Within the first few months of dealing with each other they had made so much money they actually exchanged first names. For my sake Benny asked the broker about where that batch of dumps would be sold. The reply was as unsettling as it was simple, "Today? Dàniao 5 [a Chinese forum, accessed through QQ]."

Identity Theft happens in three stages: Acquisition, Use, and Discovery. Different cybercriminals do different things with the dumps they acquire. If the average Identity Theft victim is lucky, all they'll have to worry about is a few stray charges on a credit card. Other times the crimes haunt the victim for years.

The best way to understand how far reaching Identity Theft can be is to continue following the path of a stolen identity. Unfortunately, I was unable to secure (or afford) an interview with an active broker. In its place I've reconstructed the rest of the process...

Let's say you're a fairly sophisticated cybercriminal that has just purchased the stolen identity database that Benny just sold to his broker. The first thing you did was go through the dump to pick which names to check out. While it's possible to run these names through Equifax, Experian and TransUnion credit reporting bureaus, some websites that deal in dumps will do the legwork for you. One of the names, Jane Doe, turns out to be a great find: a single, 34-year old woman, working for a mortgage company, lives in Alexandria, Virginia, and has an impressive FICO score of 804 (out of a possible 850). Because of her ethnically-generic name, line of work, age, and credit score, she's almost perfect.

Jane's Social Security Number starts with 231, a number within a range of codes that means it was issued in the state of Virginia. Based on the fact that she lives in Alexandria and a Zabasearch turns up two more Virginia addresses, you deduce that she was probably born in Virginia, too. Contact with the state's Division of Vital Records proves to be fruitful. Posing as Jane's half-sibling, you pay a few dollars and breeze through the process of obtaining a certified copy of Jane's birth certificate from an overworked, underpaid clerk.

A big part of using a stolen identity revolves around convincing yourself of one main principle: you are who you say you are. Once armed with Jane's credit profile, SSN, home address and birth certificate you are as much Jane Doe as Jane is, at least to anyone online that doesn't know her. And if you happen to be female (or at least a damn good female impersonator), you can go to most places as Jane Doe. You've got everything you need to rapidly breed a clone of Jane's identity in much the same way that we all do in our formative years: A driver's license, SSN card, and other forms of legit ID like a library card, membership cards, bank accounts / ATM cards, department store credit cards, business licenses, and on up to a passport, the ultimate form of legal identification. It's a jackpot of limitless possibilities for you... and Jane has no idea that her nightmares are just about to begin.

The first thing to consider is Jane's bank and credit accounts—they are now yours. The downside is that fraud investigators are on top of it. Draining her accounts will have to happen in one of two ways:

► *Steal as much as possible as fast as you can. While this is the best way to get most of her money, the chances of the accounts suddenly being flagged for investigation also increases. This also increases the chance of the accounts being suspended, too.*

► *Gradually bleed the accounts. The idea is to withdraw money so slowly and in such minimal amounts that neither the person nor the bank notices the abnormal expenses on the report. This method takes much longer but it increases the likelihood of not getting caught.*

In any case, the minute the compromised accounts are discovered all the work put into breeding her cloned identity will be shot. By the end of the day Jane will be busy notifying creditors, filing reports with law enforcement, and cursing your existence to anyone that will listen.

Next consideration is opening up new lines of credit in Jane's name. This could be tricky. If her debt-to-income ratio is already too high, any attempts you make to open new credit lines will get declined—and possibly alert account managers that something is wrong. In the pursuit of getting money from a cloned identity, you have to determine whether or not you'll get more from draining the existing accounts (including tax returns) or establishing new lines of credit THEN maxing out all of the credit limits.

The real beauty of Jane's identity is that she has taken care of her name. With the exception of a few parking tickets, her criminal record is spotless. No judgments or liens. Her name was as well-groomed as a Bonzai tree. You already know from experience that possessing her identity, or any identities like hers, has a value far beyond their credit limits. There is a fortune to be made selling identities to people who need to hide out for several years, just long enough for the statute of limitations to expire for most crimes. This doesn't include dealing with serial killers, rapists and other psychopaths. Aside from the fact that they don't tend to have as much money as other career criminals, these monsters can't help themselves. Their sick ways will surface again and again until they die or get caught. The last thing you need is to get busted for aiding and abetting their deeds.

Beyond hiding out, there are those who would rather leave this country to escape their criminal, civil, or financial problems. Some just want a way to disappear and live under the radar without Uncle Sam knowing they are gone. In 2010, U.S. Marshals arrested more than 36,000 federal fugitives and over 81,900 state and local fugitives. Of all those people, who wouldn't pay you top dollar for your services? Since law enforcement agencies always check airports when anyone goes on the run, using Jane's identity to straw purchase pre-owned vehicles for fugitives would be a cash cow along with providing them with enough of an identity to travel under. A road trip into Tijuana is a great way to kick off a new life.

Jane's identity also has unlimited possibilities in the commission of other crimes. At the top of the list is the ability to rent an untraceable vehicle, take a road trip to other states and make straw purchases of guns, booze, and regulated chemicals that will be resold on the black market. Beyond shopping sprees, these crimes can get more elaborate and sinister, such as kidnapping, armed robbery, drug trafficking, terrorist attacks, and more. Even the vehicle itself can either be sold to a chop-shop or ditched as part of evading the law. By the time the Feds contact the real Jane Doe she'll be connected to more felonies than John Dillinger... all of which will dead end with her name, months after most of the evidence trails have gone cold.

Stolen identities, especially one like Jane Doe, would be the perfect cover for all kinds of high-end white-collar crime: money laundering, non-profit donation scams, medical scams, real estate scams, corporate espionage, political bribery, and investment fraud. When large sums of money are involved, some people (before they become victims) will do some basic research, often little more than a simple $50 dollar criminal background check—most of which are only as accurate as how current their state is technology-wise. These types of criminals often get caught only after agencies like the Federal Trade Commission, FBI, or Secret Service get involved and the paper trails lead right back to their own identities. Imagine the surprise everyone has when the money is gone, the secrets exposed, and they discover they've been doing business with a mirage... someone they've never met. Had many white collar felons such as Martin Frankel and Bernie Madoff made use of clones of stolen identities in their scams, the authorities would probably still be trying to catch them today.

The core of each of our worlds is based mostly on records stored in a handful of reporting bureau computers. It doesn't take much to duplicate that information. And as a cybercriminal, one of the great advantages you have is that the people who maintain those records are not legally responsible for the accuracy of what they type in. Mistakes happen all the time. Due to this lack of checks and balances with credit reporting, some forms of identity theft can go on for years without being discovered. And as long as you exercise a little discretion with your endeavors, you'll probably never get caught unless you're really stupid, get ratted out by someone, or you royally screw up. Until the system changes, the future is bright for buying and selling stolen identities on the black market. Welcome to full access to Jane Doe's life—her world is yours.

By my estimates, Benny had to be earning kingpin-style money. Figure a conservative limit of $300 dollars on each credit card, 300 cards on a skimmer can easily yield at least $90,000 dollars of credit and inventory. A dozen skims can take down a little over $1 million dollars.

Back at the house we found Benny's roommates huddled around one of the computers, browsing Craigslist posts with snapshots of women in lingerie and freaky poses. With the talk of having a party later that night they were hyped up like college freshmen. My thoughts drifted back to my estimates. I knew the math was solid but something still didn't sit right. Who makes that kind of money yet still needs roommates?

Benny walked out of the kitchen with a couple of cans of corned beef hash. A twist of a trick lid revealed they were secret containers full of credit cards. MasterCard, VISA, American Express, Discover, and even Paypal. "All these cards are blanks!" I said, marveling at the quality and detail. Fake scratches lined some of the cards to mimic the stress of heavy use. The logos and embossed text were a flawless match. Even the holograms on some of the VISA cards were good enough to fool the typical cashier. "Where'd you get these?"

"I got 'em from Shinjen. PVC with the magnetic strip on the back, some with the [RFID] chip inside. Send them the artwork and they'll screen [print] it right on the card, glossy or matte, add barcodes—you name it."

After returning home I spent a week trying to find Shinjen, figuring it was either a person or some crime ring on the come up. It turned out to be neither. "Shenzhen",

on the other hand, is a huge port city in southern China. Benny and his cohorts used the name as a reference for both the city itself and slang for any source in Southeast Asia that widely disregards U.S. intellectual property laws, willing to sell and ship just about anything to anyone. If you've ever purchased a pair of Lebron X Nikes or a Burberry purse at rock bottom prices from a flea market, or got a bargain on a TAG Heuer watch from some guy in the mall parking lot, there's a good chance at least one of those products was shipped overseas from Shenzhen.

The Shopping Spree:

When most people discover they've been the victim of Identity Theft, the news comes in the form of a call from their bank or a grossly violated credit card statement. Unlike the Orwellian horrors of the Jane Doe scenario, most credit card theft ends up being part of something much simpler: The Shopping Spree.

Credit card fraud is nothing new. As soon as businesses started swiping plastic cards back in the late 1950s, someone else started trying to figure out how to steal the card numbers and buy things. It was called "carding" by the time the 1980s-era computer underground had emerged. Valid numbers often came from discarded credit card carbons retrieved from garbage dumpsters. Programs appeared in the underground that could generate valid numbers on the fly. Most carders back then didn't have access to credit card blanks nor the means to create credit card duplicates using the stolen info. Due to the lack of a physical card, most carding fraud had to be done over the phone, usually buying products through mail order and having them delivered to unoccupied houses. The carder would often leave a note instructing the delivery driver where to put the package (e.g. – behind a bush, around back, etc.). If all went according to plan the driver would take the note in lieu of an acceptance signature and leave the package in the requested spot. Later the carder would come retrieve the package, only to be long gone by the time the cardholder contacts the credit card company about the unwanted item(s) on their bill. Since some merchants used better verification methods than others, theft by carding was a hit-or-miss affair. Carding was also used to buy intangible things like long distance calling card numbers to trade or steal access to online services like CompuServe or America Online (the closest things to public Internet access at the time).

By the 21st century, the quirky days of carding had given way to interna-tional intrigue—digital crime waves so far-reaching and mind-boggling they seem like the dystopian imaginings of a Philip K. Dick novel. Internet globalization had cross-pollinated credit card fraud with identity theft, causing all of it to mushroom into a multi-billion dollar industry. Scores of other products, technologies and services have risen up to support (and combat) this type of cybercrime.

To prepare for a shopping spree the first step was to take the credit card info of several stolen identities and imprint them on matching cards. Benny sat down at his desk, plugged a piece of equipment into his Dell laptop and began to thumb through his selection of PVC card blanks. Between the magnetic card reader writer encoder, embosser and tipper, the steps were simple enough for any 3rd grader to follow. In about the time it would take to cook a frozen pizza he cranked out several credit cards, all practically identical in quality to the originals. He offered me a couple of Platinum American Expresses with the ease of a salesman giving away a business card. Resisting the inner buzz of temptation I handed them back.

Benny never used any card numbers stolen by his skims. It wouldn't take much for any of the recruits to start double-dealing, plus he didn't want to risk anything being traced back to his sources. The cards he used were dumps from a high quality batch put together by the broker, insuring that the numbers haven't been abused. Even if he didn't take such precautions this type of fraud was so rampant that he had a better chance of getting caught for speeding.

ZOMBIE TRIVIA

Q: Which Post-Apocalyptic scenario does not belong in this group: DAY OF THE DEAD, RETURN OF THE DEAD, 28 DAYS LATER, or THE HORDE?

(answer on page 384)

Transportation was the next consideration. To get the most out of the endeavor, Benny swore by using a van, preferably a cargo van like the Ford Econoline. Anything like a U-Haul truck uses too much gas and it draws attention; people instinctively associate U-Haul with the mixed emotions and drudgery of moving. People see white or blue cargo vans so often that they're practically invisible in most environments. Passenger vans and mini-vans were to be avoided due to their large side windows. During a routine traffic stop, boxes in a dark cargo area are just shadowy shapes to a police officer. Side windows let in ambient light; the instant that cop glances in the back to see stacks of shiny unopened boxes with logos like iPad, Xbox, or Samsung, the situation can go to Hell real quick. This is why he has business casual Polo™ shirts and several sets of car door magnet signs, each with the name and address of a different independent courier service.

The next was step was the most important: testing the cards. Some people will get cards in hand and immediately go attempt to make big ticket purchases. A huge mistake, Benny claims. Upon walking into a department store, by the time they go through the aisles to pick out those Bose speakers, COACH handbag or that or 65" Sony, if they go to use the card and it has been flagged, they're done. They've been made—recorded on at least a dozen different cameras—and probably less than a minute away from being detained by store detectives until the police arrive. This is why most savvy thieves test their cards by making a few small purchases at places like gas stations, convenience stores or bodegas. The charges don't stand out as much, security is more relaxed, and if the card is declined it doesn't look as suspicious.

Benny never tested his cards anywhere within an hour of home. He never spent more than $50 dollars during a test so if the card didn't work he just paid in cash and left. For every card that worked he knew it was going to be anywhere from 4 to 48 hours before the charges would be applied to the cardholder's account. "A shopping spree shouldn't last more than 18 hours from start to finish", he said as he plotted out his route. "I start out at the farthest store and work my way back in. Sometimes I go as far south as Virginia and as far west as Ohio."

The distant 17-year old in me was mildly excited at the idea of being invited on the spree. During my rogue hacker days I would have been the first one in the van, all-in to win. Back then my crew and I had dabbled in more than a few carding stunts. The risks were like juggling eggs while jogging home every morning to make breakfast—a fun and thrilling challenge until you realize the risks were rarely worth the reward. At that moment, the middle-aged geek in me didn't know if I still I had the stones to take such a trip. As a man with a small business and well-maintained beer gut, the last thing I needed was to be on a spree with their crew when they got busted.

The spree never happened... and no explanation was given. Even though his roommates were rumbling about another party later that night, I suspect the real reason had to do with my presence. If I were him, I wouldn't have taken me along either. The only thing more dangerous than introducing a guy to a criminal enterprise is to turn him into a witness.

The doorbell interrupted our conversation. Benny went to the foyer and all I could make out was that he was dealing with an irate woman. After a few minutes he left with her to go take care of the problem. The other guys had already gone somewhere. Alone in a house that hadn't been quiet since we arrived, I took a nap.

Some hours later I woke up to a dark room and thunderous beat of loud Latin House music. I wandered out of the room to find the air thick with booze and smoke, the house packed with people in full party mode again. Most of the women looked like call girls on the stroll—literally. They were the women that the roommates were raving about earlier that day, escorts from the Craigslist adult classifieds.

Cheers soared as a busty woman wearing a thong and clear-heeled stilettos captivated a packed room. Booze and bad lighting smoothed out the stretch-marked maturity of her hips as she did a hula-hoop dance on the pool table. On the wall behind her was a flashing lightshow—a glowing television with its screen fractured beyond repair. The party rallied on as if that smashed Samsung was some hip cat psychedelic prop. Figuring that Benny or one of the roommates needed to know, I started looking around for them.

Down a dark set of stairs in the basement is where I found Benny, talking with two guys amidst a clutter of boxes and forgotten furniture. Dimly lit and dusty, it was an oddly comfortable refuge from the madness upstairs. At first I thought I walked in on a private discussion but they didn't seem to mind my presence. One of the guys slipped something into Benny's palm with a handshake. When he offered them a drink for the road they declined, picked up a couple of shopping bags and left.

Telling any party host about damaged furniture is touchy, so I offered to take that drink with him. When I mentioned the TV he got upset yet still remained much calmer than I expected. "No sweat man," he sighed. "I just hate people breakin up my s**t. It's not that serious."

Not that serious? Regardless of how he paid for it, that Samsung was still worth over thousand dollars. With a faded grin he shook my hand and patted me on the back, drunk and appreciating my attempt to look out for his interests. He moved a few boxes of old porn video tapes and then pulled back a musty tarp, exposing a dark space beyond a false wall partition. The yank of a light switch string revealed more of the basement—practically another room—with boxes stacked almost to the ceiling, all shiny and brand new. Video game consoles, Blu-ray players and discs of all kinds. Car stereos. Assorted digital cameras. Top of the line earbuds and headphones. iPods, iPads and various tablets. Laptops and notebooks. Cigarettes and cigars. Cases of Cognac. Watches and jewelry. Sports apparel. And enough pairs of sneakers to outfit an entire NBA basketball team. He slid out another Samsung TV to replace the smashed one; there were several more in waiting. Suddenly it made sense why the Shopping Spree didn't happen—they were already sitting on enough stolen merchandise to get half of Brooklyn locked up. He chuckled then answered my question before I could ask: "It'll all be gone before Wednesday."

Every item in this carefully selected inventory was in demand, easy to stash, and next to impossible to trace. And he wasn't like some flunky in the movies that only sold this stuff out of the trunk of a car. Most of it was earmarked to be sold into a loosely-knit distribution channel that supplied various legitimate online vendors, corner bodegas and flea markets around the city. Some vendors sold these products at a discount, using them as loss leaders that were irresistible to customers. As the conversation progressed, a bottle of Jameson whiskey appeared and seemed to start filling our glasses every time they got a little low. Listening to him break down how this supply chain worked brought on flashbacks and old temptations. For me, the addiction to the rush of pulling off such capers never went away; it merely became part of my penance to protect the networks of my business clients.

Booze makes fast friends. The whiskey and mutual familiarity with cybercrime made it seem like Benny and I were fraternity brothers, alumni that graduated from the same academic program in different decades. Without thinking I let it slip that I was thinking about writing a book about cybercrime. Much to my surprise he loved the notion. He began lecturing as if he figured we were co-writing a how-to guide. As he bragged about supplying Macbook Air notebooks to a local radio station as promotional giveaways for a charity fundraiser, someone upstairs called his name.

A couple of attractive young women emerged from the dark stairway. At least one had the vibe of a masculine lesbian; disdain for the debauchery upstairs was still lukewarm in their eyes. Dressed in the height of bohemian fashion, everything about them screamed East Village millennials, definitely more comfortable at a wine-n-cheese gallery opening or walking on the wide side by taking in a slam at the Nuyorican Poets Café. Benny offered them food and drinks but they declined, stumbling over their words while mentioning that a car was waiting for them outside. It was obvious they had no intention of staying but had worked out that excuse just to keep things pleasant. Happily dismissive of their airs, he pulled a gangster knot out of his pocket and peeled off several $100 dollar bills for each of them. In return he was handed a portable external hard drive. And after giving him half-hearted hugs of appreciation they disappeared back up the steps. They didn't look my way or say hello.

"They seemed friendly enough," I mumbled. "What's up with them?"
"Natalie and Ashley," Benny shrugged as he plugged the portable hard drive into a laptop. Apparently their aloof attitude was nothing new. "They're my beautiful selfie sirens. Just like those chicks on the rocks, if

you ever see them on Facebook you better sail your boat in the opposite direction—and don't look back."

"Why? What are they?"

"Bait."

Since the 90s, American companies had become a huge target for cybercriminals abroad placing orders with stolen card numbers. Unwary domestic retailers would process payment for an overseas order, send the products, and eventually fraud investigators would get involved. If the company was negligent in verifying the identity of the cardholder it would be held responsible for refunding that money back to the cardholder. Since the cost tracking down and prosecuting the overseas scammer often cost far more than the value of the merchandise, the company got screwed from both sides. This is a predominant reason why most retailers stopped shipping outside the U.S. altogether. Along with that, the old "empty house mail drop" tactic had been rendered obsolete in many areas. Factors such as rising cybercrime, advancements in anti-fraud measures, Internet evolution and social media created the perfect storm that gave rise to the Parcel Mule.

A Parcel Mule is a low-level variation of a Money Mule, which is a high-tech reinvention of someone tricked into participating in a Confidence Scam. It is comprised mostly of three primary concepts:

1. **The Drug Mule,** someone who gets paid to smuggle drugs out of one country and into another.
2. **The Prison Inmate Pen Pal,** where a convict writes letters to any number of women (or men) with the intention of eventually winning their love, sympathies and support to get money, packages and other goodies.
3. **Catfishing,** the practice of establishing and maintaining a relationship using a completely fabricated online persona.

The Money Mule is variation of a money launderer where a criminal sends illegal funds to the mule's bank account and then the mule transfers those funds to another bank, usually in another country. The Parcel Mule receives products that were purchased with stolen credit cards and then ship the merchandise somewhere else—almost always another country. Herein, the participants will be referred to as "Money Mules" or "mules".

The mules are unaware that they are being used as middlemen for illegal activities. Whether they are transferring funds or reshipping stolen goods to a foreign destination, they are almost always convinced these ventures are legitimate and their participation is for a good cause. Sophisticated operations have been known to use several mules strung along to make it more difficult for investigators to track down whoever is at the top of the supply chain.

"The Nigerians [scammers] mastered the methods but there's more money in dealing with the Russians," Benny said. He prided himself on having blended the functions of a Money Mule and Parcel Mule using the methods from both countries. Some schools of thought advocate seeking out mules in job classified ads; he began his hunt on dating websites, seeking out men with certain personality traits. "Grooming good mules takes work. It takes the diligence of a college basketball recruiter, a flair for sweet talking erotic writing. Over time you hypnotize the mules. You get them to convince themselves that they're in love with her. And you want them so deep that they'll do anything to get to her."

When Benny first broached the subject of money mules I had never heard of them. As he described the scheme I thought this was more like a half-baked idea he was still working out, maybe based on some type of scam that had already seen its heyday. It seemed like something that would've worked back in the early to mid-90s. Back then, for every cyber romance that blossomed into something real there were easily a dozen or more that went terribly wrong. Some lonely heart traveled to meet a long-time long-distance love interest for the first time and discovered that s/he was completely different than originally portrayed. Horror stories were so rampant they gave online dating a stigma that still lingers to this day. And in this age of social media, smartphones, Skype and high speed Internet I couldn't imagine anyone falling for those old tricks. I was wrong.

Enter the age of Catfishing—and both of Benny's bohemian girls. Natalie provided the fresh-faced beauty of Katiya, a 23-year old Russian aspiring model and student who has been searching for her American Prince Charming while working to save up enough money to move to New York City and pursue her studies at NYU. Ashley lent her brawny-n-tawny good looks to Asja, a 25-year old waitress living in Hungary after escaping war-torn Bosnia, struggling to save up enough money to get herself and her elderly grandmother back to America. Both women had taken countless photos of themselves (selfies) over a period of a couple of months and sold them to Benny. These selfies captured a range of moods and occasions, various stages of dress and undress, and even their proverbial bad hair days. The first few weeks of photos were upbeat and full of social events and partying with friends around Manhattan. The post-deportation selfies were more somber, usually dimly-lit snapshots taken with a laptop's webcam while sitting in bed or on a couch. Photos were categorized into folders based on time of day; if a selfie was sent to a mule around 5pm EST it would be picked from the late night folder to match the six hour time difference of Eastern Europe.

Attention to detail didn't stop with the selfies. Taking the Prison Pen Pal game to new heights, Benny and his crew had created incredibly detailed personas for Katiya and Asja based on female friends, acquaintances and characters from romantic comedies. These cheat sheets and documents contained all kinds of background stats, physical attributes, personality traits, and meaningful life milestone dates (such as birthdays, anniversaries, places lived and etc.). Witty comebacks, slang, teenage crushes and any other life story highlights—anything that can be cut-n-pasted into emails and chat windows. Every email and cybersex chat transcript was saved. All of this information is stored on a single USB flash drive, enabling an operator to manipulate the mules from virtually any computer with a live network connection.

Any attempt by a mule to engage in video chat almost always ends up failing. This is intentional. In this case it's because Natalie and Ashley were only available for their photos and the operators that wrote correspondences to the mules were all male. To make the lack of real-time chat believable, her explanations all come back around to a lack of high speed Internet: forced to rely on dialup or stealing access through a neighbor's connection. The excuse for no phone calls relies on her living with a jealous ex-boyfriend she plans to leave. All of this gently forces the mule to get accustomed to a routine of emails and cybersex chats. The photos are released to the mule one or two at a time to convince him she is real and experiencing little snapshots into her life (e.g. - new hairstyles, favorite food or drink, showing off her shape after working out, etc.). By restricting the conversations to text with the occasional photo and/or rare pre-recorded video/audio clip, any operator involved with the scam can handle her responses—and the materials can be used simultaneously on multiple mules across multiple scams. For the mule, the experience becomes a kind of personalized interactive wet dream, complete with enough timely glimpses into her life to convince him that everything happening between them is real. All of this contributes to the "damsel in distress" illusion, assuring his cooperation because he's fallen in love with a woman that desperately needs his help.

Here's a simplified overview of how the scam works:

▶ The character backgrounds for Katiya and Asja are prepared. In this case it is Benny and his people providing the personas, the stolen credit card numbers, scoping out the mule(s) and handling most of the correspondences.

▶ When the mule first begins corresponding with Katiya (or Asja) he is introduced to a woman who lived in New York City for a few years. As the story goes, she was going to school while working a minimum wage job and earning side money as a purchasing agent for an overseas distributor, taking orders for American products and shipping them back to their native countries. An expired student visa and a "terrible mix up" resulted in her getting deported.

▶ The cyber relationship progresses rapidly until the mule is in love. At this point he is at his most receptive. The woman asks for his help with the business venture and he accepts. His logic—she wants to be with him and this business is the fastest way to help her earn enough money to cover the legal and travel expenses to bring her (and those other family members) back to America.

▶ At this stage, the mule's romance reaches its pinnacle. In some scenarios the funds are transferred to his bank account to cover the cost of reshipping those products overseas. In other scenarios he regularly received wire transfers and then transfers them to different offshore bank accounts. Everything the mule sends or transfers overseas ends up in the hands of a transnational organized crime ring. Regardless of what he does, he receives commissions for his service which makes it all more exciting and seemingly legitimate… and his woman is talking like she is practically ready to marry him.

▶ From the start of the mule's activities within 3 to 6 months he receives a visit from the FBI. The minute a mule begins asking certain questions it tips off the operators that he's been busted and someone is coaching him on what to say. The events that follow go something like this: The romance for the mule is shattered by reality. Every point of contact or online presence associated with his woman gets dropped or goes dead, including her name. If INTERPOL or some other agency tracks down the shipping destination they usually find unoccupied apartments or empty storage spaces. Even the woman's name turns out to belong to a totally different person—usually a foreign exchange student that was completely unaware that her stolen identity was being used in a scam.

> "...Everything the mule sends or transfers overseas ends up in the hands of a transnational organized crime ring."

As if the sting of recovering from a fraudulent romance wasn't enough, law enforcement usually holds the mule completely liable for his participation along with any money that touched his bank account during the scam. And by the time he finally faces a judge and takes his fall, somewhere else another mule has already been lured in to take his place.

Back upstairs the party was deep into a Reggaeton vibe, so saturated in flavors of Spanish and Soca remixes that I couldn't make out any of it. The crowd was still dancing in high gear as if the party had just started. Whether it was the booze and a lack of sleep, being in my 40s, or all of the above, I couldn't keep up with the pace. The bedrooms were occupied. A live sex show was happening in the bathroom. People were smoking God-knows-what in the kitchen. I finally asked Benny if there was somewhere I could go crash for a while; he took mercy and gave me the keys to his SUV and promised to wake me up when the party quieted down. Parked behind the brownstones and blocked in six cars deep, driving was out of the question. I decided to walk up the street to an all-night diner to grab an early breakfast and wait for the party to end.

Daybreak was less than an hour away when I finally paid my tab and headed back to the house. The cool early morning serenity of the walk was ruined for me once I reached the bloody stoop. Inside, every room was trashed. There were still several women hanging around; one was coherent enough to pass on the message that Benny and his roommates had taken someone to the hospital. Once I was reasonably sure the place wasn't about to get raided by a SWAT team I grabbed some cleaning supplies and got to work cleaning up the blood. Between the hot merchandise and the drugs and the leftover hookers, all I cared about was making it back to Virginia without getting locked up.

The next person that arrived was my associate. Together we finished cleaning the stoop as I filled him in on everything that transpired overnight. I demanded another change in plans and he agreed to them. My associate left a thank you note on the fridge before we took a cab over to that hotel over in Jersey.

My associate won his court case. We didn't get the full story about what happened at the house until we were on the train headed back to Virginia. A couple of guys came to the front door, upset about the party and instructing Benny that he had to shut it down. A larger guest decided to play bodyguard, intervening on Benny's behalf. Heated words ensued and one of the guys swiftly responded—by smashing the guest in the face with a bottle and throwing him off the stoop. The two guys then went through the house, kicking people out with ferocious impunity.

They turned out to be bulls with a crew that answered to a well-known underboss with an American arm of the Izmaylovskaya Bratva, one of the oldest syndicates in the Russian criminal underworld.

The enigmatic nature of the house suddenly made sense: Just like every vampire has a more powerful maker that is further up the supernatural chain, it became clear that Benny wasn't the head vampire. He wasn't the ruler of the house. He and his roommates (his crew?) were merely earners and caretakers. And all that money they were pulling in? Most of it probably went straight to Little Odessa.

Less than a year later the New York Times ran a story about a sting operation that took down a major Identity Theft ring. Some of the details related to credit card fraud seemed more than coincidental. Benny and his crew came to mind. Curious whether or not they were caught in the dragnet, I reached out to my associate; we hadn't been in touch since he paid me for my services in New York. When I called his mobile a woman answered, informing me that no one was there by that name. Several emails went unanswered. Even his business website had lapsed to a point where it came up as not found. I took all of this as a hint not to dig any deeper. That's when I started putting together the notes that would later become this chapter.

Years ago, cybercrime had a barrier to entry. You had to be a hardcore programming-guru SQL-by-hand X.25 PAD jumping network hacking badass in order to have a shot at cracking into a mini or a mainframe on a corporate network to find and steal a database containing credit card information without insider help—and make it happen over a connection that was a tiny fraction of the speed of dialup Internet of the late 90s. To pull it off required practically being a Michael Jordan among NBA All-Stars. Today, technology has dissolved most of those barriers. Almost anyone with a computer, the right software, and at least a 4th grade education can snag hundreds, even thousands, of credit cards within a month or two—more than most malicious hackers prior to the 1990s could have ever dreamed of scoring in a lifetime.

As of this writing, estimates on annual cybercrime revenues vary, ranging from as low as $10 billion to as high as $1 trillion—numbers on par with world military spending. In comparison to the illegal drug trade that brings in $320 billion annually, many security professionals predict that cybercrime will outgrow that industry by 2020. Some believe this has already happened. At this point, determining the accuracy of the statistics is almost irrelevant. The shadow is cast… and there is no turning back.

What to do in the midst of a zombie outbreak?

According to the Zombie Dispatch Commission (ZDC), written accounts of real world zombie outbreaks are rare. Those who survive (and are willing to talk about it) will usually recount a helter-skelter tale of days spent on the run while evading hordes of flesh-eating ghouls, witnessing unspeakable horrors while seeking safe places to hide out. Upon making contact with someone outside of the infected perimeter, they often reached safety shortly after the ordeal.

One handwritten journal, recovered from a Las Vegas estate sale in 1978, tells the account of a handful of people that survived a Class 3 outbreak that occurred in the desert near Nye County, Nevada, in 1950. The safe haven was a brothel owned by a retired Vaudeville dancer-turned-madam and her nephew, a World War II veteran (who also authored the journal). Originally a gambling roadhouse, the three-story building had no ground floor windows and reinforced exterior walls and steel doors. The basement had a fully-stocked food storeroom and a cistern that was still connected to an old freshwater well. Along with being in the perfect fort, the author boasted that they had "enough guns and ammo to win Iwo Jima all over again."

Even more unusual is the fact that this journal provided a glimpse into the monotony of survival during such an outbreak and insight into ways to deal with it. Instead of sitting around going slowly insane due to fear and the constant clamoring of zombies trying to break down the walls, the people kept each other entertained. They practiced ballroom dancing, told stories, sang songs, played cards, billiards, Monopoly, and performed weekly skits inspired by characters from their favorite broadcasts like

The Jack Benny Show and The Colgate Comedy Hour. Ironically, the one activity that wasn't on the pastime list was sex. The madam put a freeze on that before the end of the first day. Feminine hygiene products had to be rationed and contraceptives were scarce. Plus, all the ladies were convinced they had witnessed the beginning of Armageddon. Repentance was a high priority and money was worthless, turning the brothel into little more than a lock-in at a co-ed dorm. The last journal entry, penned on Christmas Day, 1950, mentioned low food and a high-flying military airplane being spotted. History shows that a Mark 4 nuclear bomb was dropped in that region on January 27th, 1951. Animanecrologists and conspiracy theorists believe the bomb was used as an aggressive quarantine tactic although the U.S. Atomic Energy Commission (now the U.S. Department of Energy) had no records of this. They stand by their assertion that it was merely the first of a string of planned nuclear tests. The state of Nevada denies having any records of the property, the business or the madam. WWII service records, however, confirm the existence of the journal's author. Like with the fates of the people in his journal, the vet's whereabouts are unknown.

Since things in cyberspace move at light speed, tasks that may take seconds (or hours) on a computer would often take months (or even years) in the real world. And just like those people in the Nye County Outbreak that were holed up in that brothel for weeks, fighting a zombie outbreak on your computer can—and will—have you tied up for hours. A single complete anti-virus removal scan can take anywhere from 30 minutes to several hours; the typical zombified computer needs at least three scans with a fourth one to verify that it is free of contagions. On some occasions there is no way to avoid the nuke approach; completely erasing the hard drive and reinstalling everything from scratch.

While cleaning up infected computers, sometimes clients ask if there's a way to speed up the process. With current technology, the answer is "Yes and No". Just like with the Nye County Outbreak, there's no way to quickly clean up a zombified computer unless you nuke everything and start fresh. This is because of the vast amounts of storage space on our hard drives, software data files, and the incredible number of hidden data files that are generated each time we use the computer. Even a new computer where the owner has barely used it for a month can easily have over 500,000 files already stored on it—and every file needs to be scanned and checked against a database of over 15 million possible contagions. To put this effort into perspective, let's say you were a super doctor with the ability to scan for every known disease, cure 99% of them, and each patient only takes one hour. If you were tasked to examine 500,000 patients, by the time you've finished with the last person your grandchildren would almost be old enough to have children.

When dealing with zombies, even the ones that have taken over your computer, the bottom line is that you have to keep your morale high. If that's your only computer, you need to let the anti-virus programs scan and clean uninterrupted. Listen to music. Take a nap. Read a book. Go off and do something else if you can. Aside from the long boring stretches of anti-virus scanning, there will be occasions where you have to do hand-to-hand combat with 'the zombie inside' as it fights to regain control over your computer. In those cases, a variant of one or more of the contagions has outsmarted your anti-virus software and is still running amuck in your system. It will fight like a hooked Blue Marlin as it continues to try to replicate itself, sometimes damaging more system files or destroying your data. If successful, it will quietly turn your computer into a zombie again, reconnect with its Botnet, and all your efforts to clean the machine will have been wasted. Without a positive mental attitude, the wrong move could end up causing you lose everything on that computer.

Characteristics Common to Most Known Species of Living Dead:

Movement: Zombies walk with a sort of swaying stumble. While some move faster than others, they have very low dexterity and virtually no reflex muscle control. This is due to a combination of rigor mortis, damage to parts of the brain that are still functioning, and any physical trauma the zombie may have weathered before being turned. Older ghouls move slower due to advanced decomposition but they are still every bit as vicious as the fresh ones. Of course this doesn't apply to the online variety. In cyberspace they all move fast.

Stamina: Humans get tired. Zombies don't. NOTE: zombie computers need electricity and connectivity. Take away power and Internet access and a zombie goes into suspended animation indefinitely, much like what happens to the walking dead when they are frozen.

Pain: Zombies can't feel pain. They don't age or heal like humans, either. Instead, their aging process can be compared to that of fried chicken. By all accounts reported to the ZDC, there are only three ways to dispatch these foes: (A) destroy the brain, (B) incinerate the body or (C) time and the elements have finally rotted the brain to a point where it can no longer control what remains of their muscles. It's not unusual to encounter the berserkers with broken, shredded or missing body parts.

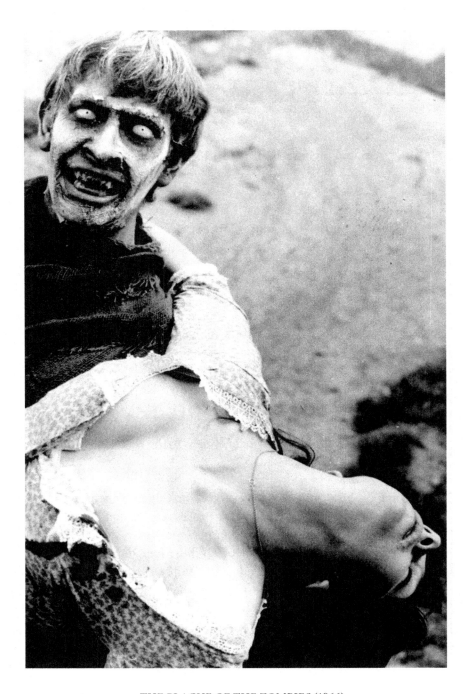

THE PLAGUE OF THE ZOMBIES (1966)

Chasin' Strange
in
Cyberspace

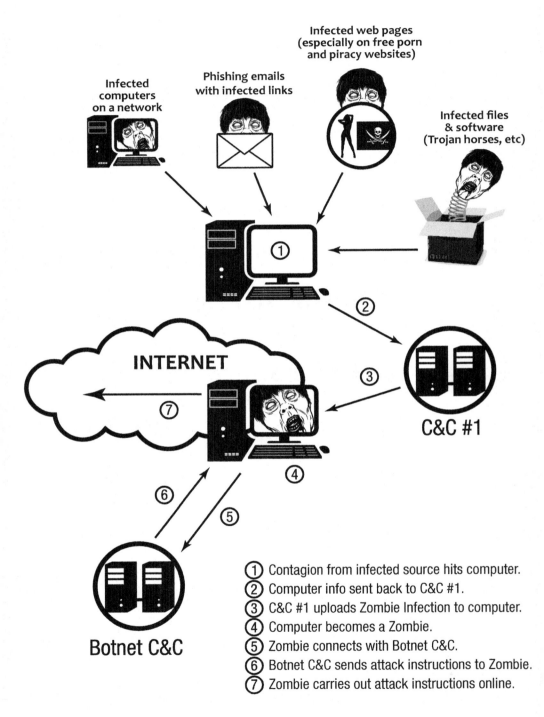

Infected web pages
(especially on free porn
and piracy websites)

Infected
computers
on a network

Phishing emails
with infected links

Infected files
& software
(Trojan horses, etc)

INTERNET

C&C #1

Botnet C&C

① Contagion from infected source hits computer.
② Computer info sent back to C&C #1.
③ C&C #1 uploads Zombie Infection to computer.
④ Computer becomes a Zombie.
⑤ Zombie connects with Botnet C&C.
⑥ Botnet C&C sends attack instructions to Zombie.
⑦ Zombie carries out attack instructions online.

My Computer Caught a Virus—
How did this happen?

Back in the late 70s, listening to my parents' vinyl records was a favorite pastime. One afternoon while playing 'Spaced Cowboy' by Sly & the Family Stone, I noticed a short static zap toward the end of the song. Thinking it was a new scratch on the record, I freaked out. I tried everything possible to clean album: Peroxide. Rubbing alcohol. Spit and a toothbrush. Nothing worked. I even hid the album for months at a time to keep from getting in trouble.

Sometime in the early 90s, while in a record store I saw that same album on sale as a cassette tape. Excited at the idea of hearing those songs with remastered clarity, I bought the tape and popped it in the cassette player as soon as I got back in my van. When it got to the end of Spaced Cowboy, what did I hear? The same static blip. It turns out the noise was a glitch on the master reel—a permanent part of the song.

The lesson learned? No matter how careful we are with technology, things can happen that are totally out of our control. Technology is always at the mercy of the technology itself, regardless of how carefully it is handled. The same principle applies to how our computers catch viruses. If you use the Internet, sooner or later you will catch a virus. It's unavoidable. At the root is one of four main causes: Infected Computers, Infected Emails, Infected websites, or Infected files.

The Carrier Website

A Carrier Website, one of the main sources of viral attacks in cyberspace, refers to any website that serves a seemingly harmless purpose on the surface but secretly serves one or more illicit objectives for its owners. These websites have three main traits in common:

► The site offers pirated copyrighted material (e.g. - porn, software, movies/TV shows, music, ebooks, and etc.) to be downloaded or traded for free.

► The site is hosted somewhere outside the U.S.
► The owner(s) of the website makes money off of its visitors.

Although the attack method changes to stay ahead of malware detection technology, the overall method remains the same: set up a website, post up a collection of stolen copyrighted content, and then do one of the following:

1. Make money by selling pay-per-view and/or pay-per-click advertising on those pages,

2. Booby-trap some of the pages. These invisible traps are tiny programs that secretly trick your web browser into installing their malware onto your computer. While the visitors are happily clicking around on the website to get their fill, their computers are secretly being infected with malware stored on that server or downloaded from a remote location. When there are booby-traps, more often than not the objective is to infect the visitor computers, turning them into zombies.

3. Trade copyrighted materials with other visitors. Sometimes these offerings are booby-trapped, too.

4. Some kind of exploitation that involves a combination of 1, 2 and/or 3.

All free websites aren't necessarily carrier websites, nor are all carrier websites intentionally booby-trapped by their owners. The problem is that even "safe" carrier websites run by security-conscious webmasters are still at risk of occasionally getting booby-trapped contributions posted by outside sources. These commonly come in three types:

Screenshots—Also known as "Screens", these thumbnails are often included with an uploaded package to give the potential downloader a sample of what to expect. The screens themselves are usually safe but they are often linked back to remote image hosting websites. Anywhere between the carrier site and the remote image host are often where booby-traps are set up. It's easy to do and in less than a second they can hit your computer with contagions that can cause anything from simple pop-ups to full-blown zombie outbreaks.

Comments—on many of these websites where users can upload contributions, they can also post comments. Booby-trapped links and malware spawn can also be posted here, too. It should be noted that this method is largely ineffective because contagions hidden in the comments are often discovered within hours of being posted. Regardless of how the website managers are capitalizing on its users, the last thing they will stand for is some scrub trying to sneak in and skim on their scam. The comment is deleted and whoever posted it is blocked and banned.

Malvertisements—Many carrier websites were set up specifically to sell ad space on their pages. Since these ads are managed by a third party ad network, cybercriminals will go through the trouble of submitting legitimate ads and then swap them with booby-trapped ads, exposing countless users to whatever viral infection it carries. With any booby-trapped website it is easy to catch multiple viral infections during a single visit.

Porn, Piracy and Minors

When it comes to home Internet access and anyone old enough to turn on a computer without adult supervision, Porn and Piracy are the third leg of a perfect trifecta for computer crashes and other disasters. I'm not condoning or advocating the involvement of minors with such activities, just stating it as a consistent observation. It's a sign of the times we live in. And before anyone out there begins firing off angry emails about me stereotyping our youth, don't bother—I'm just the messenger sharing a little information. To put it into perspective, between 2010 and 2011 I took a random sampling of 30 residential visits, all with infected computers where there was at least one child over the age of 10 that lived in the household. All 30 residences had direct evidence of Porn and/or Piracy activity.

And when it comes to discussing the matter, I tend to treat it the same as I would about alcohol consumption—both are activities that I wouldn't condone or advocate for minors. It's a subject for the parents to discuss with their youth in accordance to their own moral, religious, and social beliefs. At the same time, for the purposes of this book I have to address the reality: If you've got at least one person living with you that is over the age of 10 there is a high probability porn going to become an issue at some point.

Porn—The Unstoppable Guilty Pleasure

When it comes to emergency residential calls to rescue malware-infected computers, I've lost track of how many times I discovered evidence of porn . It's comparable to visiting a home where the owner has a pet; somewhere there will be pet poop. Erotica and computers are so irreversibly linked it is almost a fact of life, regardless of age, gender or religious inclination.

The numbers back this up. Major free porn sites such as Pornhub and YouPorn pull in more than 1 billion page views a month. And even though these are owned by legitimate businesses they are also constantly guilty of allowing registered users to upload copyrighted material. If these sites were charging half a penny per page view they would bring in more than $5 million dollars a month in revenue. According to data compiled by Family Safe Media, more than 68 million Internet searches for porn happen daily. More than 40 million people admit to regularly visiting porn sites with roughly 70% of them being men. The backgrounds of these visitors are as diverse as drivers on the road. The stats are very telling and since people don't often openly admit to their freaky fetishes, I'd wager that the actual numbers are much higher.

Cybercriminals have been taking advantage of this for years by setting up free porn websites. To bait these sites they post up pages of photos and videos, usually copyrighted material stolen from legal sources. These days, the contagions are so sophisticated it's the pages themselves that are booby-trapped—exposure to them can infect a computer without a single click. While horny visitors are "distracted" their computers are secretly infected with malware. The malware quietly installs itself, grabs passwords or whatever identity-related information it's programmed to seek, and sends it all back to an untouchable server in some country. Although this kind of trap is nothing new, cybercriminals continue to scoop up countless unsuspecting fish like trawlers on the high seas.

Baron Samedi says

"Free porn, like promiscuous sex without a condom, will eventually lead to your computer catching a virus – it's not a matter of if but when. If you have to indulge, stick to the porn websites where you pay a subscription fee."

"Evidence of adult material" is something I commonly say to a client if I have to elaborate on the source of malware found on their computer. It's my gentle way of saying someone has been looking at porn, especially if I don't want to spark up any controversy about who was at fault. Where there are people and at least one computer with unrestricted Internet access, there's a 3 in 4 chance that someone has used that computer to view adult material (or will do so eventually). It's a little like finding an empty potato chip bag at a Weight Loss Camp; this wasn't an accident and the culprit didn't indulge in just one chip.

Contrary to what some people believe, the problem isn't the porn itself. Computers cannot catch or transmit STDs. Smut has no effect on machines whatsoever because they don't "see" porn. An image or video could be of a sex act, a circus clown or a giraffe and to the computer it is all the same: binary data.

This is the porn we see on the screen...

(Okay, so it's not porn - just go with the example for now.)

...and this is what the computer sees:

```
    78 79 7a 85 8
 9  9a a4 a5 a6 a7 a8 a
   c4 c5 c6 c7 c8 c9 ca d4
 5 e6 e7 e8 e9 ea f4 f5 f6 f
08 01 01 00 00 3f 00 b4 cc fd
53 88 1c f8 dd 88 49 c8 8a d6
7d 95 1e ce c1 22 d3 56 ee 2c
d5 ec dc 3c ab 77 57 1a 4f d3
cf 75 35 2d 64 95 54 c0 47 36
25 ad 21 b1 45 d6 a4 29 fa e9
4 26 3f 2d b3 ab 03 52 b4 95
 5 8c 18 e1 40 ff 00 6c f2 9
  d8 06 07 d9 18 ce ee 2a
   82 26 9d 15 b5 a5
    2f a7 d4 b6
```

This is actual data sampled from inside the zombie girl image file. These alphanumeric pairs are called Hexadecimal digits, a human-readable representation of how your computer processes everything you see on the screen.

There is a connection between porn and those infected computers: the <u>source</u> of the porn. In those cases, it almost always turns out that someone had visited a free porn website in the hours/days/weeks prior to the infestation that eventually crashed the computer.

The Pastor's Zombie

Based on my initial conversation with the man of the house, a few days earlier his computer was overrun with pop-up ads, causing it and their home network to freeze up. Usually when I got such calls it turned out one of the computers had been turned into a zombie and assimilated into a Botnet. The fact that the pop-ups featured busty co-eds, horny singles, and webcam fantasy freaks wasn't that big a deal. I see all kinds of things on peoples' computers, including glimpses into their erotic fetishes. The fact that the man was a well-known Pastor at a mega church and his wife was connected with local politics wasn't a big deal, either. I meet all kinds in this line of work. What I found strange was the whodunit tension since the couple was in their late 60s and the only two living in the house.

A low stream of denial spilled out of the Pastor as he palm-shunned the screen. The wife crossed her arms and looked away. "What could have possibly caused this?" she asked.

I explained that this type of pop-up infestation was caused by malware, typically contracted from a person visiting a website with booby-trapped links. It's a tactic commonly used on free porn sites to promote other subscription websites of a similar nature. I assured them that this situation would be handled with the utmost discretion. Regardless of the cause, my job was to preserve his data and make sure his computer was 100% free of viruses, pop-ups and anything else that didn't belong there. The Pastor's wife thanked me and as she left the room she shot him a kind of look I'd only seen in gangster movies.

Most of the time I refer to these types of residential visits as Ghostbustin' Calls—I'm faced with a computer so infected with invisible mayhem it acts as if it's haunted by all kinds of evil spirits. And even in bizarre situations like this I do my best to remain objective.

I have to. Aside from the forensics and prevention aspect, I've seen how my assumptions can be wickedly incorrect. Sometimes it's hard not to pass judgment. This was one of those cases. The Pastor's wife struck me as being so straight edge she made Martha Stewart look like an outlaw biker chick. With the Pastor, however, it felt like we were standing on the Guilty Gallows and every question he answered put another loop in his noose: By the time their email reached the house it had passed through several outside anti-spam filters. The couple lived in a 6-bedroom house with a great security system. The afflicted computer was upstairs in the Pastor's study; the wife's laptop was downstairs and working fine. There were plenty of relatives and grandchildren but most of them lived out of state and hadn't been there to visit in over a month. No recent guests or gatherings, either. There was hired help; a cleaning lady (who was so averse to the Internet she didn't even have an email address) that came once a week and a landscaping company that never set foot in the house. Short of hiring SEAL Team Six to break in there was no way anyone could've used that computer without the Pastor or his wife being present—or so I thought.

Tiny greening blinking lights caught my attention from atop the armoire; a wireless router. A little more detective work revealed that it was less than a year old and not password protected. Anyone within range could've been using the couple's Internet connection. Several gigs of pirated games in a hidden folder, the most recent of which had been downloaded a day before the pop-ups started. When I asked the pastor if I could see his game controllers, he had no idea what I was talking about; confirmation that the games definitely weren't being played on that computer.

Our culprit turned out to be their neighbor's 14-year old son—and the outbreak of nasty pop-ups had nothing to do with browsing free porn websites. From his bedroom nextdoor, the teen had been using his laptop to connect to the unsuspecting Pastor's computer, piggybacking on their Internet through the unprotected wireless router. With the exception of being able to physically turn the computer on or off, the teen had full access to all the files on Pastor's computer. Secretly the boy had been using that PC as a stash for trading pirated games and bootleg movies through Limewire, a popular underground file-sharing network. Had either the boy or the Pastor been running a current anti-virus on their computers, one of them might have detected the game with the infected files. When the boy installed the game it unleashed some malware that opened up a bunch of ports, turning both computers into zombies. Their machines practically became radioactive overnight, trying to infect other computers with viruses and worms while sending out spam emails and pop-up porn ads.

Digital Piracy

Piracy and anti-piracy measures make up one of the continuums in cyberspace that will live on like Police and Thieves. On the surface, digital piracy is an underground pastime, social scene, illicit economy, and gateway vice all rolled up into one. Each media type, whether its software, audio, video or ebook, has its own set of technical disciplines used by the players within each one of those scenes. Their supply chains are every bit as efficient as any of the old school organized crime syndicates, filled with an international menagerie of geeks, rogues and brilliant miscreants. The Catch-22 is that most participants wouldn't be interested in giving interviews until well after they've left the scene and the Statute of limitations has run out. All of their warez are eventually made available to casual Internet users through torrent websites, P2P networks and IRC chatrooms. People are visiting those sources 24-hours a day, freely taking what they want.

Pastime

Digital piracy in the physical world would be the equivalent of collecting knockoffs; illegal reproductions. The popularity (or rarity) of whatever you're into collecting will determine how much of it you'll find. The key difference is that everything in the collection represents a copyright violation; stolen merchandise in the eyes of the law. For example, if you're into games, it's possible to download pirated games for every gaming console and popular computer platform since the early 1980s. Did you grow up on the Atari 2600 or playing Pacman in the arcades? There are entire websites dedicated to trading copies of the ROMs for every Atari game cartridge and stand-alone arcade game that ever hit the market since Pong. Same for every variation of popular home computer, Nintendo, Playstation, and everything right on up the Wii. If you set out on a mission to download and play one pirated game each week, you would have enough to keep you occupied for decades without worry of any repeats. And when it comes to movies, music, and TV shows, the numbers are incalculable. Some entities have even set up advertiser-supported websites and started streaming their stolen content, making them almost indistinguishable from legitimate sources like BBC, HBO, Netflix or satellite radio.

Although the Internet has ushered in an unbridled era of illegal duplication unlike anything seen in history since the invention of the photocopier, none of that can parallel the boom that is happening with Porn. Basically, if you can imagine a person doing it during the act of sex and it turns you on, someone out there has started paying people to perform it on video, someone else has started distributing that video on DVD and Blu-Ray, and still there are thousands of other people distributing pirated copies of these videos throughout the underground. Unless you're into some real demented freakmonster stuff, anyone in search of porn will find their preferred genre to be as prolific as weekly sitcoms on TV—and most of it will make your local strip clubs look as tame as the lingerie section at Wal-Mart.

Baron Samedi says:

"Many file sharing websites and porn websites are deeply interconnected and completely wide open. Where you find one vice you'll generally find the others are just a click away. What this means is that when a child tells mom that they're "just downloading music" from some somewhere like Limewire, Bearshare, or Vuze, it actually means they are a keyword search and a click away from full-length porn videos, pirated games, bootleg movies (many of which are so new they are still in the theaters) or downloading PDF bootlegs of books on illicit topics such as improvising munitions, hacking, fraud, and etc. The Underground has almost no censorship."

After I explain this, sometimes people go on a tirade about how come this isn't controlled or regulated. I usually respond with "it is... but it isn't". Most ISPs here in the U.S. will do their best to identify and/or block out known sources of illegal activity. In many ways it's a bit like tapwater in that even with decent processing standards there's always some kind of contaminant getting through. There's always a tradeoff involved: if they don't filter the water it can be cheap and flow freely but there's no telling what contaminants might be in it. If they do filter the water to its ultimate purity it will become too cost-prohibitive to distribute through the normal water system.

The same applies to data traffic. In order to filter everything to eliminate possible access to illicit materials would require extremely strict controls on many levels. For most people that would mean a fully-censored Internet experience. And if the heavily censored Internets in countries like China and Iran are any indication, computer hackers and cybercriminals will always find ways to break through the digital blockades.

Underground Social Scene and Economy

Software Pirates have traditionally enjoyed their own weird subculture, largely hidden from most of the world except for those who use and trade in pirated wares. These digital cliques are usually referred to as "Warez" groups. Most operate by a code of conduct often referred to as "The Standard", not too dissimilar to the Pirate Code that was part of 17th and 18th century Caribbean pirate tradition.

Most commercial software, movies, music and ebooks are released with some form of copy protection to prevent illegal duplicates. New movies and music releases has to be leaked, stolen or ripped. Software has to be cracked in order to make it freely distributable. Cracking is usually a sport for young gun programmers because it requires a knack for reverse engineering someone else's code, the drive of a medical school student, and ridiculous amounts of free time. As a result, warez groups divide up the labor. Along with those who do the dirty work there are packagers, distributors, and couriers to get the warez out there. Top pirate groups commonly have their cracked version out in the wild within a few days of the product release. And with music and movies, often the pirates have the latest releases out before your local stores do.

On that same note, for every buccaneer like Bartolomeu Português or Blackbeard, countless others that sailed with them never achieved the same notoriety. They anonymously passed through the pages of Caribbean history like gentle waves on the seashore. Today's Warez Scene is the same way, and the mystique of the infamy has appealed to a predominately male subculture in their teens and twenties. Almost every hacker I've ever known (ethical, opportunist or malicious) has passed through the Warez scene at some point. The transition from fledgling pirates into deeper cybercrime is similar to how there are plenty of Rappers and Pop Music stars who cut a few albums, dabbled in film and television, and walked away from the music industry once they found success as actors.

Here's how the criminal nexus comes together:

► Somewhere in the chaos of cyberspace, someone decides to set up a pirate website. Prior to the late 90s, this was traditionally done by a young computer geek or hobbyist who wanted to offer a friendly place to various underground pirate groups to share their latest warez (cracked software), much like Tortuga during the days when pirates sailed the Caribbean. Today, the origins behind many pirate sites aren't as roguishly altruistic as they once were. As twisted as it may seem, many of them are now thinly-disguised transnational businesses, making money by providing access to content they don't own.

► Among all the offerings of movies, music, software, and ebooks, more than half the major sites also have sections dedicated to porn. And the typical selection on any given site is would dwarf any of the old school adult book stores. Hundreds, if not thousands, of releases that range from brand new high-definition videos all the way to loops and XXX films originally shown in theaters back in the 1970s. It should also be noted that these sites refuse to allow child porn, bestiality or snuff, because anything on that level will usually get them banned from their host and bring almost certain doomsday punishment from the police in that country.

- ► These offerings bring in a constant stream of traffic; for every person who offers up something for people to grab, there are probably dozens of people leeching (downloading) it.
- ► The hosting companies and data centers make trailer loads of money off of these pirate sites because they charge them based on monthly traffic and storage space.
- ► The network service providers make a healthy cut off charging those data centers and hosting companies for the high bandwidth usage.
- ► To pay the hosting bill, the pirate site operators sell advertising space on their pages. A good portion of those advertisers are for adult-oriented content like matchmaking websites, weight loss, sexual enhancement products and online games.
- ► Some of the more high profile pirate sites sell their ad space through different "blind" advertising networks. Aside from taking the pirate site operators out of the loop of having to sell their own ad space, by using blind ad networks the advertisers save money by relinquishing control over where their ads are being displayed.
- ► Some ad networks do not host the banner ads on their own servers. As a result, cybercriminals have figured out how to exploit this. They pose as a legitimate company and pay for a real ad to run for weeks, sometimes months. Then, when the ad network least suspects it, the fake company will swap out their original banner ad for a malware-infected advertisement that gets pulled into the ad network, instantly distributed and displayed on countless websites. The malvertisement might only be up for a couple of days before being discovered or taken down. Anyone who sees the malvertisement is at risk of having their computer infected. With file-sharing websites, a single exposure can easily be responsible for creating thousands of zombies.

All of this begs the question might be posed "Well, how come the feds don't shut down these sites?" The answer is "they do... when they can".

Most of these file-sharing websites and networks tend to be based in well-connected countries with data centers that will host any website as long as the money is right. Places like the Russian Federation, China, and the Ukraine where U.S. lawyers trying to shutdown these distribution sites would find it easier to send a man to Jupiter. Among them was Demonoid (2003 to 2012), originally based in Serbia. Not only did this invite-only "secret" underground website rise up to become one of the biggest sources of pirated software on the planet, but according to a Dec 2010 Alexa.com report it achieved a rank of 538th in overall popularity, making it more popular than the online edition of the New York Post newspaper. This John Gotti of pirate websites had message forums, spawned countless associations and friendships, and had a following so huge they even started selling Demonoid merchandise. While writing this chapter I was unable to confirm how much this website earned in revenue before they were shut down. To put it into perspective let's look at ThePirateBay.com, a similar high-profile advertiser-supported pirate website. This site averaged about 11.5 million unique visitors per month (Source: eBizMBA.com). If the site operators charged as little as $0.02 per daily unique visitor, that means they were easily earning *at least* $2.7 million dollars a year in ad revenue. With that much money coming in, there will always be friendly hosting companies in obscure countries that will gladly accept their business and turn a blind eye on suspected cybercriminal activities.

ZOMBIE TRIVIA

Q: In WHITE ZOMBIE, what created the zombie outbreak?

(answer on page 384)

The Truth Behind Popular Misconceptions about Viruses

1. Viruses can physically damage your computer:

Contrary to some wild legends and claims that a computer was permanently damaged by a virus, this isn't possible. While it is true that there are some viruses that can infect the BIOS, EFI or some types of firmware, a virus cannot infect hardware. This is because no virus (or any other kind of software) can make physical changes to hardware. Such notions are the equivalent of claiming that watching certain types of TV shows will cause your television to explode. And in the rare event of contracting a virus that infects your computer's BIOS, EFI or firmware, they should be taken to an IT professional to be cleaned and reset to factory default.

2. Doing a System Restore or Reinstalling Windows / Mac OS X / Linux and copying my files back will get rid of a virus:

This is a mistake commonly made by gifted amateurs—people who know just enough about computers to be dangerous to the public. It's a cleansing tactic that was once somewhat dependable... back in the early-to-mid 90s. Today, even the most archaic viruses floating around were programmed to thwart this simple removal method. They all hide hooks in various parts of the system and memory. Any attempt to delete a virus in one part of a live system will usually cause hidden copies to spawn more and spread.

NOTE: the System Restore that came with some computers will delete all personal files before reinstalling the operating system—and this still does not insure virus removal. Double-check your documentation before considering this as an option.

3. _____ anti-virus software will protect you from all viruses floating around online:

Generally speaking, the fight against viruses and malware is an arms race, and anti-virus programs are behind the curve. According to Kaspersky Labs as of December 2012, their software is detecting and blocking more than 200,000 new infections a day. Granted, these numbers vary wildly between anti-virus software providers but one thing is consistent: none of their packages should be treated as if they provide 100% protection.

4. _____ firewall will protect you from viruses:

As of this writing, the firewalls that came with your computer aren't sophisticated enough to protect your computer from most Trojans, viruses, and forms of malware. This is especially true of malware that gets introduced to your computer or network because someone clicked on an infected email or link. Many infections are smart enough to disable the built-in firewalls to get around them. High end firewalls can capture some types of contagions but because of the sheer numbers that get introduced to the wild every week it's not safe to assume they can all be stopped this way. Firewalls help, about as much as washing your hands regularly can prevent the average person from occasionally getting sick.

5. The Windows "Blue Screen of Death" means your computer has been hacked or infected with a virus:

Although it's true that some viruses can cause a Blue Screen of Death (BSOD) on a PC, more often than not the cause is either due to faulty hardware, a hardware conflict, or problems with the drivers. If you're troubleshooting a BSOD error, assuming the cause is a virus will only cause you to waste time scanning for viruses that might not be there.

NOTE: Anytime a BSOD occurs there will be some kind of error code on the screen (also called a STOP code). It'll generally start with a "0x" and an alphanumeric string of some sort (e.g. – 0x8E or 0x0000008E). Write down the entire error code and then Google it.

5a. Mac OS X or Linux/BSD users don't experience Blue Screens of Death:

Every desktop and laptop has at least one Screen of Death (also called a Kill Screen). The color and behavior of the screen depends on the operating system.

For Mac OS X users, according to the Apple support site: If you see a blank blue screen or a blue screen with a colored pinwheel when you try to start your computer, but starting up doesn't progress, you may have a problem with damaged or incompatible startup items or software. Details can be found here: **http://support.apple.com/kb/PH4190**

For Linux users the Screen of Death is called a Kernel Panic. Sometimes you see nothing, other times you see a core dump or a bunch of cryptic codes and numbers on the screen. In any case, everything freezes and the computer has to be hard rebooted.

6. A bunch of error messages means the computer has been hacked or is infected with a virus:

This is far from accurate. The unfortunate truth is that there are a number of ways that files can get corrupted on your computer—without any viruses whatsoever. This can happen as a result of faulty memory, faulty software, sectors on the hard drive that have gone bad, sometimes even your anti-virus can be the culprit. This can happen on any system running Windows, Mac OS X, Linux, Android, or iOS. If you're faced with error messages about a file that can't be opened, run an anti-malware scan before jumping to conclusions.

What to do if you've been the victim of Identity Theft?

Contact local police, your bank and creditors, and then the Federal Trade Commission: **http://www.ftc.gov/bcp/edu/microsites/idtheft2012/**

Another awesome resource is the Identity Theft Resource Center: **http://www.idtheftcenter.org/Help-for-Victims/document-catalogue.html**

The Key Secrets to Freeing your Computer from a Zombie Infection

When it comes to any kind of computer problem, one of the things we often forget to do is not panic. Keep a cool head. The problem could be as simple as not being able to open an email attachment, or as dire as your laptop going on the fritz less than an hour before a major sales presentation. When we panic, we get mentally fatigued quicker. When that happens we don't think things through. We make bad calls, and they usually lead to more bad calls.

To put this into perspective, everybody panics during a zombie outbreak. The surprise of cannibalism has that effect on people. In the middle of all that we have knee-jerk reactions to almost everything. We forget that we're experiencing a completely unnatural disaster. For example, during a Class 4 zombie outbreak like one seen in episodes of "The Walking Dead", given the option between seeking refuge in a police station or a graveyard, which would you choose? One place is full of people with weapons that are trained to protect and shoot to kill; the other is full of people that are already dead. On the surface it seems like an easy decision, right? Maybe not.

At first, a police station would seem like a great place to go; a bastion of safety. The problem is that a lot of people living in that area would have the same idea, too. Thanks to years of budget cuts and low pay, most police stations have limited space, barely enough for all their officers to be present at the same time. The building would fill up pretty fast. It wouldn't take long for them to be forced to turn people away. Each time one of the cops blasted a few zombies, that gunfire will echo brightly—a beacon of hope for frantic unarmed citizens—and an unintentional dinner bell for every footloose zombie within a few miles. As a result, scores of hapless refugees would arrive outside the station expecting police protection only to find barricaded doors and horrors. For zombies, it would be like walking into brunch at the local buffet. For those inside the station, their biggest risk would be running out of food and water… long before running out of ammo.

By contrast, a graveyard would be a sanctuary—the perfect place to escape the mayhem long enough to plan your next move. People naturally steer clear of cemeteries. Add the news reports of flesh-eating walking dead and they will <u>really</u> stay as far away as possible. The sole instinct that a zombie possesses is to feed on the living, particularly humans. Where there is no sign of living people, there won't be any zombies. It's just that simple. And as for the recently interred that may still be intact enough to reanimate, contrary to Hollywood depictions, they can't climb out of their graves. They were laid to rest in metal caskets that are locked and buried beneath a few tons of dirt. Even with the increasing popularity of green burials, the grave-emerging zombie is still impossible. Biodegradable coffins are made of wood, wicker or recycled paper; if the container was in the ground long enough for the occupant to be able to claw through the lid, the tons of the dirt would have already crushed it. On the remote chance the occupant somehow reanimated, it would be completely encased in hard dirt and immobilized, reducing the snarling fiend to little more than a confused capsule of squirming fertilizer.

Between the police station and the graveyard, once you get past the "normal everyday" mode of thinking and analyze the situation based on a new set of abnormal factors, it becomes clear which choice is the safer bet. The same kind of pretzel logic applies to dealing with a zombified computer.

Whether it's a walking corpse or that infected computer, zombies have the moral compass of a hive-minded insect—a killer bee. There's no good or evil, no right or wrong, no sense of compassion or guilt. They just exist to do what they do. Once your computer is infected with malicious code and turned into a zombie, you're not in control of the situation. Forget about depending on cause and effect; most of those principles don't apply. Beyond an understanding of programming logic, system processes and how data is handled in cyberspace, the strongest weapon against the zombie is that a human can outthink it. It starts with asking these questions: "What can I do?", "What can I read?", and "Who can I talk to about this?" Those answers will point you towards a solution.

Freeing your computer from a zombie is a bit like a murder investigation. All the clues are in the details, scattered about deep inside the machine—and very easy to overlook if your mind isn't clear, calm and focused.

Good Anti-Virus Info Resources:

http://www.securelist.com
http://www.gmer.net (English)

Zombie Infection: Understanding Rescue and Recovery

In any area under siege by a Class 2 or Class 3 zombie outbreak, the government is always faced with the decision to start with one of two types of operations: (1) Rescue or (2) Recovery.

Regardless of what country a zombie outbreak occurs, rescuing survivors while protecting the surrounding uninfected areas requires a massive containment effort with assistance from at least four entities: a world-class military force (e.g. - NATO forces, The U.S. Army, Special Forces, etc.), the local militia (e.g. - the National Guard), and a public health agency (e.g. - World Health Organization, Centers for Disease Control, etc.). The problem is that each organization achieves its goals in a very different way. Military forces like The U.S. Army and the Marines is trained to sweep and clear; if it looks, acts or smells bad and can't speak, kill it. Trying to use them as a policing force to keep the living outside the perimeter and the undead inside is like trying to shave with an electric hedge trimmer. The National Guard is much better suited for civilian policing, riot control, and preventing looting—perfect for guarding the perimeter around an outbreak. And the CDC has to be involved to make sure everyone follows basic safety protocols to prevent the spread of the contagion as they study it to determine the cause and find a cure (if we're lucky).

During every Rescue Operation there is a point where the top brass makes the final judgment call where anyone that has not been rescued up to this point is probably no longer alive. This is where the operation shifts from Rescue into Recovery mode. In the aftermath of most disasters, this is commonly a matter of going through all the debris to recover and identify the deceased. In the event of a zombie outbreak, an entirely different protocol is necessary. While it's true that the cadavers are easier to find, the problem is that many of them won't stop wandering around attacking anyone on sight. Those ghouls will continue to be a vicious threat until they have all been rounded up and properly neutralized or dispatched. This is why a Recovery Operation after any Class 2 (or higher) outbreak often requires bombing the hell out of the affected area until nothing moves. The Zombie Dispatch Commission recommends anything from Lockheed Martin's Paveway II line of laser-guided bombs, 500-lbs or greater. Although these missiles strike with surgical accuracy, precision engagement is not necessary. When the smoke clears, everything will either look like rubble or burnt scrambled eggs.

Anyone that has ever had to rescue a zombie-infected computer quickly learns that this will require the same kind of approach: (1) Rescue the System (and its data) or (2) Recover the System by erasing everything on the computer and either rebuilding the desktop environment from scratch or restore the system from a backup.

Zombie Infection:
Rescue Discs and Rescuing your Data

NOTE: In this chapter, the reference to "disc" is a catch-all for CD and DVD discs as well as USB flash drives. Most stand-alone rescue suites started out as programs that were meant to be put on a 3.5" floppy disk or burned to CD or DVD. Many of these packages now provide a version that can be installed on a bootable USB flash drive, too.

Baron Samedi says

"Using a bootable rescue disc is often the first approach. When scanning and removing malware from an infected computer, expect it to take a minimum of 2 or 3 hours."

With the advances in storage technology, the price-per-megabyte is constantly getting lower. Back in 2004, a 120 GB hard drive cost a little over $100 dollars. As of 2014, that same $100 dollars could buy a single 3 TB hard drive—the equivalent of 26 of those 120 GB hard drives. With rapid advances in technology and increased demand for solid state drives, the result has been hard drives with much greater storage capacities at lower prices. This is a mixed blessing.

The upside is that consumers benefit from the bargain prices. The downside is that these hard drives take much longer to scan. For small businesses that have upgraded older machines with newer hard drives, this means that backing up their computers has gone beyond a simple act of pragmatism to being a necessity. Every time a computer gets infected with malware it's practically a coin toss as to whether or not the Operating System is corrupted and needs to be reinstalled. Paying a Geek-for-Hire service to remove malware and/or rebuild a system gets expensive quick. With the hourly rate for most IT services (and the fact that it can take up to several hours to scan and disinfect), the bill can skyrocket past the value of the computer... and that's just to restore enough stability to retrieve the personal files.

For most small companies, this expense could be chalked up as part of the cost of doing business. Some can afford it, some can't, and all of them could write it off on their taxes. But for home computer users, a zombie-infected system often represents a different kind of crossroads. The average middle-class household can't afford the spontaneous expense of a few hundred dollars (or more) to repair/rebuild/recover their computer, let alone buy a brand new system. And if anyone living at that residence is under the age of 18, the chances are very high that one or more computers in that household will be virus infected and/or zombified at least once a year. Children, computers and computer viruses seem to go hand-in-hand like youth and mischief.

The following list should be considered merely a few highlights of the free rescue discs and antivirus solutions that are available in a pinch. as of this writing, Linux has purposely been omitted from this list because it holds less than 2% of the desktop market.

For the PC (Microsoft Windows Vista, 7, 8, and later):

NOTE: As of this writing, Microsoft has stopped providing updates for Windows XP. It should expected that more and more anti-virus programs will also stop supporting XP, too.

Microsoft Malicious Software Removal Tool:
http://www.microsoft.com/security/pc-security/malware-removal.aspx
From the Microsoft website: The Microsoft Malicious Software Removal Tool is a [free] anti-malware utility that checks computers running Windows 8, Windows 7, and earlier for infections by specific, prevalent malicious software-including Blaster, Sasser, and Mydoom-and helps remove malware and any other infections found.

Comments: This is not intended as a substitute for having a real-time anti-virus software installed and running. Think of it like an Asprin: good for dealing with immediate aches and pains but not a permanent solution for any underlying problem.

Microsoft Security Essentials:
http://www.microsoft.com/en-us/download/details.aspx?id=5201
From the Microsoft website: Microsoft Security Essentials provides real-time protection for your home or small business PC that guards against viruses, spyware, and other malicious software.

Comments: With Windows 7 and newer, if there is no anti-viirus installed on that computer it will default to using this program to provide real-time protection. It should be considered a "baseline" form of protection, in much the same way a handgun might protect you from one or two zombies but it won't do much if you're attacked by a horde.

Kapersky Rescue Disk:
https://support.kaspersky.com/viruses/rescuedisk
Comments: Kaspersky Rescue Disk is designed to scan and disinfect PCs in cases where the infection is so severe that it is impossible to clean the computer using normal anti-virus programs (e.g. - McAfee, Norton, AVG, etc.) or malware removal utilities (e.g. - Kaspersky Virus Removal Tool, Spybot S&D, Malwarebytes' Anti-malware, etc.) while Microsoft Windows is still running. Most of the time this is my first choice when I know a PC is a zombie that's crawling with viruses and malware. It is relatively fast, taking roughly 45 to 90 minutes to scan and clean most PCs. After this scan usually I can boot normally and run any additional spyware/malware removal programs to clean out and immunize against any remaining contagions.

Anti-rootkit utility TDSS Killer:
http://support.kaspersky.com/5350
Comments: I often run this after using the Kaspersky Rescue Disk.

Hiren's Ultimate Boot CD:
http://www.hirensbootcd.org/download/
Comments: Hiren's BootCD is a boot CD that has a compilation of a dozens of computer management and repair utilities. Think of it as somewhere between a digital first aid kit and a Swiss Army knife that can be used to diagnose and fix many different kinds of computer issues. It's a must-have.

F-Secure Rescue CD:

http://www.f-secure.com/en/web/labs_global/removal-tools/-/carousel/view/142

Comments: Although this is a great rescue tool to have handy, I rarely use it on professional rescue calls. It's best to start this scanner and let it run overnight. As of this writing, I've never seen it take less than 3 hours to run.

GMER (Rootkit scan and removal tool):
http://www.gmer.net/

Comments: This is an awesome rootkit scanner, particularly for finding hidden processes and services. When used to do a scan of every possible source on a booted PC (memory, registry, or files on the hard drive), it can easily take several hours. Also, the results may require the interpretation of an IT professional; some files may produce false positives and deleting them can potentially damage your system.

For Mac OS X:

NOTE: The comments and criticisms regarding these selected anti-virus programs are noticeably more brief than their PC counterparts. This is for two reasons: (1) I've worked on more Windows computers than Macs and (2) while writing this book, every Mac owner I came in contact with believed in the myth that Macs are immune to computer viruses—and as a result they didn't believe anti-virus protection wass necessary.

Avira:
http://www.avira.com/en/download/product/avira-free-mac-security

Comments: Very good free real-time anti-virus solution. The downside is that it will noticeably slow down your computer while scanning.

Sophos Anti-Virus for Mac (home edition):
http://www.sophos.com/en-us/products/free-tools/sophos-antivirus-for-mac-home-edition/download.aspx

Comments: Among the top anti-virus protection programs for Mac, very thorough and good at weeding out false positives.

ClamXav:
http://www.clamxav.com/download.php
Comments: This free, open source anti-virus program has a pretty good reputation among reviewers. The only drawback is that because it is open source, it doesn't get updated as often as its commercial counterparts. Versions of ClamAV are also vailable for Linux and BSD.

Rootkit Hunter:
http://www.rootkit.nl/projects/rootkit_hunter.html
Comments: This is primarily for Linux and BSD users, which includes Mac OS X because it is based on BSD.

For Android (tablets, smartphones) and iOS (iPhone and iPad):

NOTE: Anti-virus apps for the iPhone and iPad are the subject of constant debate. The claim is that there is virtually no way to introduce malware into the device unless it has been jail-broken (i.e. - removing the limitations set by Apple so the device can be customized at will).

Avira, McAfee, and Trend Micro are among the commercial anti-virus software vendors that provide free downloadable apps for mobile devices. They're all worth checking out, especially if you already subscribe to their services for your PC or Mac.

AVG (Android):
http://www.avg.com/us-en/antivirus-for-android
From the website: AVG AntiVirus FREE for Android™ combats viruses and malware, and also provides loss and theft protection through the ability to track and control your smartphone remotely if you should become separated from it.

Zombie Infection: Data Recovery

NOTE: In this chapter, the reference to "disc" is meant to be a catch-all for CD and DVD discs as well as USB flash drives. Most stand-alone rescue suites started out as programs that were meant to be put on a 3.5" floppy disk or burned to CD or DVD. Many of these packages now provide a version that can be installed on a bootable USB flash drive, too.

Data recovery is the process of salvaging files that has been lost due to a failing storage device, malware corruption, or by human action (e.g.—accidentally deleting a file). If you've ever experienced a computer hard drive crash or SD card crash and lost some irreplaceable photos or work documents, you already know how painful this loss can be.

PhotoRec (runs on Microsoft Windows, Mac OS X, and Linux):
http://www.cgsecurity.org/wiki/PhotoRec
From the website: PhotoRec is file data recovery software designed to recover lost files including video, documents and archives from hard disks, CD-ROMs, and lost pictures (thus the Photo Recovery name) from digital camera memory. PhotoRec ignores the file system and goes after the underlying data, so it will still work even if your media's file system has been severely damaged or reformatted.

PhotoRec is bundled with Testdisk, a data recovery program geared more toward system repair. Both programs are free and can be downloaded individually or found on a variety of Live CDs:
http://www.cgsecurity.org/wiki/TestDisk_Livecd

ZOMBIE TRIVIA

Q: What sci-fi horror novel served as inspiration for the 1932 film ISLAND OF LOST SOULS?

(answer on page 384)

Hiren's Ultimate Boot CD:
http://www.hirensbootcd.org/download/
Comments: Hiren's BootCD is a boot CD that has a compilation of a few dozen computer management and repair utilities. Think of it as somewhere between a digital first aid kit and a Swiss Army knife that can be used to diagnose and fix many different kinds of computer issues. I've included it here because it also has data recovery tools, including Testdisk and PhotoRec.

Recuva:
This file recovery program recovers lost files from your PC, digital camera or iPod.
http://www.piriform.com/recuva

Disk Drill:
http://www.cleverfiles.com/
From the website: No matter what type of storage device you've lost data from, if you can normally connect it to your Mac and view the contents, Disk Drill can scan it. Even if you're currently having trouble accessing your hard drive or external device, there's a good chance our free data recovery software for Mac will be able to rescue data from it.

Wikipedia has a good starter list of Data Recovery software packages for Windows, Mac OS X, and Linux. Some of these programs are to be run from their own bootable media; others have to be installed on your system while it's running. Prices for most of these packages ranges from free to $200, depending on the features. The list can be found here: **http://en.wikipedia.org/wiki/List_of_data_recovery_software**

Baron Samedi says

"Get at least one data recovery program that is on bootable media (e.g. – TestDisk LiveCD) and one that can be installed on your system (e.g. – Recuva, Disk Drill, etc.)."

Whatever you finally choose for data recovery, have copies of these programs stored on media and kept in a cool, dry place (e.g. – with other CDs, a media safe, on the shelf, etc.). Test them out once or twice in a non-emergency situation so you're reasonably comfortable with how they work. I recommend this because when an emergency happens it's easy to panic and when people panic they tend to do far more damage by inadvertently clicking on options they don't understand. I've seen this mistake often, after someone has lost one or more files, panicked and then screwed up while trying to retrieve it. They end up hiring someone like me to fix the problem, often pretending like they hadn't touched their system at all.

Lost Microsoft Word Documents

One of the most common data recovery calls I get is from someone who was typing up a document using a program like Microsoft Word and somehow they lost their work before they had a chance to save it.

NOTE: Since more than 80% of the computer users out there either have or use some version of Microsoft Office (or comparable clone), the tips in this section will be focused on Microsoft Word. Most of these tips are universal.

1. Stop what you're doing and don't type anything else. Every keystroke at this point matters.

2. Compose yourself. Take a deep breath and think—freaking out will only make things worse.

3. If Word didn't crash but suddenly the page space went blank, mentally walk back through every single thing you did right up to losing your unsaved document. Try clicking on "Undo" a few times in case you accidentally highlighted all the text and hit the spacebar or backspace.

4. For all the other possible tips to check, no one breaks it down better than Microsoft. Visit:
   http://support.microsoft.com/kb/316951

Although no one wants to hear this when they've lost an unsaved document, here's the reality: Anything short of the computer exploding at your fingertips, losing that unsaved document was your fault. Sometimes you have to own the mistake in order to learn how to prevent it from happening again. The last time I lost an unsaved Word document was sometime in the 90s. Following these simple rules has saved me plenty of headaches:

▶ If you think you're going to spend more than five minutes writing something, save your document before you type the first word.

▶ If you plan to type anything longer than 50 words (about the size of the NOTE paragraph at the beginning of this section), save your document before you get started.

▶ If you're writing anything of significant length and importance (e.g.—research paper, thesis, book manuscript, etc.) then save multiple copies of the document. The number of copies is solely up to you. For example, while writing this book I maintained at least eight working copies spread out over four computers, two USB flash drives, and two secure remote storage locations. I usually made sure all the copies were current at the end of each writing session. On three occasions Microsoft Word ccorrupted the manuscript, setting me back less than two hours worth of work. Without the backups that loss would have been months, if not more than a year.

▶ Enable Autorecover. From within Microsoft Word, click to File > Options > Save then set the Save Autorecover information to 5 minutes. If Word closes unexpectedly for any reason (e.g.—crash, power outage, etc.) this setting will insure that you never lose more than 5 minutes worth of work.

Zombie Outbreak Classifications

The first signs of a real world zombie outbreak in your area will likely begin with one of two things: the Emergency Broadcast System alert or a weird, violent commotion somewhere within a few blocks of your home. Sometimes sirens and maybe something on fire off in the distance, too. Unfortunately, in cyberspace it won't be that obvious.

For the sake of this book, the classes in this section are used to categorize the types of zombie activity. The first paragraph refers to zombie outbreaks in the physical world and the second is dedicated to its cyberspace equivalent. The comparison-contrast between the two is meant to help characterize the severity the cyber outbreak.

It should also be noted that most cyber outbreaks are very rarely just one class. This is because the damage from a real-world zombie outbreak is easy to measure. 10 bodies found means there were at least 10 casualties—the math speaks for itself, no need to speculate. When zombie outbreaks occur in cyberspace, area of effect isn't necessarily a factor. There's no such thing as "here" or "there". Gauging the scope of damage requires knowing approximately how many computers and networks were affected. A single zombified computer might attack a handful of machines, hundreds or even thousands, and do so within a small area like an office, a network on the other side of the world, or all of the above. That same zombie might also be part of a Botnet tasked to hit a single target or cause widespread mayhem affecting countless people across the planet. The only way to know a zombie's mission is to capture the malicious infection and study it in a controlled environment like a living virus. Thankfully, as of this writing, no one has figured out how to make a zombie computer commit the kind of attack that leaves behind a physical body.

Class 1:

This low-level outbreak often occurs in isolated areas such as islands, rural towns, or geographically remote areas with low populations. The total casualties, including zombies, is less than fifty. This outbreak will usually occur within a 20-mile radius and last less than 2 weeks, possibly longer if zombie footage makes it to YouTube. Viral video clips bring wannabe hunters and curiosity seekers to the area, most of which briefly become zombie snacks before joining the ranks of the walking dead.

In the IT world, this kind of outbreak usually applies to the typical home computer virus infestation; always one computer (desktop or laptop) and rarely more than three machines. The severity, however, can be extreme because these infestations may go unchecked for months. Different types of contagions will accumulate to a point where they're strangling each other in memory and bringing the infected computer(s) to a crawl.

Class 2:

This outbreak occurs in densely populated areas, such as cities or their surrounding suburbs. Sirens are constant due to fires and alarms in the distance; there's a strange pungent smoke in the air. The total casualties, including zombies, are less than 500. This outbreak will usually occur within a 50-mile radius and last between 2 and 6 weeks, rarely longer. By the end of the second week a state of emergency would have been declared for an outer perimeter around the affected radius. The Center for Disease Control (CDC) will quarantine the area, calling it something like a cholera outbreak. Full media blackout will have occurred; Internet, cable, and cell phone transmissions will have been suppressed in order to "protect" the population outside of the infected radius. The National Guard will perform sweep-and-clear maneuvers only if the Pentagon thinks they can't contain the outbreak using the surgical bombing practices.

In the IT world, this kind of outbreak usually occurs in a small office with a few infected workstations at any given time (often less than 3% of the entire network). Generally, when these office computers are managed by an integrated suite such as Windows Server 2012 and have some kind of client-server protection in place, the outbreaks are contained to their individual workstations.

Class 3:

This outbreak occurs in an area of a few hundred square miles. It often captures international media attention because the death toll is high, often in the thousands, and commonly covered up with some kind of industrial accident like the Chernobyl Accident of 1986. Looting and widespread panic may be part of the event. FEMA will not get there in time. Experts debate the number of zombies involved in a Class 3 because it could be as low as 500 and as high as 5000. Once the outbreak has been contained, separating the dead from the re-dead is not as much of a priority as the cleanup, which includes eliminating all evidence of zombie activity. Survivors that escape the area before final containment will be monitored by government agencies for decades after the event.

In the IT world, this kind of outbreak applies to server infestations. Only on rare occasions do these outbreaks reach national epidemic proportions, such as the Code Red worm and Nimda virus of 2001. At the individual network level, this type of outbreak is best compared to a Patient Zero scenario—spreading an unknown contagion to countless people before finally catching the attention of the medical community.

Class 4:

This is a Zombie Apocalypse in the truest sense, an outbreak that has reached a point where the contagion has surpassed all containment efforts. Widespread panic in major cities has given away to pockets of martial law to combat anarchy. Utilities have begun to shutdown in many areas. Casualty levels are incalculable because communications between any government agencies still in operation are sparse at best. Preppers will rejoice in having been proven right. They, along with politicians, the very rich and any other lucky souls will hide out in underground military bunkers or remote locations. Other popular refuges include tropical islands (since walking corpses will tend to decay faster) or near the North and South poles, figuring that frozen zombies are too slow to present much of a threat.

In the IT world, this kind of outbreak hasn't happened—yet. We're talking about a sophisticated contagion so powerful that computers around the world succumb to it, causing a cascading series of crashes of global proportions. Millions of industries and organizations will be impacted. In isolated nations, cyber warlords rise to power. Those businesses without working disaster recovery plans will die overnight. Communications networks fail. Satellites go rogue. Stock markets around the world plummet, causing weaker economies around the world to collapse. Martial law ensues in some places, widespread pandemonium and stupidity in others. The only thing missing would be Terminator cyborgs, Skynet and bad Schwarzenegger quotes.

While it should be noted that my Class 4 description may sound far-fetched, it is rooted in a reality that most people are better off being unaware of. Just covering all the cyberthreats that have been introduced into the wild within the past month would require a book larger than this one. As most IT Security people can tell attest to, cyberspace is full of invisible battles and secret wars that take place around the clock. A few of those secret weapons of cyber mass destruction, such as the Stuxnet worm of 2010, have managed to gain limited media attention in recent times. And as of this writing, stories have surfaced that the Center for Strategic and International Studies (CSIS) and the China Institute of Contemporary International Relations have been engaging in war games against each other, primarily as a way to pacify accusations that each side is launching cyber attacks against the other.

Another ugly truth is that the distinction between common contaminants and cyber assault weapons has been blurred. They're becoming one in the same. Contrary to the lingering misconception, anti-social computer whiz kids aren't sitting around creating these pieces of malicious code anymore, at least not for fun. Governments and transnational criminal organizations have taken the lead—and each new generation of cyber assault weapons grows more complex than the previous. More and more incidences of these attacks require removal processes that are beyond the scope of any one particular anti-virus/anti-malware software packages. Unlike nuclear missiles that require yellowcake, uranium, and other rare components with gazillion-dollar price tags, the cyber weapons of mass destruction are built with components based on knowledge, security vulnerabilities, and decent programming prowess. Every laptop with an Internet connection is a potential missile silo and detonator. The things that will bring about a Class 4 outbreak are commodities that no customs agent, TSA officer, or bomb-sniffing dog can detect. At least with a Zombie Apocalypse we would see and hear (and smell) the threat coming.

Understanding Protection during a Zombie Apocalypse

When it comes to the best zombie movies, one of the things I've always appreciated is that the story doesn't mess around. There are few opening credits. They don't waste time with romantic plot development; no drawn out introductions. All we see is someone going about their daily business and then BAM—zombies! Every good zombie story feels like waking up in the middle of The Running of the Bulls in Spain... and the bulls are on parade.

The human-zombie transformation erases all evidence of past memory, personality, and intelligence. They do, however, seem to retain many of the base functional principles associated with Gestalt psychology, especially continuity. Translation: if you're being chased by zombies and escape by ducking into a building and barricade the door, that's not necessarily the end of your troubles. Zombies are much like sharks in the fact that they don't need sleep like they did prior reanimation. Their need to feed will drive them to bang on the structure indefinitely, trying to break in to devour you... at least until something else draws them away.

During a Class 1 outbreak, the number of zombies would be relatively low. Your primary concern would be whether or not you had enough food and water to outlast the snarling stinky savages outside. With all that in place, it's time to find something to use for earplugs and maybe a John Grisham novel because you'll have time to kill. You're in for the kind of boredom on par with waiting for the return of Halley's Comet.

If this happened during a Class 3 outbreak, however, a whole new problem surfaces—the combined weight and mass of the zombies becomes a threat. The typical zombie body is roughly 45% water and has the agility of a 15-month old. A deluge of zombies in pursuit of prey will collectively take on the destructive force of a 6-foot high flash flood. Anything in their path will get pulverized—including slow zombies. The impact and crushing weight of the herd would eventually bulldoze most standard brick walls to collapse, possibly demolishing the entire structure... a gruesome fate.

Zombie computers act the same way: mindless, highly infectious entities that relentlessly seek out and attack the uninfected. And when a zombie computer reaches out across the Internet and makes contact with its Botnet, it joins a hostile mass of hundreds (sometimes thousands) of other digital zombies, marauding through cyberspace engaged in some of every kind of attack—all while the machine itself sits quietly on its owner's desk. People can't see or hear them coming, only experience the effects after the damage is done.

Baron Samedi says:

"Think of your layered approach to security like the walls and moats around a castle. The policies define the rules of who can come in and out and what they've got permission to do while inside."

Zombie-Possessed—How Will I Know When My Computer is Infected?

The symptoms of a zombie-infected computer, like its undead counterpart, tend to become more obvious as time goes on. People that have just returned from the dead will look reasonably normal from a distance (aside from any noticeable trauma experienced before their demise). Up close you'll notice the glazed eyes, stiff lumbering gait and runaway case of gingivitis as they try to eat you. With time, decay, and a few unsuspecting meals they become the shambling, blood-stained beasts we all love to hate.

This is where zombie computers differ. They always look the same on the outside, no snarling or bad eating habit. And what you see on the screen will basically look the same, too. It's the behavior that changes. Although there are all kinds of things happening in memory, the following are some symptoms you'll see on the screen. They're listed in no particular order mostly because they usually happen at random:

- System won't boot properly (e.g. - Blue Screen of Death on Windows, missing startup files, endless boot loops, etc.).
- Prankish screen displays pop up. NOTE: Even though this isn't impossible, this occurance is more Hollywood myth than reality. Most dangerous viruses and malware are intended to remain unseen and undetected.
- System is running slow or your CPU stays up near 100% even if you don't have any programs running.
- System's built-in Firewall is mysteriously disabled (especially with Microsoft Windows).
- Anti-virus software has been disabled.
- Any attempts to install or run anti-virus or anti-malware programs fail.
- Most of the screen is blocked by a fake anti-virus or some other warning that will not allow you to click on icons, run programs or access the Internet.

- ► Web browser hijacking (e.g. - you try to go to Google or a known anti-virus software website and the browser takes you to a completely different place).
- ► The homepage in your web browser has changed.
- ► Your Internet connection is slow or cutting out at random.
- ► Uncontrollable pop-up ads (not as common but they still happen on occasion).
- ► Web browser crashes at random.
- ► Unable to run system-specific monitors and configuration programs (Windows Task Manager, Activity Manager, etc.).
- ► System freezes and/or crashes at random.
- ► Some programs close unexpectedly.
- ► Your mouse pointer acts like it has a mind of its own.
- ► Motion trails happen as you move things on the screen.
- ► Your friends begin complaining that they're getting junk emails from you.
- ► Your Internet Service Provider informs you that your computer is infected. NOTE: Usually when this happens they are close to cutting off your connection.
- ► Some (or all) of your files disappear (common occurrence with ransomware).
- ► System files turn up missing or corrupted (especially certain .dll files).
- ► Computer shuts down or reboots for no apparent reason.

For lack of a better way to put it, your computer starts to feel like its haunted. This is why I often refer to virus and malware removal as "Ghostbustin".

The Dangers of Dead Computers

Characteristics Common to Most Known Species of Living Dead (cont'd):

Sound: Zombies can't speak but they tend to be easy to hear as they approach. Aside from their flat-footed shuffling, they make sounds ranging from throaty, uncontrollable moans to vicious, indescribable snarling. Based on most accounts, in a normal setting the Lurches are easy to hear as they approach. The snarling is usually a sign that they are dining on someone or they've spotted their next meal. NOTE: As zombies get older they tend to get harder to hear as they approach. Their vocal cords turn to beef jerky and with advanced decomposition their loss of body mass makes their footsteps lighter. In cyberspace, zombies don't make a sound until you see a popup ad.

Odor: Corpses stink. So do zombies. Survivors of zombie outbreaks have often attributed their luck to finding themselves downwind of the hordes. Smelling the ghouls long before being spotted by them gave the living a chance to hide and wait for the Stenches to pass. NOTE: The recently deceased that have just reanimated may take a few days before they start to smell.

A Computer's Life: From New to Disposal

Computers, like people, have a life-cycle. This cycle is the usefulness of that computer to you (or your company) from the time you purchase it through to the time you dispose of it.

The current industry standard for the life-cycle of a desktop computer is 4 to 5 years, while that of a laptop computer is 2 to 3 years. This is based on a series of statistical expectations, such as heavy usage, the likelihood of hardware failure over a certain period of time, and the ever-present advances in technology. While it looks great on paper, these standards were set to give people a timeline to buy new computers more often. Using this standard as a guide for how often to replace your computers isn't cost efficient, nor it is practical. The average person never comes close to pushing their computer to its limits. Computer manufacturers know this, and if they could have their way we would all be buying computers every 2 or 3 years like we trade in cell phones. With most computers made after 2004, the potential length of a computer's life has been radically extended, thanks to memory and storage becoming cheaper by the day. This section is dedicated to some possible ways to do get more use out of your old computers after you've replaced them.

Most home users have never heard of this 2 to 3 year standard, let alone attempted to stick to it. Most people are never told much of anything beyond what might prompt them to buy more software and accessories. Basic computer maintenance is also overlooked, resulting in computers getting more and more bogged down. This usually continues until the computer becomes "so slow" it's unbearable, causing the owner to think it's time to buy another computer, often regardless of whether or not the computer is outdated. This is like buying a new car, never doing basic maintenance to it (e.g. - oil changes, tune-ups, new brakes, rotating tires, etc.) and then getting rid of the vehicle once the engine starts to run rough or the tires go bald.

When is it time to get a new computer?

The answer isn't a simple one. It's best handled on a case by case basis. Upgrading your computer is worthy of a book unto itself. In the interest of simplifying it for this book, determining whether or not it is time to get a new computer starts with your time, your budget, and figuring out the answers to a series of "IFs".

If your computer has plenty of hard drive space, you've added the maximum amount of memory (RAM) that it can handle, you've installed the best graphics card it can support, you've done all the updates to your operating system (e.g. - the latest version of Microsoft Windows or Mac OS X) and you've done all the routine maintenance (e.g. - defragged hard drive, cleaned up registry, removed temp files, etc.), and the computer still turns out to be too slow for your tastes, more than likely it is the CPU itself that is the problem. While it is possible to upgrade the CPU with some computers, with others this isn't an option; check with the manufacturer's website. If after all that checking and/or cleaning and your computer is still too slow for your tastes, it's probably time to buy another computer—especially if your computer is over 4 or 5 years old.

New Life for Old Computers

Ask me about what you should do with an old computer and I'll always tell you that you should find a way to reuse it if it still works. And while I do believe in donating to worthy causes, I also believe that if you don't have time to properly clean your data off that computer, don't let it go unless you're 100% sure the person you're giving it to is computer savvy enough to know how to scrub the hard drive. Always remember to check for important files before wiping your old hard drive.

The cool thing about getting a new computer is that you've now got an old computer. A mistake many people immediately make is to treat that old computer like a piece of junk to be thrown out. Ever since I was a child, I always wanted to be a Mad Scientist... and every time I get my hands on an old computer I can hear the distant thunder of creative potential. You can be Frankenstein creating his next monster, turn that computer into music studio to become the next Rick Rubin, or come up with something wild that belongs in a Steven Spielberg flick. The choice is yours, and the biggest pre-requisite for most of the following ideas is that you've got to be in touch with your Inner SuperGeek and ready to try something a little out of your comfort zone.

The following ideas are the types of projects that are usually reserved for seasoned Geeks, people needing to study IT practices outside the classroom, mad scientists or ambitious novices that are interested in reusing an old computer for something fun and interesting. Each set of project descriptions has been kept vague on purpose; in great detail, this section would be worthy of an entire book unto itself. Instead, this is where it's time to put Google to good use.

Experimental Linux machine:

Most people have been conditioned to think that they have to either be on a PC (running Microsoft Windows) or on a Mac (running Mac OS X). The truth is, these days all the hardware is more alike than dissimilar. The computing world is bigger than Microsoft and Apple.

For the purposes of this book, Linux is being used as a catch-all term for any one of the free Unix-like operating systems available online for download. Along with Linux, FreeBSD is another popular alternative. Most small business owners and managers that I've worked with tend to look at Linux with the same optimistic-skepticism that most people look at electric cars. I've found that the only way to introduce them to the concept of a Linux network is to ease them into it. Linux is perfect for repurposing old computers. As an operating system, Linux comes in distributions (often referred to as "distros") and most distros have a Live CD version, allowing you to test drive different flavors of Linux by running solely off a disc (or a USB flash drive). If you find one you really like, you can then install it.

For anyone studying computers and networking in school, old computers are excellent for practice. If you can take a computer apart, put it back together, install any given operating system or network three or more computers together, you effectively have the basic know-how to administrator a SOHO environment network with any number of computers.

On a personal note, this is what I've usually done with my old computers. Aside from keeping me intune with what is happening in the Linux world, it satisfies my inner 10-year old Mad Scientist—plus it's definitely safer than a chemistry set.

Make a Hackintosh:

For those who have a PC and feel adventurous, it's possible to turn that PC into a Mac running Mac OS X. Yes, it's true. I've seen it and just might do it myself if you catch me bored and housebound on a rainy day. Crazy world, right?

To see if you can use any parts of your old computer towards a Hackintosh, check out **http://www.hackintosh.com/** or **http://www.hackintosh.org/** .

With a hard drive that is at least 1TB or more you can get real Frankensteinian and turn that old computer into a machine that runs Hackintosh, Microsoft Windows, and some flavor of Linux all built into one.

The cool thing about the Hackintoshes is that there's a whole subculture behind them. They're friendly, helpful and they don't get into all the PC vs Mac fanboy stuff. Keep in mind that Apple's End User Agreement for Mac OS X is pretty boilerplate. If you even think about building and selling Hackintoshes you'd be better off breaking the Oath of Omertà; at least the Mafia won't come after you with lawyers.

Web server:

By installing Linux on any old PC or Mac made after 2007 it can be turned into an in-house web server. If the Internet connection for your office has a static IP address, you can register yourcompanyname.com and have it point to that machine. Aside from setting up your own website, having your own web server is useful for things like setting up an FTP server or even your own private cloud, both providing a private space where you (and your customers) can exchange files from anywhere online. NOTE: if your website attracts a lot of traffic, you may want to move this server to a suitable co-location center or move the website to a professional hosting service like HTML.com or GoDaddy.com.

If you're not sure whether or not you've got a Static or Dynamic IP address, check with your Internet Service Provider.

Network Honeypot:

During a zombie outbreak, often a key strategy is not to go hunting for the zombies. Instead, let them come to you.

Zombies of all kinds are creatures of instinct; purely pre-programmed reaction to stimuli. Fire a single shot, zombies come running for food. Make noise walking through deserted city streets, zombies will come out in droves to seek out the source.

A Honey Pot is a computer set up on your network that serves as a decoy. Simply put, it's an early warning system that someone or something has intruded your network and is either snooping around or launching attacks. Because the Honey Pot shouldn't have any legitimate users on it, all kinds of traps and monitoring software can be installed. Generally they are purposely set up to get into than other production systems, specifically so that whatever gets in can be logged, tracked, and traced. If it's a human intruder, there will be multiple visits trying a few things each visit. If it's an automated attack or a zombie, it'll try to scan every port and use every known attack.

While there are a number of free and commercial Honeypot software packages out there, here are a few free ones to check out:

LaBrea (free Honeypot that runs on Linux, FreeBSD, and Windows):
http://labrea.sourceforge.net/labrea-info.html
NOTE: The FreeBSD version *should* be hackable to work on Mac OS X; as of this writing I have not tested this program on a Mac yet.

HoneyBOT (free Windows-based Honeypot):
http://www.atomicsoftwaresolutions.com/honeybot.php

To read more about Honeypots in general, check out:
**http://www.sans.org/reading_room/whitepapers/detection/
hands-honeypot_365**
(that is an underscore between "reading" and "room")

Automate your Home:

This one is as cool as it is easy to do. LinuxMCE is a free and open source PVR/Hone automation system that uses Bluetooth technology to support many devices handled by a gyroscopic remote control and automate different systems in the house. It will allow you to do everything from changing the setting for your air conditioner, set up motion-sensitive video cameras, turn off lights around the home, or record your favorite TV shows. The software can be downloaded here: **http://www.linuxmce.org/** .

Build your own Arcade Console:

For those that aren't familiar with gaming emulators, you're in for a treat. Emulators are programs that emulate gaming consoles, old orphaned computers, and even hundreds of those old stand-alone video games that were in the arcades back in the 80s and 90s. If you can think of it and it involved some kind of a computer, someone has probably made an emulator for it. Want to play some games that were out on pre-Macintosh Apple computers? You can do it. Missing your old Commodore 64 games? You can play all of them without pulling that old C64 out of the closet. Think of that old game you used to play in the arcades and you can probably find the ROM for it. Since many of these were running on systems with a fraction of the power of today's machines, the average old computer is beyond perfect for this purpose. These two links have information resources for practically every kind of arcade/computer system/gaming console emulator out there: **http://www.emulator-zone.com/** or **http://en.wikipedia.org/wiki/List_of_computer_system_emulators** .

The most popular arcade emulator out there is Multiple Arcade Machine Emulator (MAME): **http://mamedev.org/** and the ROMs themselves (games extracted from the original media) can be found with a quick Google search.

Disclaimer: The copyright status of the game ROMs for MAME vary, ranging from Abandonware to actively enforced. Neither the author, publisher, or anyone affiliated with this book can be held responsible for any actions taken on the basis of this information provided. Download and play at your own risk.

Convert it into a stand-alone firewall:

Adding this to the list was a bit of a Catch-22 for me. There are plenty of tutorials online that cover this topic, plus the instant I added one to this book it'd be outdated. On the other hand, if I omitted the mention of turning an old computer into a firewall, I'd probably get scores of scathing emails chastising me for not including one of the most fundamentally useful projects for an old desktop.

Set up a file server:

For other computers on your home network. This is especially handy if your SOHO or home network has a bunch of important files that everyone needs access to, regardless of whether they're on a PC, Mac, tablet or smartphone. Aside from documents it's also great for storing everyone's photos, video clips, audio, etc.

While it's possible to simply take an old PC or Mac and simply turn on file sharing to make it a file server, it's better to have much more control over the file server settings, particularly for security purposes. FreeNAS is a nice package for the high end SOHO environment and allows for additional plugins. It's based on FreeBSD, open source and best of all it's free. Check it out: **http://www.freenas.org/**

Another file server package is Open Media Vault. It's free, open source, based on Debian Linux, and has plugins for expanded functionality. I personally like this package because it is a bit simpler to install and has web interface to manage all the settings.
http://openmediavault.org/

Another option is the Windows Home Server. It's a Windows-based, media-streaming server, designed specifically for home networks or SOHOs with 10 computers or less (more licenses available from Microsoft). It's a little easier to set up than FreeNAS and Open Media Vault and aimed slightly more towards the home user, but it's not free (starts at around $50 dollars, more if you want to buy it pre-installed on a PC). A free trial is available for download; check out:
http://windows.microsoft.com/en-US/windows/products/
windows-home-server

NOTE: All three packages may require adding memory (RAM) or storage space (another hard drive). If you intend to use them on an old computer please confirm that your machine meets their minimum requirements before installing.

Donate your CPU power:

Although a good portion of this book focuses on defending against globally distributed zombie outbreaks, there is a way to take the same principle behind vicious Botnets and apply it to the common good: Volunteer Computing.

Also known as Grid Computing, this is where you donate your computer's idle time to academic, engineering, medical and/or scientific research. This is done by allowing your computer to be joined with many other individual computers spread out all over the Internet. Together, they create a huge system with incredible computational power that surpasses most institutional supercomputers. By breaking up the work into tiny pieces and having them processed across many thousands of computers, research time is reduced from years to months. One such organization is the World Community Grid (**http://www.worldcommunitygrid.org/**), dedicated to various humanitarian causes such as fighting cancer, AIDS research, and projects that combat world hunger. The software used to power many Volunteer Computing projects is called BOINC (Berkeley Open Infrastructure for Network Computing). It is free, compatible with PC, Mac and Linux, and can be downloaded here: **http://boinc.berkeley. edu/** . More info about BOINC-based distributed research can be reviewed at **http://www.boinc-wiki.info/** . BOINC can be installed on any old or new computer. I mentioned it here because this option will also work along with one or more of the other ideas outlined in this section.

The following projects all require a person with either (A) better-than-average computer savvy or (B) a lot of computer fearlessness and unshakable patience.

Media Projects Using Old Computers:

- ► Stream media throughout your home
- ► Create your own Internet Radio Station
- ► Build your own DVR—MythTV

Projects Using Old Routers:

- ► Extend coverage by using it as another wireless access point (AP)
- ► Relieve wireless N routers from supporting G
- ► Convert it into a Wi-Fi hotspot

Firmware Projects Using Old Routers:

- ▶ Experiment with aftermarket firmware
- ▶ Make it a repeater to take the signal further
- ▶ Use it as a wireless bridge or gaming adapter
- ▶ Offer VPN connections or connect networks together

Cybercrime Potluck:
Dangerous Secrets from Dead Computers

First and foremost, old computers should NEVER be thrown away in the garbage. None of it is biodegradable and some of the metals and plastics inside the machine are toxic and bad for the environment. Beyond that, if the hard drive in that computer gets into the wrong hands before it gets buried in a landfill, ALL the data on it can be retrieved, including usernames and passwords to your banking website, credit card numbers, and other types of sensitive information that should never be released into the wild.

Sound crazy? It's not. It happens every day.

The saying "One man's trash is another man's treasure" is a reality. People go through other people's garbage, especially in situations where there is little or no food, lawn cuttings or other perishables in the bin. It could be a person searching for recyclables to sell. Or a junk collector that knows good stuff is regularly thrown out on that route. Somewhere in between there is the possibility of the Identity Thief looking for documents containing exploitable information. In any case, it's a jackpot payday if they find your computer's intact hard drive—potentially a winning lottery ticket with the payout coming straight from your wallet.

To put it into perspective, according to a study done by New York-based computer forensic firm Kessler International, an estimated 40% of all hard drives sold on eBay contain data that is retrievable. In general terms this is probably a conservative estimate that fluctuates. It could be as high as 4 out of every 5 old computers that are thrown out, resold, or donated to charity have personal data on their hard drives that can be easily recovered. From my own experiences, with the few dozen used computers that I've checked out for potential buyers, I've found personal and confidential data on <u>every one of them.</u> While it's true that someone had deleted the personal files in most cases, they always left the operating system (usually some version of Microsoft Windows) and the installed programs intact.

There are a few dozen free data recovery tools that are available for download that can retrieve any files that weren't properly erased. Anyone with a little tech knowledge and a knack for snooping could recover all the personal and confidential files on that computer and start building a reasonably accurate profile on all its users. I put this to the test by going to a couple of flea markets, a thrift store and a pawn shop and purchasing two old laptops and two hard drives that were once in desktops. The following results were gleaned after about half an hour of poking around with each one:

- ▶ Hard drive #1: appears to have been in a computer that had two homes: first, it was owned by a freight company, second it was owned by a woman. Either the woman received the computer as-is from the company or the computer was stolen and came into her possession. There was an old unprotected Microsoft Access database that contained all sorts of client info, including some 14-digit numeric entries that were plaintext (unencrypted) and looked conspicuously like authorization codes of some sort. The woman was unmarried; she frequented several popular matchmaking websites, used MSN Instant Messenger regularly, often shopped at Dillard's, and made the common mistake of using the same username and password for everything.

- Hard drive #2 (still in the laptop): Contained product photos and accompanying descriptions from a man who sold used products on eBay. His payment ledger was a simple Excel spreadsheet; several pages of Paypal accounts, check numbers with bank account and routing info, and full credit card numbers along with the full cardholder names and addresses. After skimming through the emails in his Outlook inbox, it became apparent that he and his wife were expecting a baby girl. Based on the number of Monster. com emails, he gave up his eBay venture, put his resume out there and went job hunting. He also collected porn video AVI and MPEG files, more than likely ripped from DVDs. Most of them were from Bangbros.com, Brazzers.com and Tube8.com.

- Hard drive #3 (still in the laptop): Previously owned by a man that played video games, listened to 90s techno music and watched enough gay porn to make Liberace blush—all of which he attempted to delete or uninstall. The lack of an Outlook email inbox indicated that he was probably accustomed to using web-based email services like Yahoo, Hotmail, or Gmail. Based on the websites in his bookmarks, he was probably a health nut: frequented jogging and fitness websites, an avid reader of articles about organic foods, and a die-hard NY Giants fan.

- Hard drive #4: Owned by a high school student that used it to do homework and frequent free porn websites. Due to some inconsistencies with the permissions, a deeper check showed that it was previously owned by a local college and used in a computer lab. The machine itself had not been properly cleaned at all. Every time the computer was turned on it would still quietly try to reconnect with a file server on campus. A few minutes of forensic scanning turned up scores of logins and passwords along with a few thousand essay papers. Judging by the cheesy topics and Twitter-style grammar they were probably English 050 students.

Need I say more?

The Bizarre Afterlife of Data

One of the most paradoxical secrets about your computer: the data saved on its hard drive is more plentiful and persistent than you'll ever know. This fact might seem strange because we're always seeing and hearing about events that point to the contrary: My computer crashed. A virus deleted my homework! I never got that email. Everyone has at least one story about typing up something important in a word processor or an email when the program suddenly bombed and they had to start all over.

For most people, the loss of photos and recordings due to a computer or device crash has practically become as predictable as puberty. Anyone that hasn't experienced at least one of those scenarios is either computer illiterate, retired from the workforce before the early 1990s, or so young they probably shouldn't be reading this book.

Electromagnetism is used to store and retrieve information on your hard drive. Because of that, Data Remanence refers to the leftover impressions of data that remains on a hard drive even after that data has supposedly been erased. The remnants found on any hard drive are caused by one of three things:

▶ **Basic file deletion**—when we delete a file, whether directly or by dropping it in the recycling bin or trash can and clicking empty, that file isn't actually gone. It is still on the hard drive, flagged in a way to let your computer know that the space it occupies is available to be overwritten if the computer needs to use it.

▶ **Basic reformatting**—because formatting a hard drive can be a timely process, there are different levels. The fastest (simplest) format level just flags all the space on the hard drive as being available for use. If you compare your hard drive to an apartment building, think of the level of thoroughness as the difference between forcing all the residents to move out (fastest) versus tearing down the entire building and reconstructing it from scratch (slowest).

▶ **The medium itself**—(e.g. - the hard drive, USB flash drive, SD card, etc.) allows previously written data to be recovered.

To get an idea of how data remanence works, think of a notepad and a No. 2 pencil. Someone can write a secret message on the pad and then decide to get rid of it. If they tore off the sheet and threw it in the garbage, you could easily go into the garbage to retrieve the sheet and read the message. If they used an eraser to remove the message from the sheet, you could look very closely at the paper itself; usually there are enough remnants of the pencil strokes to figure out the message. And if you're really determined to know what that secret was, you can look closely at the sheet that was beneath the top sheet, study the impressions from the pencil point and simply reconstruct the message.

Should your hard drive (or other storage media) fall into the wrong hands, anyone that knows how to exploit data remanence can easily recover all sorts of sensitive information that has been typed, viewed or processed on your computer. Think about how many login names and passwords you've typed to access various websites. How many times you've connected to your online banking and all the account information on the screen. Each time you've typed in the credit/debit card while purchasing something online. Unless you know how to thoroughly clean the data remanence from your hard drive (on a regular basis), effectively there's some kind of a digital snapshot or footprint of almost everything you've typed, looked at, listened to, purchased with, or done using your computer.

The top malicious hackers know this secret—and their zombies love it. Sophisticated coders design their zombie contagions to include searching the data remanence on an infected computer's hard drive in much the same way that CSI agents will search through a murder scene for fibers and DNA evidence. And just like with any criminal investigation, the information recovered from the remnants all become part of what they use to take you down.

Shoot it in The Head—Safe Data Destruction (digital)

Due to data remanence, the single most effective way to insure the erased data on your hard drive cannot be retrieved is to physically destroy the hard drive itself. This can be done with a drill, hammer, shredder, degauss, or some other destructive method. DISCLAIMER: Neither the author, the publisher, nor book seller can be held responsible for any damages that may occur from (or during) the process of destroying your hard drive. The following methods are provided mostly for those that are very paranoid or easily entertained:

- **Drill**—bore several holes into the top of the hard drive (the flat surface, usually with a label with all the manufacturer info printed on it) and into the bottom (the circuit board on the underside). If you can drill clean through from one side to the other, definitely do so. Aim for inside the circular impressions, as this is where the actual storage platters are inside the hard drive. Any standard power drill should do. Protective eyewear, gloves and facemask should be worn during the process.
- **Hammer**—To bite off of one of my favorite Marvel comic book characters, "Hulk, SMASH!" While this approach may be fun for demolition junkies, this should be done with caution. The bigger the hammer, the fewer the strokes needed to get the job done. Since the hard drive is made of various plastics and metals, keep in mind that pieces <u>will</u> fly everywhere when you start smashing it. Protective eyewear, gloves and facemask should be worn during the process.
- **Shredder**—most computer recyclers have hard drive shredders on site. In operation, it looks and sounds like something out of a James Bond movie.
- **Degaussing**—also known as demagnetizing, is a process where the magnetic media inside the hard drive is erased by a powerful magnetic field. When properly implemented, it makes any data formerly stored on the drive impossible to read. And while professional hard drive degaussers are the most "safely convenient" solution for cleaning your old hard drive, they can cost anywhere from $2000 to $30,000 dollars USD.

> "...there's some kind of digital snapshot or footprint of almost everything you've typed, looked at, listened to, purchased with, or done using your computer."

▶ **Other destructive methods**—can be almost anything. I've seen hard drives destroyed with low-grade explosives, run over with monster trucks, shot with guns, steel wool scrubbed on the platters inside, and dropped into an [outdoor] homemade smelting furnace. If you happen to be one of those pyromaniacs that likes to burn things, I would recommend against using fire to destroy a hard drive. There are plenty of materials inside a hard drive that will give off noxious fumes when burned, the kind that can be dangerous when inhaled.

To get rid of a SSD, Flash drive, etc, use physical destruction.

Wiping your Hard Drive Clean (non-destructive, for selling or donating)

Since you'll probably be cleaning the computer yourself, it's best to use some system cleaning software to delete your trash folder, delete documents (and other personal files), delete emails, contacts, and your Internet browser's cache, history and cookies. All software with non-transferable licenses should be completely uninstalled, too. Whatever utility you use should not only delete your files but overwrite them first so they can't be recovered.

When you begin looking at different programs to wipe your hard drive clean, you'll probably see references to different standards. The plain truth is that there's enough on these standards to fill a few chapters and most of it can put you to sleep faster than any short-acting anesthesia. To simplify your search for a good file eraser or hard drive cleaner, your choice should meet or exceed at least one of the following data sanitization standards:

- ► Secure Erase (minimum form of data sanitization)
- ► DoD 5220.22-M (US Department of Defense - very popular)
- ► AFSSI-5020 (US Air Force)
- ► AR 380-19 (US Army)
- ► NAVSO P-5239-26 (US Navy)
- ► NCSC-TG-025 (US National Security Agency)

Microsoft Windows hard-drive wipe:

For Windows, there are plenty of disk cleaning utilities, including Wipedrive System Saver (**http://www.whitecanyon.com**) and Paragon Disk Wiper (**http://www.disk-wiper.net**). Wipedrive System saver has become a favorite because it many PC manufacturers these days ship computers without Windows media and this version of Wipedrive allows you to wipe your personal data off the drive but leave Microsoft Windows intact, making it safe to donate.

Mac OS X hard-drive wipe:

For Mac OS X, although there are disk-wipe utilities out there like SuperScrubber, the built-in disk utility does a great job at securely erasing any hard drive. There are several modes: Don't Erase Data, Zero Out Data, 7-Pass Erase, and 35-Pass Erase.

- ► The Zero-Out-Data mode writes zeros over your hard drive once to erase data on the computer. Granted, it's not up to government security standards but it's good enough for most home users.

- ► The 7-Pass Erase mode meets the U.S. Department of Defense 5220.22-M standard. It writes over your data seven times, an excellent solution for businesses.

- ► Forget about Don't-Erase-Data. It does the bare minimum to "clean" your hard drive and, although it may look empty, there are dozens of programs that can recover all of your files with the click of a button (see "The Bizarre Afterlife of Data", page 171). And the 35-Pass Erase mode is more of a psychotic joke than a useful feature. Even though it is 99.999% effective, it will take 35-times as long to run as Zero-Out-Data—possibly days to complete (depending on the speed of your Mac and size of the hard drive).

Data Shredders

Should you decide against destroying the hard drive and need all data removed, the other alternative is to use a Data Shredder.

Baron Samedi says

"There are digital file shredders, your computer's equivalent to a paper shredder. Most of them are either cheap or free. Get one and keep it handy."

Simply put, a data shredder goes through the extra steps to overwrite the data with useless data before actually deleting the data, making it irretrievable. Also known as file shredders, is the software equivalent of running a document through a paper shredder and then burning the confetti.

PC:
http://www.fileshredder.org/

Mac OS X:
http://www.apple.com/downloads/dashboard/business/shredder.html

And once you've got your info cleaned off the computer…

Sell the Computer or Give it Away

Once your hard drive has been properly cleaned, you should be good to go with the rest of the transaction. Just be sure to turn the computer over to the person as promised (i.e. - if they're expecting a PC with Windows pre-installed on it, make sure you re-install Windows and check with Microsoft and transferring the license. Same with Mac OS X. For more details on how to do this properly, please refer to the following sites:

Transferring license ownership of a used PC:
**http://www.microsoft.com/OEM/en/licensing/sblicensing/Pages/
transfer_oem_licenses.aspx**

Transferring license ownership of a used Mac:
https://discussions.apple.com/docs/DOC-5641

Donate or Obliterate—
What to do with that old computer

When it comes to donating your computer, the easiest route may seem to be to just drop the computer off at a school or charity. The problem is that most of the time they're not equipped to repair and upgrade them… but refurbishers are. A nonprofit refurbisher (or a school-based refurb) will replace any potentially faulty parts, making sure that computer is 100% factory-grade and all the installed software is legal, and then send the machine on to a school, nonprofit, or charity. As of this writing, most refurbishers work with computers that are Pentium-III or faster—in non-Geek speak, basically any usable computer manufactured after 2003 and is Internet-capable. If your computer is older than that, you'll probably end up taking it to a recycler instead. To find a list of refurbishers geared toward nonprofits, check out **www.techsoup.org** or contact your city dump.

Recyclers, on the other hand, are a service that is essentially the end of the road for that computer. Unlike the inhouse recycling I addressed previously with reusing a computer for another purpose, Recyclers will take the computer apart, set aside the usable components, safely remove hazardous materials, and break down the remains. At the end of their process nothing left. A quick Google search for "computer recycler" and the name of your town should turn up listings for recyclers in your area. If all else fails, call your city landfill.

Whether you're sending your computer off to a Recycler or Refurbisher, always check their website before you donate. They have designated drop-off locations and often provide specific instructions for how the computers should be delivered. If you're still not sure about whether or not they'll accept your computer, give them a call. Although Recyclers will accept and scrap any computer, there are plenty of computers that Refurbishers can't accept. Also, be sure to include all the accessories (mouse, keyboard, documentation, all the CDs and DVDs that came with the system, and anything else that came with it). Be sure to include the proof of license, which will help with the legal transfer of the operating system. Most refurbishers only accept complete computer systems.

When donating a computer with Microsoft Windows pre-installed (i.e. - there weren't any installation CDs or DVDs that came with it), keep in mind that its license is only valid on that OEM machine. It's a bit of a headache but, in the interest of keeping things legal for the charitable organization, please be sure to do a legal transfer. Computers running Mac OS X and Linux have different license requirements (and usually have installation discs). While some sources may recommend that you provide the operating system that came with the machine, I have to stick by my caveat: if there's no way you can wipe that hard drive and reinstall the OS then just do the wipe. It's better to make sure all your personal data is erased and let the refurbisher work out the missing OS details. As far as I know, recyclers won't care.

On the remote chance that your computer is still under warranty, you can contact customer support to find out how to remove your personal files. Outside of the rich and famous, this is very rare. By the time most computers are old enough to be sent to a refurbisher or recycler, the original owners can't even remember when the warranty expired.

For tax purposes, you'll definitely want to keep a list of what you donate to a nonprofit refurbisher. They'll provide a tax receipt upon request. Although businesses can deduct the un-depreciated value of the computer, individuals can only deduct the current market value.

ISLAND OF LOST SOULS (1932)

Corporate Zombies:
Living, Dead and Unemployed

The Sleepwalkers

(l. Homo Sapiens Animata Mortuus Karloff-Lugosi):
These Voodoo-influenced golems, usually the mindless minions of an evil arch-villain, were introduced to the world in films like WHITE ZOMBIE (1932) and virtually every zombie movie made prior to the 1960s. Their trademarks are being wide-eyed, slow moving, brain dead, and rigor mortis stiff with "sleepwalker" style outstretched arms. Compared to the other zombie types, Sleepwalkers are the easiest to outrun, making them seem almost innocuous—unless they get ahold of you.

Among the living, this best describes most Internet users that are technology illiterates, including many users who got online later in life. This is actually a plus because they don't often go to websites that might harbor links to infectious malware. If this doesn't make sense, ask yourself when was the last time you heard of a syphilis outbreak among senior citizens?

The Strollers

(l. Homo Sapiens Animata Mortuus Romero):
The archetypes for modern zombies, these creatures were made famous by films like NIGHT OF THE LIVING DEAD (1968) and most recently through the TV show THE WALKING DEAD (2011). These ghouls are stiff and have the functional intelligence of a mosquito. Aside from their speed, Strollers are deadly and relentless in their pursuit of feeding on live human flesh.

Among the living, this best describes the average adult users that are reasonably comfortable browsing the Internet, mostly because they won't give any thought to what they're clicking on before they click on it.

Anything related to Information Security and Risk Management is worthy of its own college courses. In a perfect world, every small business manager should know this stuff. Conventional information security practices dictate that the policies in this chapter should be part of a larger Information Assurance (IA) policy document. The reality is quite different. For every business client that followed my advice to start an IA document there were at least half a dozen others that agreed the document was necessary but never bothered to follow through. Candidly speaking, I can't blame them. All the ins and outs of the ISO/IEC Security Standards are enough to make anyone revert back to using the pencil, paper and abacus.

In an effort to find a rudimentary middle ground between functional policy documents and realistic expectations for the typical small business, I've decided to break a few rules. For the purposes of providing you with an easy (but useful) introduction to policies, procedures and plans, I've trimmed away much of documentation and reporting. This chapter focuses on the basics of an IT policy, BYOD policy, Security policy and some key points related to Information Security in the office.

The Truth about Digital Privacy in the Office

In the late 90s, my business partners and I were riding high on the Dot Com rush, so much that we were able to purchase a small web design in Richmond. Twice a week I had to drive about an hour to spend the day there. On two occasions I arrived to find the new web designer curled up fetal position and asleep under his desk; the second time I fired him on the spot. He turned hostile after I took his key, threatening to sue if I didn't let him get to the files on "his" computer. I welcomed his threats, even taunting him a bit. A little digging finally explained his sleeping habits: He spent his nights as a submissive male in a show at S&M club, brought in on a leash and whacked with a riding crop. He had been exchanging photos with other people in the BDSM scene using his Yahoo email address and saving them to that PC. Compared to what I've seen on various computers since then, his activities were pretty tame.

I use that example to bring up the fact that digital privacy in the workplace is mostly a false sense of security. It's comparable to the notion that you can ask an undercover cop if s/he is a cop and they have to admit to being law enforcement or it is Entrapment. Undercover agents lie about their line of work all the time. Jails and prisons are full of people that learned the truth the hard way. The purpose of this chapter is to enlighten business managers and employees alike on the truths about digital privacy in the office.

1) **My email is private.**

The typical email message is about as private as passing a handwritten note to someone. This is because most of the time the messages we send and receive are sent as 'cleartext', the digital equivalent of a postcard—anyone who intercepts the message between Point A and Point B can read (and understand) its contents without using any special descrambling methods.

At first thought you might shrug your shoulders and say "Who cares?" After all, the U.S. Postal system processes around 554 million pieces of mail every day, a little over 6400 pieces per second. And in cyberspace, an estimated 3 million emails are sent rocketing around the world every second. Either way, who would be insane enough to go digging through all that mail in transit to find a postcard you sent or received?

In most cases it's not about you but the keywords and types of information that are in your messages. Just like you can use "Find" in your favorite word processing program to search for a word in a document, it is possible to search through everything on your computer as well as doing what is commonly referred to as "sniffing"—intercepting data as it passes real-time through that computer's network connection. This data may contain your name, a password, a credit card number, anything. The typical zombie, unlike their walking dead counterparts, can be designed to seek out types of information with the accuracy of a top thoroughbred sniffer dog.

Baron Samedi says:

"Never send anything over email that you wouldn't send on a postcard through Snail Mail."

There are exceptions to this advice but unless you're familiar with public key encryption then I suggest sticking to the Baron's tip. This is especially true with sending sensitive information like passwords and credit card numbers. The reason for this is because some contagions, once they've zombie infected a computer, will search it for valuable data such as email addresses, address books (full names, addresses, etc.), personal identity info, credit card info, access codes, and even images (yes, images). Anything it finds gets sent back to its Botnet command center. Seconds later the stolen information can be on the other side of the world. Stolen data gets compiled into databases that are bought, sold and traded between cybercriminals like stocks on the NASDAQ.

Remember, standard email messages are essentially postcards. No matter how secure your computer might be, you can't vouch for the security of the other person's computer or anywhere in between. Although the chances of having one of your emails intercepted are usually pretty remote, all it takes is one exposure in the right place at the wrong time. According to an annual study conducted by Javelin Strategy & Research, Inc., between 2005 and 2011, over 56 million people were the victims of identity theft. The sad truth is that those people all shared the same remote chances of being exposed, too.

2) My company can't read my email because I'm using Gmail (or Yahoo, MSN, Mac, etc.).

This one is tricky. While it is true that you can use https to make your connection to Gmail encrypted and unreadable by any one in between, this doesn't mean your employer has no say in the matter. Through their IT policies, many companies spell out that they reserve the right to review all communications that pass through company equipment. That means anything that passes through your desktop/laptop computer, phone, voice mails, emails, smart devices and anything else transmitted over the network. It a company wanted to put data-taps on their employee computers, however creepy it may sound, they would have the right to do so.

The legal perspective is that you're being paid on company time while on company property and using company's hardware/software over an Internet connection being paid for by the company. Not only is this the conventional wisdom, that's the way many courts are ruling when faced with situations where the policy isn't expressly written.

3) I created the files; I have a right to make copies of them when I leave my job.

Regardless of how it might feel when you receive (or create) company materials, you don't own them. They belong to the company. When you're at work on company time, the company owns anything you output that's related to work. Every document, spreadsheet and email is theirs. If you're producing creative, such as designing t-shirts or brochures, they own the design and the master files. Not only is this normally covered in most "work for hire" agreements, this is also addressed in Employer-Employee agency law within U.S. Copyright code.

When you leave a company you're expected to leave behind anything that is company property—laptops, tablets, books, credit cards, keys, company vehicles, and etc. Most of people have worked enough jobs to instinctively know this protocol without having to refer to the company policy manual or any agreements signed in the beginning. This also applies to digital materials such as emails, documents, memos, proposals, reports, confidential specifications—basically anything you can print, duplicate, or send over the Internet.

On a personal note, I've seen both sides to this scenario. When I was 19, I landed my first internship with a small 5-person startup. I designed graphics for Point-of-Purchase advertising systems, a predecessor of today's business website. It quickly evolved into my first professional Graphic Design job, lasting for about two years. On a Tuesday afternoon my boss informed me that he had taken another job and the company was permanently closing its doors on that upcoming Friday. Everyone else was going their own way. As the only college student, he assumed I would go back to regular life as a student. What he didn't understand was how personally invested I had become in the company. The use of computers for Graphic Design was so relatively new that my school wasn't teaching it in the classroom yet—and I had spent the past two years creating more computer graphics than everyone else in my entire department. While on the clock I had created a great portfolio of work. When I asked if I could make copies of my work, he said "No". Even worse, he declined my offer to buy the production computer from the company. It didn't matter that the company's owner was a geriatric multi-millionaire that spent most of his time competing in Bridge tournaments around the world.

News of this closing felt like first heartbreak. Once he mentioned that a co-worker was coming in later to box up the production equipment, I put my anguish aside and quietly went into action. With less than two hours and no blank floppy disks, my only option was to print my samples. Due to a disorganized project filing system and a painfully slow color printer, I was only able to smuggle out three pieces.

For several years I held a grudge. The experience left me with deep, unspoken fears of putting my creative energy into design work and having nothing to show for it. Everything I designed after that ended up in my portfolio, without permission and regardless of any Copyrights or Trademarks the employer may have established.

About 10 years later I was a partner in that high-riding Internet web design company. One of our sales reps had gone rogue and we had to fire him. The next thing we knew he was out in the marketplace doing his best to imitate some of our biggest offerings that my partners and I had originally created. And what he couldn't imitate he tried to pass off as being one of his ideas, regardless of the fact that he had no design or technical background. A few cease-and-desist letters from our lawyer helped, but not much. As a business manager and partner, that turned out to be among the first of numerous times that my Intellectual Property was exploited or blatantly ripped off. It taught me that the other side of the business equation couldn't be ignored, either.

These days, any time I mentor young graphic designers, programmers or writers I stress a middle ground—collecting samples for your portfolio is super important—but it has to be done the right way. Get permission from your employer or, better yet, write it into your employee agreement to where you reserve the right to keep a copy of your work that isn't confidential or proprietary in nature.

4) If I leave a company (i.e. - new job, get fired, etc.) I have the right to erase all the files on my laptop or desktop.

On occasion you'll hear about people having to learn this the hard way. As spelled out in #3, your company owns the works you produce on company time. Just like you don't inherit the right to copy your files, you don't have the right to erase them either.

The other side of this equation deals with business continuity. When you leave, someone will be hired to replace you. It's not fair for your former employer to have paid you for your work only to have you leave and then they have to pay someone else to remake everything because you deleted it. That would be like you hiring an architect to design your dream house only to have her destroy the plans after you paid her. Of all the situations in this chapter, this one can have the most unpredictable consequences.

One scenario that comes to mind involves a small advertising boutique where the head of sales got into a terrible fight with the owner. The sales rep was fired and told to turn in her laptop. A few days later when the owner tried to use it, the machine would freeze on a black screen shortly after boot. I was brought in to fix the problem. As it turns out, everything on the laptop had been wiped out except for an AAC music file named 'ClickMe'. Since my scans for booby-traps came up clean, I clicked it. "Dirty Work" by Steely Dan played from the speakers.

At first the former employee adamantly disavowed all knowledge of how this happened. "It said it caught a virus" she claimed with coy cluelessness. And I might have bought her innocent act if she hadn't done such an amateur wipe job on the laptop. Not only was I able to recover all the files, I also found forensic evidence in her web browser files that showed activity in her iTunes account right before everything disappeared. Working off of speculation, I claimed I had retrieved all sorts of evidence against her, topped off with her purchasing the Steely Dan song. Once I rattled off the fines and prison time for her criminal charges she confessed to all sorts of things—expensive meals on the company's tab, secret side deals, stealing a copy of the client list. She even confessed to an extramarital affair with her neighbor.

Keep in mind that you may be asked to give up your desktop or laptop at any given time. This prevents the need to ask to copy your files and delete them from the machine before it is taken away. The instant you show any reservations about turning over your computer, people will get curious and go digging. Whatever they find on that machine, no matter how insignificant, is now subject to review—personal letters, chat transcripts, cached copies of those forgotten photos from Spring Break on Facebook that someone tagged you in. The solution is simple: Avoid using company computers for personal affairs or, if you absolutely have to (and it's not against policy), store all your personal files either in the cloud (e.g. - Google docs, iCloud, etc.) or store them on a USB drive (hard drive, flash drive, etc.). As an employee, the only time you <u>might</u> expect some digital privacy in the workplace is if:

- ► Your company allows you to use your own device (i.e.—a BYOD policy),
- ► You're getting online with a data plan that you pay for (e.g.—mobile broadband on a laptop, smartphone, or tablet), and

▶ You're doing either of the two in full compliance with the company's policies (i.e. - you're on break, there's no conflict of interest, and you're not sending out anything company-related).

Anything else should be considered private only if your company doesn't know about it or they just don't care.

The Company IT Policy: A Necessary Evil

Baron Samedi says:

"If you're running a business with eight or more employees (and as many computers), start an IT Policies document. Consider it a living document that will grow and evolve to reflect the current computing and web browsing trends. Over time it will become your best friend. It will save you money and, sooner or later, it will save your business."

NOTE: IT Policy documents range in size from a few sheets to manuals that are hundreds of pages in bound notebooks. For the sake of this book, I will refer to them all as an IT Policy document, regardless of size and scope.

There are templates for IT Policy documents all over the web. I've seen some commercial-grade templates that are extremely thorough and cost around $500 to $600 dollars. For those of us who can't afford anything like that, here are a couple of awesome links to check out:

http://www.sans.org/security-resources/policies/

http://humanresources.about.com/od/internetpolicysample/ Internet_Acceptable_Use_Policy_Internet_Policy_Samples.htm

It's pretty easy to use one of these as a starting point. When people know the boundaries of how they can use the network resources it actually makes life a little easier. With the small companies that have hired me to fix problems, most (if not all) the following was true:

- ► The person that was designated to handle IT had little or no IT experience in their background before they were saddled with the responsibility.

- ► Management didn't appreciate the value of their network unless it was offline.

- ► Their network was relatively open and unrestricted.

Since we're talking about IT Policies, it would be easy and self-serving of me to speak of this topic in all kinds of lofty, management-friendly pseudo Geek-speak. The truth is, putting together an IT Policy from scratch sucks rocks. There's nothing interesting about the process; it's a blend of legalese with IT jargon, all basically defining management's expectations about how employees shall and shall not use the computers, data, and network. In the grand scheme of IT achievement, the observable payoff is about as exciting as establishing the rules of engagement for a high school prom. On that same note, once an IT Policy is in place it adds other strengths to the network that the technology itself cannot provide: Governance.

One of the key benefits of an IT policy is that it establishes boundaries. There's no way to maintain a secure and productive network without boundaries. People need parameters. It's not much different than the way we tested our parents and teachers when we were teens. Given the opportunity, people in general <u>will</u> try—and do—some of everything using their work computers, regardless of how inappropriate, crazy or downright stupid it may seem. Many of these boundaries also tie into conduct and protocol in other areas of the business, including the penalties for breaking those rules.

Generally speaking, the sooner a company adopts some kind of IT Policy, the better off it will be in the long run. This is especially true for small businesses in fast growth industries. The following is an example of what happens to a company network when the company hits the jackpot, no one is babysitting the kids, and the gate is left wide open...

Saved by Zombies

I was teamed up with another consultant; both of us tasked to audit and grade the IT infrastructure of a television production company. There were also intermittent speed problems with their Internet access that neither their ISP nor their IT people could track down. Unlike the typical small business, they had over 200 core employees spread out in offices between Washington DC, New York City, and Los Angeles. Within the first hour of being in their conference room, I'd already been hacking around on their no-security network, snooping through folders like a hungry dog while my partner conducted the interviews. Their IT guys seemed like dependable team players but they had been there for less than a year. Each had previously worked in a completely unrelated profession, hired because the offered salary didn't attract any qualified IT candidates. Their Chief Technical Officer had never fixed a computer in his life. By lunch there was no need to continue with the audit—their network had already flunked.

For businesses of this size, speed problems on the network were often due to hardware issues, like a hub somewhere that should've been replaced with a switch. The company president, who admitted to that he knew more about life on Mars than his understanding of computers, claimed their network problems were caused by noise (in his mind, any problems involving "wires" were caused by signal distortion)—and it turned out he was correct. There was noise on the network, but not the kind he suspected. Electronic interference isn't capable of repeatedly transmitting the same deliberate, errant data... only zombies do that.

This turned out to be the first Class 2 level zombie outbreak I'd ever fought on my own. Tracking it down was a tedious nightmare. Whoever originally set up the network took a smart approach to organizing the topology; they included the floor and room numbers in the ID of each computer. Since then, the company had experienced rapid growth and many changes. Employees came and went, along with a revolving door of underpaid IT staff. Computers had been moved around or replaced, leaving only a handful of machines still in their original offices. And since there was no IT Policy nor network documentation in place, every incoming IT guy learned about the network terrain from a few sparse pages of chicken scratch notes left by their predecessors. The IT guys only knew the computers by who occupied the office it was in, not by their computer name or its documented location. Their network had evolved into its own organic ecology—and no one was in control.

To find the first few zombies I had to hunt floor by floor, room by room, and sometimes even desk by desk. One zombie turned out to be a print server device about the size of a Kleenex box under a table in an executive copier room. Based on the Pentium III label it had probably been there since the 90s. Another zombie turned out to be a forgotten intranet server that apparently should have gone with the team that went out to Los Angeles. And yet another zombie was an account exec's desktop that he only used as a file server while on the road. In every case, the forgotten machines had been sitting quietly on the network for years, vulnerable to the next virus outbreak and trying to spread all kinds of contagions, some of which were archaic by Internet standards. In total, I found and eliminated ten zombies. For almost a decade these rabid machines had been actively attacking other computers on the network, some of which were attempting to reach Botnets that were long gone. In addition to the vicious circle, the attacks from the forgotten zombies were largely ineffective because the IT guys were constantly cleaning up infected computers and updating anti-malware packages. Only the new outbreaks with the latest contagions were causing damage.

As luck would have it, those zombies also provided the clues that helped rescue the company network. The various contagions they had been infected with acted as a sort of fossil record of the kinds of outbreaks that had occurred on the network over time. Evidence pointed at this network being under siege at least once every few months, probably crawling with dozens of zombies at the peak of an outbreak. Once the IT guys went from

*floor to floor cleaning up infected computers that were "moving slowly"
or "acting funny", the number would then dwindle back down to the ten
forgotten machines. And since the remaining zombies weren't able to get
outside of the office network, this pointed to the fact that someone was
inadvertently introducing new contagions into the network.*

*A week of further network traffic analysis revealed even more mayhem.
Close to 30 employees had been using the network in their spare time to
do whatever they wanted: download pirated music and movies from P2P
sites, share pirated music and movies, and cruise MySpace (which was
popular at the time) which often led to browsing unauthorized websites
(including free streaming porn sites)—all excellent sources for every kind
of imaginable computer virus. With all the piracy that had been going on,
it was a miracle the MPAA, RIAA, and the Feds hadn't already kicked in
the doors and raided the place with extreme prejudice. And since there was
no centralized Endpoint [anti-virus] Protection solution on their network,
the IT guys stayed busy cleaning up after the outbreaks, which explained
why they rarely had time to be proactive about upgrading their network.
All of this was going on behind the scenes while the company was churning
out numerous multi-million dollar TV productions.*

A big part of their problem involved two major factors: (1) As much as
60% of the threats to any business come from insiders and (2) they were
a small business that experienced several years of incredibly fast growth.

Contracts came in and revenues skyrocketed. The company ramped
up staff and equipment at an unprecedented pace—but they neglected to
reinvest in their IT infrastructure. Management had taken their network
for granted even though the business couldn't function without it. Along
with that rapid growth, there was no IT policy or any form of acceptable
use agreement. As long as the employees kept producing great work,
they could basically do whatever they felt like doing on the network with
impunity, including bringing in unauthorized computers. The network
had grown into a chaotic parasite-infected dragon and the inexperienced
IT guys were barely hanging onto its tail, doing what they could to keep
it under control. If it wasn't for those zombies causing enough network
latency problems to warrant bringing us in to help, there's no telling how
long that viral snake pit would have gone on.

Among small businesses, implementing an IT policy is becoming more and more of a necessity instead of just being reserved for big corporations. A few years back I had a brief foray into the construction world, mostly to use my business experience to help a cousin grow his home improvement services into a real company. To get the contractor license for the business I had to take an 8-hour course at a community college. The class was pretty long and intense, complete with a textbook and a workbook. I found myself taking notes like a madman until about halfway through the day when the instructor made it clear that our final tests at the end of the class weren't going to be graded.

"So what's the purpose of the test?" I asked.

"It's up to you as contractors to learn and adhere to building codes and ethical business practices," he said as he studied our faces. "But the reason for the class and the test is to eliminate all possible excuses—including ignorance. If you are found guilty of code negligence or engaging in illegal or unethical business practices, you will lose your license and be fined. That's it, no room for discussion. You... Were... Told."

Those last three words graced me a new understanding of the true power of an IT Policy. Regardless of how simple or detailed the policy document is, the guidelines themselves won't prevent employees from abusing company network privileges. The impact of a good IT Policy comes with the fact that the fear of loss is greater than the sense of gain. Having each employee sign a copy of an IT Policy and taken through awareness training will make them more accountable for how they use the network resources. Most won't bother to memorize the policy details. The promise of getting penalized $500 dollars for improper network use is the kind of punishment no one will ever forget. For that kind of potential fine, you can bet they'll be inspired to either stick to the fundamentals (i.e. - work-related activities only) or bring in their own devices (if allowed).

At first glance, a $500 penalty for improper network use might sound steep, maybe even Draconian. Truth is, as far as the actual costs to the business, it's actually lenient. Let's say your employee, John Doe, was browsing some sports blog and inadvertently infected his workstation with a nasty Trojan that caused a Blue Screen every time it boots up. Removing that malware can easily cost between $300 and $800 in labor just to get that computer back to normal. Disinfecting the computer can take 25 to 90 minutes per scan (depending on the software, amount of data and speed of the machine). Cleaning and removal can take up to three scans, not including the final scan to make sure the computer is clean. With the complexity of some of the more recent infections, the malware attack is so well-entrenched that rollbacks and backups cannot be trusted at this point. The only way to be sure the machine is clean is to slick the computer and rebuild it from scratch. That means format (erase) the hard drive, reinstall the operating system (e.g. - Windows XP, 7, 8, Mac OS X, etc.), reinstall all the drivers, reinstall the OS updates, and then reinstall all the productivity software to get that desktop back to normal. The entire reinstallation process alone can take 4 to 9 hours, depending on the requirements of each software package. This also doesn't include the time it will take to back up all the user's files to an external hard drive or flash drive (usually up to 2 hours, depending on amount of data being recovered). Figure in John Doe's lack of productivity while his workstation is down along with the hourly rate for your IT person's labor (at anywhere from $30 to $90 per hour) to get the computer back to normal. The bill adds up quick. Suddenly that $500 penalty becomes a fair assessment.

Baron Samedi's Top 5 Tips for Writing your own IT Policy:

1. *If you're in charge of writing the IT Policy and not sure where to begin, start with writing the Internet Acceptable Use Policy. Make use of those templates at the SANS Institute.*

2. *If you're in charge of writing the IT procedures, don't make any assumptions. Once you're no longer involved with the*

company, there's a good chance that whoever comes along after you will be starting from scratch with learning the company's IT infrastructure—everything from all the computers, the network topology, software management, user management, maintenance schedule, workflow, and etc. Since they may not be able to consult with you, the documentation you leave behind will essentially be the only legacy they have to pick up where you left off. Not leaving good legacy documentation is an awesome way to have your replacement blame everything on you until they get it all figured out.

3.   *If you're in charge of writing procedures, be very thorough with the processes and descriptions. The next person who comes along may not have anywhere near your IT knowledge and expertise. This especially applies in small business environments where the ownership side of management is very politically charged when it comes to the network. There's a need to keep all the gods and demigods pleased.*

4.   *Whether you're writing policy or procedure, don't be afraid to put your research digging gloves on. Invariably there will spots where you'll have to rely on the knowledge of others. Seek it out in books, on reputable geek-xpertise forum websites, or other IT professionals that aren't afraid of information exchanges. Approach it like you're in college writing a thesis… because effectively you are.*

5.   *Again, treat this as a living document. Think of these policies and procedures as an ongoing conversation with the future between management, staff, IT, and the business.*

BYOD - Bring Your Own Device Policy

Depending on whose commentary and statistics you read, mobile device sales may or may not overtake desktop computer sales one day. Regardless of the numbers, the presence of these devices in the marketplace will definitely force most companies to rethink their approach to IT and their current infrastructure. As a result, many companies have begun to explore or implement a BYOD policy.

In a nutshell, a BYOD (Bring Your Own Device) policy is a variation of the typical Internet Acceptable Use policy where companies offer a level of access and support to desktops, laptops, tablets and smartphones that are owned by employees. It's not uncommon to find a BYOD incorporated into a company's current IT Policy document.

A BYOD policy may take on different objectives, depending on the company and the needs of its employees. In most cases, a BYOD is an agreement between the company and employees where (1) the company will provide some level of support for the use of personal computing devices on the network and (2) the employees will agree to adhere to acceptable use policies with these devices while they're connected to the company network. A lesser common use of the BYOD policy is where companies cut back on corporate-issued computers and allow employees to purchase and maintain their own.

In either form, the rules within the BYOD policy tend to vary depending on a particular employee's role, the device(s) being used and any other dynamics set down by the company and the employee.

Among the main reasons BYOD policies have become more of a necessity is because employees are using their own computers and mobile devices for business tasks, regardless of any support from their company or IT department. If not anything else, a BYOD policy can help reduce security risks to the other workstations—as long as the personal devices are restricted to using an isolated network.

To use one of my larger SOHO clients as an example, BYOD seemed like the best way to go. It would reduce the exposure risks to the production workstations. Because of the specialized requirements of each computer in their environment, deployment couldn't be streamlined like with most other small businesses. Malware was still a constant threat, even with firewalls in place and extremely expensive Endpoint Protection installed on every computer. Just one inadvertent click on an infected website could take down a workstation, costing the company upwards of a thousand dollars a day in lost productivity and recovery. Since the wireless router had a protected guest network I advised the principals to offer BYOD to their employees. Aside from being good for employee morale, my intent was to increase the security of the internal environment by taking away any possible reason for the staff to use their workstations to visit non-business websites. Management agreed with my logic and decided to allow employees to use their own devices on the guest network—without a BYOD policy document in place. When I offered to spend an afternoon drafting up a BYOD document, they declined. "Our people know better than to misuse the network" was the explanation I was given. Since I bill them hourly, I couldn't help but wonder if their decision was driven by hubris or frugality. Looking back on it, their assessment was correct... but so was mine.

Once employees began using the guest network, the first few months were uneventful. Then one Thursday afternoon I received a rash of complaints: Email overall was working fine but outbound messages to certain companies were being rejected and bouncing back. Weird email problems like this often start off small and mushroom. My first step was to load up on Chinese food and cancel my plans for the weekend.

Throughout cyberspace there are dozens of Domain Name System Blacklists (DNSBLs), used by many networks to filter out sources of spam. Also known as Real-Time Blackhole Lists (RBLs), all it takes is one zombie-infected computer in an office to get the entire corporate network blacklisted. What starts out as being flagged on one blacklist can turn into dozens within a few days. A widely blacklisted company will find itself unable to send email to its clients, a fate as detrimental and embarrassing as getting the business phones temporarily disconnected. There was a zombie loose somewhere on my client's network—and the clock was ticking.

It took almost a week to find the first domino in the chain reaction. One of the employees had an older laptop she occasionally plugged it into the guest network. Everything on it, including the anti-malware, was a few years outdated. An obscure Trojan was also lying in wait. While copying some files from her laptop to her workstation she inadvertently introduced the Trojan to the office network. For whatever reason the

$400-dollars-a-year Endpoint Protection didn't catch the Trojan before it installed its payload: a variant of the infamous Cutwail spam module.

This Cutwail mutant turned out to be more like a sleeper agent. At least three different anti-virus programs couldn't detect it. Most zombies, like their undead namesake, are easy to spot because they make "noise" on the network, constantly sending data back out to the Internet. In contrast, this mutant bot seemed to come to life just long enough to carry out its spam attack and then shut down. Many blacklists also receive the equivalent of "anonymous tips" from the email services they protect, making it easy for the DNSBLs to detect if a network is still infected. Inside this network the zombie was so sporadic that it was impossible to find if I didn't catch it in action. Without the software to continuously monitor the network, finding the infected computer was comparable to a World War II-style hunt for an enemy submarine. It took more than 72 hours of frustrating caffeine-fueled Cat-and-Mouse to track everything back to the infected workstation and laptop.

How to Create a BYOD Policy

The employee with the infected laptop wasn't penalized for her actions. She wasn't doing anything wrong. That scenario was a perfect example of how a seemingly harmless move could have caused widespread damage. All of it was completely preventable by enforcing a few simple policies, whether in an IT or BYOD document, and a little more basic security.

If your office has wireless Internet access and there currently isn't an IT Policy document in place, it may be advantageous to start with drafting the BYOD policy first. The BYOD's objective is to put a set of controls in place to where the company mitigates many of its security risks by giving employees what they want—a less restrictive network environment and empowering them to take on a greater degree of responsibility for their computing habits. A signed BYOD policy document reinforces that personal responsibility and eliminates the "I didn't know" factor.

The details of any BYOD policy will be specific to a given organization, but most policies cover the same basic questions:

- What applications, websites and data can and can't be accessed?
- How should users protect their devices?
- Is there a need to implement "remote wipe" capability on their devices?
- Is there a need to implement data encryption on their devices (especially laptops)? NOTE: The answer should be "Yes".
- What happens when a user loses a device?

BYOD can be confusing because it involves different kinds of devices, use cases and users. To create a clear and simple BYOD policy, IT and other business decision-makers should consider these issues:

- **Acceptable use**—It is vital to specify which functions a given user can access, and what general behaviors are acceptable. It's important to protect the organization from users who may have, for example, illicit materials on their devices, or information that may be proprietary to another firm.

- **Device selection**—It's probably not reasonable to allow just any arbitrary smartphone or tablet on the enterprise network. The sheer number of devices on the market makes it cost prohibitive. A relatively broad range of platforms—such as Mac OS X, Windows, Android, iOS (iPhone, iPad, iPod Touch) and BlackBerry—is usually sufficient, enumerating devices and versions as appropriate.

- **Reimbursement**—Some organizations will pay for their employees' devices and monthly services, either partially or in full. A BYOD policy should explain exactly what charges the organization will and won't reimburse. Third-party services and software can provide detailed accounting of phone (and sometimes data) usage, but it may be easier to simply reimburse a pre-specified percentage of users' monthly bills. Your organization may need to modify its accounting systems to support this critical function.

▶ **Applications and security**—Whitelisting and blacklisting apps is a popular technique that helps to maintain the security and integrity of enterprise IT resources. It should also be noted as not being foolproof. If your organization takes this approach, the BYOD policy should explain that IT has the authority to prohibit the use of certain apps. The overall software configuration of the device is a key variable in successful mobile IT operations, so the BYOD policy should also cover the mandatory use of anti-virus apps, other security software and firewall settings.

With most small businesses, I'm often surprised to find that security policies (when they exist) don't address mobile at all. A security policy specifies what information is sensitive (or at least defines classes of sensitive information), the circumstances under which approved users may access sensitive information, and what to do in the event of a security breach. Such rules are essential. When creating a BYOD policy it might be a good time to revisit your overall security policy as well.

▶ Mobile device management—Mobile device management (MDM) software lets IT configure, secure, monitor and wipe smartphones and tablets. MDM is a rapidly evolving technology with little in the way of standards or even a widely-accepted definition, but IT should become familiar with the wide range of tools and services now on the market. MDM is also one element of a larger set of functions, often called Enterprise Mobility Management (EMM). Both can enforce BYOD policy and other requirements.

▶ Agreements—Once you implement a BYOD policy, it's important to have a written agreement in place with every mobile device user. An agreement raises consciousness about the critical nature of mobile IT operations, and it protects organizations in the event of a BYOD policy violation. Like your BYOD policy itself, this agreement should be as clear as possible, to prevent misunderstandings that could generate a wide range of problems and IT headaches—most of which tend to get expensive quick.

BYOD Policy Challenges

One challenge in developing a BYOD policy is in defining personal use vs. business use. Some technologies, such as mobile virtualization, attempt to separate the two on the same device, but fine points clearly remain. For example, the aforementioned device wipe: What if purely personal information is lost in the process?

Because of these potential problem areas, a solid legal review of your BYOD policy and agreements by appropriate counsel is vital. The law surrounding BYOD is far from settled at this point, and applicable law can vary from jurisdiction to jurisdiction at every level, including internationally. Regular reviews of policies and agreements (at least twice per year) are also essential.

Developing a BYOD policy can seem complex, especially in larger organizations, but BYOD's inherent savings on capital and operating expenses can easily pay for the required policy development, legal review, training, education, tools and systems. The convenience of BYOD is undeniable for users, and with a little work, BYOD is poised to become a key to more cost-effective IT operations.

...and if it's not implemented well, BYOD can also turn into Bring Your Own Drama.

Fortifying your Network against Attacks (Basic Network Security)

For most people, computer security is a neglected practice. The typical mindset is that if there's anti-virus installed on the computer and the computer is physically safe then the computer itself isn't vulnerable to anything. When it comes to buying a new computer, most people approach it with the same excited naivety they had when buying their first car. Cars don't get sold on oil changes, tire rotations and tune ups. They get sold on the wonderful features, great gas mileage and the glorious idea that all a buyer needs to know is how to enjoy driving it. Everything we know about car maintenance comes from advice, observation or suffering some very expensive but completely preventable misfortune.

Unfortunately the same applies to computer security. For the purposes of this book I've outlined three simple processes that can be done by anyone with a basic understanding of their computer. While it's true that no online computer is 100% safe from zombie attacks, the following steps can go a long way toward taking your network from being an exposed ranch on the prairie and turn it into a mini-fortress:

(I) Secure your wireless router.
(II) Block out known sources of infection with a HOSTS file.
(III) Use blended anti-malware protection.

(I) Secure your wireless router.

With residential and SOHO Internet connections, wireless routers come standard these days with most (if not all) DSL and Cable Internet subscriptions. And for some older connections, if there is a wireless router it is often a separate device plugged into the cable/DSL modem. Either way, there are several things that should be changed in order to provide better protection for your network. Those steps include:

(A) Set up your wireless router to allow guest network access
(B) Change the default username and password on the wireless router
(C) Make sure your router's firmware is current
(D) Change the wireless router's SSID
(E) Choose the strongest security setting
(F) Set a strong password

NOTE: When going through these steps (especially updating your firmware) it's a good idea to be physically present where the router is located. Although it is possible to do these changes through remote access, some changes to the router settings can cause your connection to drop before you finalize them. When this happens you'll have to access the router internally (i.e. - using a computer on the premises).

(A) Set up your wireless router to allow guest network access.

Most wireless routers come standard with a guest network option. If you have a wireless router made before 2010 that lacks a guest network, I'd advise buying one as soon as possible. If you don't intend to buy one or set up some kind of guest network structure, plan on not allowing anyone to use your wireless connection for plugging their outside computers or devices to your network. If you're not sure, here is a list of wireless routers that come standard with a guest network feature: **https://openwireless.org/routers**

The guest network will allow you to provide secure Internet access to anyone visiting your home or office without giving them access to the computers on your internal network. Because it is an isolated subnetwork, one of the key benefits is that it protects your computer(s) from any viruses that may be on their computer. Another benefit is that the guest network has its own passkey (password), eliminating the risk of exposing your network indefinitely by sharing your internal network passkey with outsiders. Even in trusting that person wholeheartedly, you cannot control where they go or prevent their computer from being compromised. One of my earliest on-call service clients was a perfect example:

Her favorite spot to meet was Panera Bread; she liked the Panini. I think she preferred the place because it was public yet always still felt very cozy. The dining area kept a steady stream of business-casual types, academics, and lunch dates, most of which were engrossed in their laptops and devices. And with both of our laptops out on the table, we fit right into the scene. Typhoid Mary, as I nicknamed her in my notes, turned out to be one of the most unusual clients I've ever serviced. After three separate consultation meetings I still had no idea where she lived or if Mary was really her name. Since she paid cash at the end of each session, I didn't press the issue.

She was blessed with Marilyn Monroe's curves, a sultry Miami bronze and shoulder-length hair that was raven one meeting and dirty blonde the next. Minus the smile lines, her face still had the kind of cheerleader quality most men fantasized about back in high school. Again, that was no connection to the nickname. During the third meeting I learned the truth about Mary. She was the ultimate road warrior—a one-woman escort service. Although her profession played a part in her nickname, it wasn't for the Biblical or stereotypical connotations. Simply put, Typhoid Mary earned the nickname because of her laptop.

Unlike her streetwalking counterparts, Mary was on the high-priced side of a new generation of tech-savvy pimpless prostitutes. She originally started promoting her services on sites like Craigslist and Yahoo matchmaking to find her dates. Now she brokers her services through discreet sources and a few adult dating services, raking up thousands of frequent flyer miles as she caters to the kind of executive clientele who "can't quite afford the Presidential Suite at the Marriott when he travels but expects to be treated like it". When she wasn't working or relaxing, she would often setup camp somewhere with free Wi-Fi, usually an airport, restaurant, café, hotel lobby or the occasional unsecured home wireless connection.

Her laptop was infected with over 300 different types of dangerous viruses. In the context of the Four Horsemen of the Apocalypse, her laptop was the Fifth Horseman—and it was riding shotgun. According to her, she jumped onto at least six open Wi-Fi spots a day. If her laptop infected at least one PC per Wi-Fi it probably infected dozens of computers a week. To make matters worse, the laptop was a gift; it was still registered to some company. For someone in her line of work I suspected it might have been stolen, which would explain why the anti-virus software had been expired for almost two years. Mary's laptop had probably infected thousands of computers along the mid-Atlantic seaboard—a one-machine roaming Class 3 zombie outbreak. I'm not sure if I should have cured it or burned it.

When it comes to outside threats and your network, Typhoid Mary isn't unique. There are countless Typhoid Marys at large, primarily using infected PC laptops with Mac notebooks on the increase. Typhoid Mary could be a visiting client that needs to download some files, a co-worker or your 16-year old niece that brings in a laptop, or your neighbor whose Internet is on the fritz and asked to borrow access to your wireless. A guest network can be used to keep all of them at bay.

NOTE: Providing guest network access should not be confused with "Enabling Remote Management Access". This feature makes the router's admin area directly accessible from the Internet as opposed to having to use remote access to connect to a computer inside your network then accessing the admin area. Enabling this feature is the equivalent of taking the keypad for your home/office security alarm system and putting it outside next to the front door. On most routers this feature is preset to disabled. It should be left that way unless you've got an IT professional actively working on your router.

(B) Change the default administrator username and password on the wireless router.

"...Even in trusting that person wholeheartedly, you cannot control where they go or prevent their computer from being compromised."

Every wireless router these days comes with a default administrator username and password. The way to get to it is to open up a web browser and go to the default IP address. It's always a private IPv4 address, meaning that you can't connect to the router from outside the home/office network using this address. Usually the IP address will be something like one of the following:

- http://192.168.0.1/
- http://192.168.1.1/ (when in doubt, try this one first)
- http://192.168.2.1/
- http://10.0.0.1/
- http://10.1.1.1/

And unless you're using some weird bootleg wireless router, the default username is probably "admin" and the password is probably "password". Regardless of what brand router you have, the default internal IP address, username and password are all listed in the manufacturer's documentation. On the off chance you cannot find the default username and password to your router can probably be found on this website: **http://www.routerpasswords.com/**

Log in, find the administrator section, and change the password to something else. This is to insure that no one can log into the router to make changes or lock you out.

NOTE: If you have to do a factory reset to your router it should only be done if you've absolutely got to get in to change some settings (like the passkey) or you've lost the username/password. Even then, it should only be done by an IT professional, someone who is very experienced with networking, or with the guidance of a tech support person at your ISP. This is because the factory reset will make your router to forget all its current settings, causing your network to go down. Every computer or device connected to your network will stay offline until you get that router reconfigured.

(C) Make sure your router's firmware is current

Today's routers are basically miniature computers whose sole job is to act as a sort of gatekeeper that connects your internal network to another network (usually the Internet). The firmware is like the router's operating system, containing all the latest security and network protocols. Upon logging in to make administrative changes, most of the newer routers will alert you when a new firmware update is available. Some manufacturers will also alert registered owners by email. If you're not sure, visit the router manufacturer's website and check with the support people.

(D) Change the wireless router's SSID.

The Service Set Identification (SSID), also called the "network name", is how your wireless computer or device will find (and connect) to your wireless router. Most routers purchased from a store come with the default name of the manufacturer (e.g. - Linksys, Netgear, etc.). This should be changed to something else. I've seen people use everything from their favorite football team to jazz musicians; anything that can be spelled with 32 characters or less. If this is for a residence, avoid labels that can be used to single out your household (i.e. - do not your first/last name, house number and address, etc.). Some routers have an option where you can hide your SSID so that anyone who wants to connect has to manually type in the SSID name. Although this is good for added security, it's no substitute for strong passkeys and good security settings.

(E) Choose the strongest security setting.

As of this writing, a major problem is that many new Internet connections come with wireless routers that are pre-configured to use WEP as a default security setting. Although the passkeys are solid (often defaulted to the router's serial number), the problem lies with the use of WEP and the fact that the installers never advise home owners or office managers to change it to a stronger setting. To put it into perspective, let's compare your wireless network to a house and its security settings are the door locks:

- ► No security setting, of course, would be the equivalent of an unlocked door.
- ► WEP is the equivalent of a bedroom door with a knob lock—good enough to keep the door closed but won't stop anyone that really wants to get into the room. As a security setting, WEP has been cracked. What that means is if you leave WEP as the security setting on your wireless router, anyone with the know-how and a laptop could tap into your Internet connection, opening your computer(s) up to be hacked into.
- ► WPA is an old deadbolt lock on a wooden front door—far sturdier than WEP and solid enough to do a good job of keeping the inside in and outside out. Unfortunately WPA has been cracked, too.

▶ WPA2 is two deadbolt locks on a steel door. The Enterprise and RADIUS versions are reserved for bigger corporate networks. If your network had what it took to use those, you probably wouldn't need to be reading this chapter.

As of this writing, the WPA2 security setting is best choice for most home and SOHO wireless routers.

(F) Set a strong passphrase or passkey.

As mentioned previously, another problem with most wireless routers provided by the Internet Service Provider is that they have a label on the bottom or back with the server's default SSID and passkey.

To improve security, your router password may have been changed to the serial number of your router if you hadn't previously changed the password from the default of "password". You can find your router's serial number on the label affixed to the bottom or back of your router.

NOTE: If you reset your router to the factory default settings, the router password will return to "password" and security settings will revert to WEP. The user name and password are both case-sensitive, so be sure to enter them in lower case.

(II) Block out known sources of infection with a HOSTS file.

With your computer, the hosts file is used by an operating system to assist routing by mapping certain hostnames to IP addresses. In plain English, the hosts file is like the contacts list on your cell phone—it helps your computer to know how to reach certain websites without having to look them up or call 411. In the IT world we call this Internet resource blocking—using the hosts file to prevent your computer from connecting with known sources of spyware, adware and malicious attacks.

Whether you're on a PC, Mac, or Linux, if there's a hosts file available your computer will automatically use it every time you do anything on the Internet. The following is a sample of how to list the hosts in the file:

```
127.0.0.1    localhost
127.0.0.1    www.007guard.com
127.0.0.1    007guard.com
...
```

The IP address 127.0.0.1 is reserved for what is known "localhost"—a fancy way for your computer or device to refer to itself on the Internet. The Internet site 007guard.com is a known source of spyware infections. Instead of allowing www.007guard.com to take you to some unfriendly website, by pointing www.007guard.com to 127.0.0.1 your computer thinks localhost is the destination so it never tries to connect with the real www.007guard.com. This not only keeps you from accidentally visiting www.007guard.com, it also prevents any malware on your computer from being able to phone home to www.007guard.com to download any contagions. The hosts file can be used to block all kinds of unwanted stuff: adware, banner ads, spyware, malware, etc. As a layer of protection, the more bad websites in the hosts file, the better. This is why it's important to keep your hosts file as current as possible.

The hosts file is almost always named "hosts" and can be found in the following folders (depending on your OS):

For Windows XP, Vista, 7, 8:
%SystemRoot%\system32\drivers\etc\hosts
(e.g. - C:\Windows\system32\drivers\etc\hosts)

Mac OS X 10.0 - 10.1.5:
(Added through NetInfo or niload)

Mac OS X 10.2 and newer:
/etc/hosts

Unix-like (e.g. - Linux, FreeBSD, etc.):
/etc/hosts

Android and iOS (2.0 and newer):
/etc/hosts

The good news is that the hosts file is just a simple text file, editable with virtually any basic text editor (e.g. - Notepad, Textedit, Emacs, etc.). The not-so-good news is that there are literally thousands of known malicious hosts out there with a count that is constantly on the rise. For the average home user and small business manager, keeping up with that list can be a chore. Below are a few easy ways to keep your hosts file updated:

▶   The first can be found on Microsoft's Most Valuable Professional website. It has a healthy hosts file that is freely available for download, complete with installation instructions: **http://winhelp2002.mvps.org/hosts.htm**

NOTE: The hosts file available from the MVPS website can be used on PC, Mac, Linux and various mobile devices (Android, iPad, iPhone, etc.).

▶   The second way to keep a healthy hosts file is through software. One such package is Spybot Search & Destroy (currently available only for the PC):

Spybot - Search & Destroy can detect and remove spyware of different kinds from your computer. Although some computer magazines have recently given this package mixed reviews, one of the reasons I still prefer to keep it handy is the fact that it has a bunch of built-in tools, including an immunizer that does an awesome job of adding thousands of known spyware and malware sources to your hosts file along with other layers of protection for any web browsers you have installed (Internet Explorer, Mozilla Firefox, Chrome, Opera, Safari, etc.). A free version of this package can be downloaded from: **http://www.safer-networking.org/**

NOTE: When you run Spybot S&D on Windows Vista / 7 / 8, some features will require you to run the program in an elevated status. This is done by using the "Run as administrator" option when loading the program. To do this, right-click on the Spybot - Search & Destroy entry in your start menu (instead of just left-clicking to start it). A menu will pop up; choose "Run as administrator".

More details on editing hosts file in various versions of Mac OS X:
http://support.apple.com/kb/TA27291?viewlocale=en_US

More details on editing hosts file in various versions of Microsoft Windows:
http://support.isoc.net/Page.aspx/117/hosts.html

(III) Use blended anti-malware protection.

Many people tend to believe that all we need to keep our computer safe and secure is the anti-virus program that came pre-installed on it. Unfortunately, those days are gone. A single anti-virus program is NOT enough. Today, computer security is an arms race—an ongoing battle, just like with survival after any apocalyptic zombie outbreak. Malicious hackers are working constantly to make sure their dangerous payloads bypass our protections to hit our computers. These hiding methods, called "packing", can take anti-virus programmers anywhere from several hours to several months to decode to a point where they can update their software to be able to detect these contagions. As of this writing, thousands of variants of the top malware infections are discovered in the wild every day. This continuous battle can be compared to how illegal drug cartels are constantly coming up with new ways to hide narcotics being smuggled into the country and Drug Enforcement Agents are coming up with new ways to detect and defeat these measures.

The following advice breaks a rule preached by every major nerd and anti-virus company: it's time to look into having more than one form of anti-virus protection on your computer.

More than one? Isn't that bad, like crossing the streams in Ghostbusters?

Yes and no. There's a caveat to this seemingly blasphemous gem of advice. To better explain the blended approach, the different types of anti-virus programs need to be clarified. There are three: on-demand, offline, and real-time.

► **On-demand anti-virus scanner**—Unlike the real-time anti-virus programs, on-demand virus scanners aren't constantly scanning everything. They scan for malware when we manually start them running. Most on-demand anti-virus scanners are also designed to compliment real-time anti-virus scanners, often providing a sort of second line of defense to catch what the primary anti-virus missed. Two popular on-demand packages are MalwareBytes Anti-Malware (MBAM) and Spybot Search and Destroy.

► **Offline anti-virus scanner**—the term for offline anti-virus scanner is a bit of a misnomer. The offline label is in reference to the fact that these scans are run from bootable media (CD, DVD, flash drive) instead of running on your computer after it has booted up normally. With the operating system offline, these packages are able to perform deep, extremely thorough anti-virus scans that may take up to several hours to complete. Some might compare it to exploratory surgery instead of the routine physical checkup. One of the biggest benefits of these Live CDs is that they will often save your skin if you find that a virus is preventing your computer from booting up. A few of these packages include F-secure and Kaspersky Rescue Disk.

► **Real-time anti-virus scanner**—when people talk about anti-virus software, most of the time this is the type that comes to mind. Brands such as AVG, BitDefender, McAfee, and Symantec's Norton are just a few anti-virus scanners that are practically household names because they often come pre-installed on new computers. These packages protect your computer against malicious attacks by running from the time you boot up to the time you shutdown. They constantly scan everything that either runs in memory or gets saved on your computer.

With all that spelled out, a blended approach to anti-virus protection should include one real-time scanner, one or two on-demand scanners, and one or more offline scanners burned to bootable media (CD, DVD, USB flash drive, etc.).

Because of the very nature of books, I've purposely omitted brand recommendations from this part of the chapter. What might be top of the line today may fall to last place by the time this book hits the shelves. As an alternative I'm recommending that you do the research yourself. An excellent source for up-to-date anti-virus brand comparisons and tests can be reviewed by AV-Comparatives. As an independent not-for-profit organization, they seem to be more impartial and reliable than most of the computer magazines. They also test anti-virus packages for PC, Mac, Linux, etc. Their reports and analysis can be seen here: **http://www.av-comparatives.org/**

Maintaining the Fort
(Working Business Network Security Plan)

This chapter is primarily for people who plan to telecommute from home or small business managers that need to establish security practices for everything accessing the office network from the outside.

The following tips and considerations can help you develop and win support for an effective network security plan:

▶ With the money you spend on protecting your network, think of it in terms of a Return on Value instead of searching for a Return on Investment. For every dollar you spend you're saving the company thousands of dollars in prevented theft or damage to your data. A breached network can also cause lost revenue and even lawsuits from litigious-minded customers.

▶ Don't approach security issues piece by piece (e.g. - using different anti-virus programs on different computers). Always have a unified strategy that provides equal protection for the entire network.

► Network attacks can come from outside or inside sources. Employees can inadvertently (or accidentally) introduce some malicious code on the network. Disgruntled employees can also open up vulnerabilities that can lead to all kinds of damage.

► Physical site security is just as important as computer and network security. There are plenty of cost-effective ways to pair up a surveillance camera with an old computer.

► Every office network requires a balance between usability and security. Too much security makes a network next to impossible to use. Too much usability makes your network insecure and a wide open target.

► Every employee in your company should have an understanding of basic security strategies (e.g. - how to choose strong passwords, not opening CDs, DVDs or USB flash drives or external drives from untrusted sources, not installing software without IT involvement, etc.). It may seem a bit common sense to some but without covering those pointers, even the smartest person in your office will make the most child-like mistakes that can compromise the network.

While I'll always advocate that every business have a Network Security plan in place, I've yet to actually see one in any SOHO environment. On one hand, it's not that necessary if the SOHO network was set up properly by an IT professional and is maintained to some degree. Small networks also have the benefit of "security by obscurity"; the smaller the company, the better the chance your network will never become the victim of targeted attack. On the other hand, it makes sense because putting together even a simple plan will help the ownership and management have a better understanding and appreciation for the basics of their network. It's a little bit like owning a car—once you have a general understanding of what is under the hood, you'll tend to be a little more conscientious about taking care of it. Those sentiments will tend to rub off on the rest of the staff, too.

A thorough policy takes time to prepare and should cover topics such as:

- ▶ **Acceptable Use**—specifies what employees can and can't do on the network. If social media sites like Facebook and Twitter are banned from access at any time, be sure to state that. If employees are allowed to access these sites after business hours, state that, too. Be as specific as possible because anything left to interpretation WILL be taken advantage of.

- ▶ **Email Use**—everything from acceptable attachments (and their size limits), inbox quotas, and ownership rights should be spelled out, too. When it comes to the average employee, most people assume because the email address is in their name that they own it. They assume they have the same privacy and ownership rights with their office email as they do with their home email. From a legal standpoint, that's often not the case. Since the company owns the computer and the network resources, employee emails are company property. By default, management has full rights to access to all of it. Putting this in writing will hopefully make employees think twice about using their work email address for personal affairs, especially the kind that may not fit with the company's image.

- ▶ **Identity**—who shall and shall not have access to the network. This is to prevent situations where employees bring in a friend or relative afterhours that might attempt to log into the network. It should also outline the parameters for guests getting access to a secondary [wireless] network.

- ▶ **Anti-Virus policy**—a catch-all phrase for software that will protect the network against any kind of malware (e.g. - viruses, Trojans, worms, etc.).

- ▶ **Password policy**—to establish a baseline of user passwords that are both difficult to crack and how they should be treated with care (e.g. - minimum password requirements, no password sharing, no passwords sent by email, no username/password info on Post-It notes, etc.).

- ▶ **Remote access policy**—to establish simple rules and methods that will allow employees to safely access the network from outside the office (e.g. - VPN, VNC, Remote Desktop, Teamviewer, etc.).

- ▶ **Encryption policy**—to establish an encryption standard that will be used to protect the network data. For most businesses, this won't require its own policy document but inclusion in other documents like Remote Access, Email, Passwords, etc.

Starting your Company's Security Policy In-house

Answering the following questions can help you develop your own policy:

- ▶ Inventory Your Current Security Technologies—do you have one (or more) of the following?
- ▶ Secure wireless network w/ guest network—providing network access to mobile employees and visitors.
- ▶ Firewall—may be built into the wireless router or software-based on a separate machine.
- ▶ Remote Access—to give employees and partners access to your network. This may include VPN, Remote Workplace, VNC, Team Viewer, Remote Desktop Connection, etc.
- ▶ Endpoint Security—to protect your network from adware, malware, spyware, viruses, and other attacks. This can also include intrusion prevention.
- ▶ Identity Management—such as a server running Active Directory (Windows) or Apple Open Directory (Mac) used to manage who has access to what resources on the network.
- ▶ Resource Compliance—making sure that devices and people accessing the network meet security requirements.

Define the main digital assets (data) on your network:

- ▶ What kind of data is stored on your network (e.g. - portfolio of client work for a web designer, drawings and specs for an architecture firm, client records, billing info, etc.).

- ▸ Where does that data reside on your network?
- ▸ How much is this data worth?
- ▸ Who has access to what data?
- ▸ Can vendors, partners, and/or customers get access to their data? If so, how?
- ▸ How to do control access to that data on the network?
- ▸ If your security was compromised, how would that affect your business?
- ▸ Would a compromised network disturb your supply chain or ability to provide services? If so, how?
- ▸ How fast can your backup and recovery system restore your network and/or website in the event of a major crash or security breach?
- ▸ If your network was compromised, what are the potential losses (financial, clients, etc.)?
- ▸ What are the potential losses or damages if your company website was compromised?
- ▸ If your network and/or website went offline, how long could you be down before you started to lose money?
- ▸ Does your business insurance cover you against Internet attacks and/or the theft of customer data?

Future Growth:

- ▸ How do you expect your business model and practices to change over the next 5 to 10 years?
- ▸ How often do you anticipate having to upgrade server software?
- ▸ How often do you train your employees on security procedures?
- ▸ In the coming years, is your company likely to need to provide more remote access to your data from employees, partners, and/or customers?

Most small businesses that I encounter don't have policies in place at all. They wing it. And quite candidly, if the company has less than a dozen employees, their network can just as easily operate without such documents. The greatest benefit of having them in place can be summarized with one word: accountability. The policies define what is whose responsibility and what should be in place for any given part of the network to be fully operational. Best of all, they also spell out what is (and isn't) acceptable use of the network and the consequences for anyone that abuses these privileges.

By clearly defining accountability within the network, things that need to get done will generally happen faster. And on top of that, with these policies reasonably defined there's no need for the team to dwell on the question of what needs to happen when or how because those things are all spelled out (or at least they should be). When the accountability isn't there, things that need to happen will tend to get put off for later or tossed around like a game of Hot Potato. If that wasn't the case, the world wouldn't need outside IT consultants like me to come in to document, repair or rebuild their network infrastructure.

Baron Samedi says

"*With every business network, the damage caused by any virus or data breach is a chain reaction that starts with two things: (1) a simple, careless, seemingly harmless act and (2) someone overlooked a policy that would have prevented it.*"

Extra Crispy Drama—
When Ignored Policies Go Bad

Whether it's an IT Policy or BYOD, the process of putting together technology-oriented policy is worthy of having a book of its own. I included the basic policy-making process in this book because they are almost mandatory for any business. Without them, the only thing that protects your business from a digital catastrophe is strictly a roll of the dice—and a higher power if you believe in one.

One such example involves an unnamed U.S. power plant. According to a quarterly issue of the ICS-CERT Monitor (published by the U.S. Computer Emergency Readiness Team), a power company contacted ICS-CERT in October of 2012 to report a viral outbreak that had infected a network of computers for a turbine control system. Further investigation turned up the fact that a technician had used a USB flash drive to upload some software updates. Unknown to him, the flash drive was infected with malware that got loose and ended up impacting about ten computers. Just by chance, the power plant had already been taken offline for routine maintenance; the virus caused it to be down for another 3 weeks.

Had the infection hit those control system computers while that power plant was active the results could have been disastrous: overheated turbines, widespread blackouts, and who knows what else. And although the bulletin didn't name the affected power plant, this kind of viral infection wasn't an isolated incident among utility companies. The events themselves aren't kept secret, just their locations and the details of the malware infection. US-CERT (http://www.us-cert.gov) publishes these cases to educate power station operators about the dangers of malware being accidentally introduced into industrial control system environments. What spooked me was the fact that this wasn't an isolated incident—and it wouldn't be the last.

In another example of disregarded policy, according to a report by Reuters in April 11, 2011, the personal records of over 3.5 million Texans were posted on a publically-accessible web server—and left there for over a year. These records included full names, birth dates, mailing addresses, Social Security numbers, and Drivers License numbers of unemployed and retired citizens.

How did the data end up on the wrong server? A simple mistake. Even worse, the person at fault didn't follow administrative policy and left the data unencrypted; anyone could read it. State Comptroller Susan Combs said there was no indication that any of the information had been misused. While there is no reason to doubt her sincerity, any seasoned IT person could show a 5th grader how to make sure the data looked untouched. And any seasoned Identity Broker would sit on those identities for months before selling them.

With the strange permanence of information online, the identities of those few million Texans will be floating around out in the wild indefinitely. Even worse, a majority of them were retirees, often easily victimized by cybercriminals. The same fate has also befallen the victims of the Target data breach of 2013. More than 100 million customers now have their personal information—including full names, mailing addresses, email addresses, and credit/debit card numbers—being sold, resold and adrift out there in cyberspace. The only reason these organizations managed to survive those catastrophes is because they could afford platoons of lawyers and paid settlements, plus the publicists to help them weather the media firestorm. Imagine how such a mistake could affect your company.

Keeping Zombies at the Gate:
The Network Operations Center (NOC)

The NOC, sometimes called other nicknames like "the Rack", is the space in an office that houses the equipment where the Internet comes into the building and gets piped to all the other computers and devices. These days, depending on the size of the company and its business needs, it may be as simple as a cable modem and a wireless router or hub, or it may have enough racks of equipment and computers to fill a room.

The Server Room, as the name states, houses the company's computer servers. Although the number and types of servers depends on the technology needs of the company, there's usually at least an email server and/or a file server. If there are only a few servers, most small businesses will simply put them in the NOC.

Baron Samedi says:

"At the very least, the company NOC should be in a locked room with adequate space, air conditioning and a CO_2-based fire extinguisher (for Class B and C fires). All equipment, cables, and power supplies should be more than one foot off the floor, preferably on a table, sturdy shelf, or 2-post or 4-post rack. The same applies to the Server room if there's a need to put the servers in a separate room. If this sounds complicated, talk to an IT professional."

Depending on the nature of company's business model (and space permitting), it might be worth it to put the heart of the office phone system and alarm system in here, too.

Lock the NOC

According to a series of studies performed by the CERT Coordination Center of Carnegie Mellon University's Software Engineering Institute, insider cybercrimes cause more damage than outsider attacks. With most companies whose business models depend on computers for production, security is paramount in two main places—the NOC and the Server Room.

Good computer security is all about access control, and that begins with physical security. In most offices with eight or more employees on site, physical security starts with putting the NOC and any mission-critical server(s) in a space behind a locked door, even if it's the size of a walk-in closet. It's no different than businesses that deal with large sums of cash usually have a combination safe somewhere in the building. Without a locked door NOC, the safety of any information stored on those computers is about as secure as trying to lock a filing cabinet with nylon rope.

With all of my past and present clients, the only NOC I've ever liked belonged to the Veterans Benefits Administration, a branch of the U.S. Department of Veterans Affairs. Their NOC itself was about the size of a cafeteria and had sealed doors, cardkey locks, a raised floor, 4-post racks and cabinets, uninterruptible power, air-conditioned, and a gas-based fire suppression system so powerful that it was rumored to be able to extinguish anything that moved. Aside from that textbook example, every NOC and server room I've seen since then has been lacking in one way or another. The problem is that most small businesses don't consult with a Network Engineer or System Administrator while planning out this part of a commercial space. As a result, the NOC and servers are often set up in open, unlocked spaces, leaving themselves wide open for insider cybercrimes. These threats fall under one of three main categories: **Sabotage**, **Theft**, or **Fraud**, with a fourth that is usually categorized as **Unintentional** (e.g. - an employee opens a seemingly legit email and clicks on a link that unleashes a contagion on the network).

Since the later part of the 20th century, we've been living in uncertain times. Among the few consistencies I've learned about most small business environments is that employee attitudes are a bit like small ponds; the waters tend to be still and relatively clear until something causes a disturbance. People may not be satisfied with their status in life but they are generally content—until someone or something messes with their money, family, or close relationships. There are two types of catalysts for these insider cybercrimes: Internal and External.

Internal catalysts happen within the course of normal business operations. They're usually something typical like being overlooked for a promotion, declined for a pay raise, a cut in hours or pay, or pending layoffs. On a personal note, I've seen how the threat of layoffs in a small company can turn any staff into a Machiavellian chess game. Our Internet Company had just completed a merger in early 2000, right before the dot-com bubble burst. By June we discovered that the new CEO had burned through our cash reserves right about the time the investors decided to walk away from the deal. On top of that, sales were flat and the overhead was horrendous. After the paycheck delays and whispery rumors of layoffs became real, fear and loathing spread through the company like a brushfire. Tribal factions formed. Equipment was stolen, including servers and routers out of the NOC. The awesome web development team I helped to put together had turned into a nightmare right out of "Lord of the Flies". As a co-owner in that business occasionally I'm still haunted at the thought of watching so many dreams evaporate.

External catalysts far outnumber the internal. They happen outside of normal business operation and, for most small business managers, they're almost always unforeseeable. These dynamics tend to be more insidious and often involve theft or fraud versus sabotage or unintentional damage.

For example, I was once hired by a timeshare rental office to track down a "super hacker in the vicinity" (to use the client's words). This hacker was reportedly committing fraud from one of their timeshares by way of their wireless network. After a week of monitoring their network and setting up traps, I never caught a super hacker. I did, however, come across activity that led back to the cubicle of one of their employees, a 38-year old married mother of two whose secret addiction to prescription meds drove her to start stealing credit card info to supply a small-time crew of identity thieves.

On another occasion, I was hired to troubleshoot a network problem that was supposedly crashing the inventory system. The network was fine; the glitch turned out to be greed. Further investigation revealed that the database password had been cracked—by someone on the inside. The culprit was a 26-year old assistant manager that had figured out a loophole with the inventory system. By directly changing the database, he was able to make units disappear by flagging them as lost in shipping. For months he sold the lost merchandise on Craigslist, using the money to catch up on his child support payments to keep himself out of jail.

Regardless of the reason, even the most reserved law-biding employees may step out of bounds and make bad decisions when faced with unyielding circumstances. Everything from simple theft to quick money schemes to revenge plots that would make Lex Luthor proud. Unfortunately, even within the most employee-friendly company with a close-knit staff, this kind of stuff happens. It's not a matter of "if" but "when".

Securing your Website

Having your own website is much like starting a farm; the more you cultivate it properly, the more crops it will bear for you. And in these times, even the simplest websites have some kind of server-side scripts within the site to give it interactivity, if not for any other reason than to let your customers click on the Contact button and send you feedback. During an attack, zombies that discover vulnerabilities in a misconfigured web server or poorly coded scripts will exploit them to turn that website into a zombie. Once possessed by the Botnet, a zombified website will be used to do anything from secretly steal sensitive data (like customer information), send out malvertisements and spam emails.

Baron Samedi says:

"If you've written the interactive parts on your website yourself, keep them all up to date. Regardless of the scripting language there are standard coding practices that are used to prevent your scripts from being exploited to hack into and take control of your website. If you've got the option, I'd recommend using a reputable Content Management System for the framework of your website. Aside from being easier to maintain, their support communities tend to stay on top of security-related code issues. Also, be sure to make all of your passwords secure."

When we talk about the Zombie Apocalypse or any Botnet outbreak, infected websites play a major role in the carnage, especially small business websites. According to estimates based on data compiled by Dasient Inc., a California-based Internet security firm, there were over 1.2 million zombie websites in Q3 of 2010—double the number of infected sites in Q3 of 2009. As of this writing, trends indicate that the numbers will grow exponentially over the next decade. To make matters worse, these infections no longer require the visitor to click on a link at the site; in some cases, all a person has to do is view an infected page and it will automatically download the malware. It's about as bad as running into a horde of zombies that are able to infect the living with just a touch instead of the traditional bite and reanimation.

For the sake of simplicity, I'm using this as a catch-all phrase for web servers as well as individual websites in shared web hosting environments. Either way, a website that's been compromised and turned into a zombie is bad news. Although it probably won't take more than a week before the infected website gets put on the Internet Blacklists and starts getting blocked, in the meantime hundreds, if not thousands, of people and/or computers will be affected by the infected pages.

Here's why: A typical business website may have anywhere from a handful to several hundred visitors per day. If left unchecked, a zombie website could infect thousands of unsuspecting users in a matter of a few hours. Fortunately, the typical website either uses space leased on a server managed by a Hosting Service Provider or its network connection is provided by an Internet Service Provider. In plain English, that means the infected traffic will be noisier than a high school house party in a quiet neighborhood. It'll catch the attention of the network admins who will either alert the site owner or shut down the site to get the site owner's attention. A typical use for a zombie website is to hijack the mailer scripts and have it secretly sending out spam. Worst case scenario is that the website has been fully engaged in a Botnet to participate in cyber attacks.

Small Business Servers

Whether it is running some version of Microsoft Windows Server or Mac OS X Server, an infected small business server of any kind would be the equivalent of the Doctor Doom of Zombies. Since these are integrated servers they have a number of special protocols (e.g. - LDAP, etc.) along with any number of server software packages (e.g. - HTTP web server, IMAP/POP3 Email Server, FTP server, etc.). Because of this combination, not only could it potentially infect each employee workstation turning it into a zombie, it could also send out spam to every email address in every employee's address book, turn the intranet into a zombie-net within a Botnet. If left unchecked, this kind of zombie can attack countless computers and spam hundreds of thousands of people inside of a day. A sophisticated contagion could be able to search for sensitive data such as banking information and employee data, making everyone's data in those computers vulnerable to identity theft. For even a medium-sized business, the potential effects could be far reaching and devastating. The downtime alone can potentially cost thousands of dollars a day.

Workstations—Desktops & Laptops

Between the desktop and the laptop, the later is almost always going to present the bigger physical security threat. Most of your account executives and upper management will have the company laptops, tablets and smartphones.

Keep the operating system up to date—for some computers this is more of a chore than others. PCs running Microsoft Windows will always have at least a few updates during any given 30-day period. Yes, I said always. Generally speaking, if you happen to check and don't see any updates it means either (1) you're system has recently finished doing updates, (2) your system isn't properly checking for updates, (3) something messed up with your last batch of updates and it needs attention, or (4) that computer isn't connected to the Internet.

When you get a new computer or portable storage device like an external hard drive or USB flash drive, take the time to encrypt all or part of the hard drive. The reason: a computer or portable storage device is a treasure trove of information, and all that data can be exploited if it gets stolen. By encrypting the hard drive, if someone steals it but doesn't have your password they won't be able to read or view any of your information—you data will look like pages and pages of gibberish. All Apple devices already enforce encryption and Android phones/tablets have an option in settings to enable encryption. And to add to the chuckle factor, in the event of computer or device theft, in order for it to be usable again someone will have to go through the steps to wipe out everything. This is why encryption is especially good to do with anything mobile.

NOTE: There are various free and commercial programs that can handle on-the-fly encryption. They have been purposely removed from this chapter for two reasons: (1) Just about any information about encryption software is outdated by the time a book is released and (2) encrypting any desktop/laptop/external storage device can be a daunting task and result in lost data if not handled properly; consult a seasoned IT professional.

ISLAND OF LOST SOULS (1932)

Do Not Feed the Animals—
Protection against Disgruntled Employees

"The Devil is that element in human nature, that impels us to destroy and debase."
                                    - Dr. Moreau, The Island of Dr. Moreau (1996 film)

Another lesson that can be taken from zombie outbreaks on film (or in reality) is one constant: when someone has been bitten and confirmed infected with that mysterious contagion, they've got to go… quick. It could be your best friend, a parent, a spouse, or even the Pope. The instant they transform into a vicious zombie you're no longer the same to them. You've become prey. What makes the difference is whether or not you dispatch them properly or they turn you into the Meal Du Jour.

In the business world, the dynamics aren't that simple—and usually not that gruesome—but the stakes are just as high. Terminating someone's employment should be handled the same way; with swift, well-thought out resolution. This is to prevent additional problems and headaches that may occur. Poorly-executed workplace firings may result in something I call *The Crispus Attucks Effect*.

Prior to March 5, 1770, Crispus Attucks led a life of obscurity as just another hard working man. On that date he earned his place in history as one of the first casualties of the Boston Massacre; an event considered to be the spark that started the American Revolution. For many employees that lose their jobs, subconsciously they long for the same kind of martyred remembrance, or at least the sweet taste of recognition for what they see as their sacrifices for their employer. Within minutes of being dispatched, these people often feel shocked and alone in the world, akin to the "I've been SHOT!" moment. They want someone to help or at least rise up to take their side in the face of this great injustice. Most managers find the firing process unpleasant; they tend to be curt but professional because they want the dismissed person gone so things can get back to normal. As tension mounts, coworkers shy away from the situation for fear of being added to the body count. These factors sometimes cause recently terminated people to have what chemists call an exothermic reaction—a fiery meltdown—and in most cases it can be as messy and uncontrollable as a kitchen grease fire.

Every successful small business I've ever worked with has at least one disgruntled employee horror story. As much as 60% of the cyber threats to any business will come from insiders or, in this case, former insiders. Like first kiss and first heartbreak, it is almost a rite of passage. Employee dismissal is the single greatest cause of law-biding citizens going rogue and abusing (or damaging) company IT resources to exact revenge for being fired. In the immediate days after being dismissed, most people will vent their anger to anyone who will listen. Once they've gotten the venom out of their system, the fact that bills need to be paid will cause them to let it go and get busy job hunting. Unfortunately, in today's society there are those among us who don't always think through their actions. Consequences are disregarded. They see sabotaging company equipment as an easy means for payback, even in situations where their own actions got them fired. They rationalize their motives in much the same way a vigilante or freedom fighter justifies breaking the law to achieve a goal. And from an IT perspective, this is where management hubris meets ex-employee bitterness, creating a kind of mental infection that turns even the most normal mild-mannered people into snarling zombies.

To put this into context, I share the following scenario: While writing this chapter I received a call from one of my occasional support clients, a national non-profit with state and local branch offices. Negotiations had broken down with one of their long-time employees, Mr. H, and they had to let him go. I was asked to help to track down some files on his computer and suspend his login account. Since the lock out process was a normal part of the IT routine, I didn't give it any more thought once I was finished. A few days later I received a desperate call from the main office. Between the frustration and incomplete sentences I was able to make out the gist of their emergency: Ugly emails were circulating throughout their organization. People are freaking out. Before I pieced together what happened I already knew Mr. H was involved.

Mr. H received his official pink slip on September 10th. And even though I had made sure he was locked out of his desktop and the office, I forgot that his Verizon email account was still active in the cloud. For reasons that were never explained to me, the employees at that local branch office had two email addresses—one with the main office and the other set up using the accounts that came with their Verizon DSL connection.

In the grips of what probably started as a Happy Hour drinking binge, sometime after midnight Mr. H accessed his [Verizon] office email from home. After typing up a bizarre, rambling email he sent it to a recently deceased co-worker—and BCCed it throughout the organization. Just after daybreak, dozens of staff members and affiliates all over Virginia found this morbid martyr's manifesto waiting in their inboxes. Had the letter arrived on the 9th or even the 12th the reception might have been different. Instead, this little surprise arrived on the anniversary of the September 11th attacks—almost to the hour. Shockwaves of confused sadness and paranoid rumors ripped through the organization. Phone calls were made. People got chewed out. By mid-afternoon someone at the main office finally called me for help. It took almost an hour to calm them down... and less than three minutes to fix the problem.

Although this wasn't a computer zombie outbreak it had all the hallmark hysteria and damage potential. There were a number of lessons to be taken away from this scenario. For starters, when it comes to letting an employee know their services are no longer needed, this shouldn't be a drawn out event. It should happen quickly. It also should also be near the last step in removal process—not the first. That brings us to the checklist:

Checklist Item #1: Have a plan.

It doesn't matter if your employee termination procedure includes armed security escorts or breakfast at Denny's. Just make sure there is a clearly defined plan to systematically remove their access to office resources and "transition" them off the premises as quickly and quietly as possible. Losing a job has emotional stages of acceptance to it, much like grieving over the sudden death of a loved one. The difference is that most of the intense phases happen faster and tend to be more unpredictable. Sometimes several phases happen at the same time with anger often the second to erupt to the surface. Generally, the longer someone is in an office where they have just been fired, the more embittered they will get. The darker side of IT services includes being a biohazard cleanup company; I've had to clean up the mess after sabotage done by disgruntled employees. Seeing this dark side of humanity has taught me (and many business managers) the importance of having an employee exit plan. The peace of mind that comes from seeing it work is priceless.

Checklist Item #2: Immediately cut off the ex-employee's access to all computers, business-related websites, phone system, and any other security codes they may have been assigned.

Suspend their access to every computer on the company network. Suspend their email accounts and/or change the passwords. Deactivate or reroute their voicemail boxes. Change or deactivate any security codes they may have been assigned (e.g. - building access codes, cash register codes, etc.). Change the passwords to any websites they may have access to that are paid for by the company, websites used to represent the company, or set up for employees only. For example, if your company has a Facebook group, the ex-employee's access should be removed. It's important that all of these steps happen as close to the same time as possible, preferably a few minutes prior to notifying the employee of their termination.

As part of the Crispus Attucks Effect, employees that have been let go tend to feel the need to make a statement. Sometimes that statement comes out in vicious emails or trying to damage the company's reputation. Other times company property is stolen or destroyed. I've even seen sensitive information sold off to competitors. They are hurt, and hurt people tend to hurt other people. Most of these stunts can be catastrophic and often seem like the stuff of tall tales—until they happen to you. The longer disgruntled people have access inside your company, the greater the chance they will take the opportunity to exact revenge. Aside from the obvious costs, this generally lowers office morale and creates unnecessary gossip, all of which is counterproductive.

As an added safety precaution, be sure to move the former employee's email inbox and any personal files to offline storage (CD, DVD or USB flash drive) as outlined in step #5. In the event the former employee decides to seek legal action against your company, this data will come in handy. Most of the time this data will just sit on the shelf for a few years until you come across it again and decide it can be safely destroyed.

Checklist Item #3: Make sure all company property has been returned.

In most cases this happens on a day between their release date and the date of their exit interview meeting. The sooner company property is retrieved, the better. Most ex-employees will graciously oblige because they know that not complying will cause the company to hold onto their final paycheck(s). For every business, this list is different but it should include things like:

- Office keys or key cards to everything from the office doors to closets, filing cabinets, lockboxes, and etc.
- Company Identification Badges
- Company vehicle
- Company-owned books, software, manuals, subscriptions
- Company cell phone, tablet, laptop/desktop or other equipment and accessories
- Company credit card
- Company-issued uniforms

While this list may seem obvious, business managers will neglect to retrieve many of these items. The rule of thumb is if it was important enough to be part of the job, it must be returned afterward. Everything on that list can potentially be abused or used to commit theft or fraud and cost the company money. Aside from the fact that these items cost money to replace, the real danger lies in what a disgruntled ex-employee can do with them.

I first saw this lesson in action back in my college days, working as a part-time bouncer at Norfolk Scope back in the late 80s. Rock concerts,

Rap concerts, you name it. One of the events I worked regularly was the basketball games for the Old Dominion University Monarchs. After each game they opened the exhibition hall up and called it "The Big Blue Room", a VIP-style beer-fest for students, alumni, sponsors and fans. All the beer was on tap, supplied by a local beverage distributor. Since the beers were served one cup per ticket, the Blue Room got packed quickly.

After work, a few of my co-workers and I used to slip into the Blue Room to have a few beers before leaving for the night. One of the beer truck operators, Chad the Beer Guy, used to hook us up by serving us our beers beside the truck, out of sight of the long lines. We loved it. Most of the ODU VIPs didn't even get that kind of treatment. This lasted for almost two whole seasons until one evening we stopped in to see Chad and he wasn't there. The other beer truck guys would only tell us that they hadn't seen him or he no longer worked for the company.

When the next season came around, after the first game I went into the Blue Room as usual. While standing in line waiting for a beer, I thought I saw Chad on the other side of the exhibition hall, working behind another one of the beer trucks. By the time I wandered over to say hello he was gone. After the next game, several of us did the usual Blue Room trip and, again, I saw that same guy. Since I wasn't alone I pointed him out to my coworkers. They thought the same thing I did: Chad was back working with the trucks. This time he was pushing a hand truck and disappeared behind a curtain into one of the back hallways. By the time we got over there he had disappeared. With that next game, just before the end of the second half, I clocked out early just to rush down to the Blue Room to see if I could catch Chad's ghost. Just by luck, I heard the hint of squeaky hand truck wheel come from the back hallway. I spotted a beer guy briskly walking away with a keg. It was indeed Chad. He greeted me, both nervous and happy to see me at the same time.

Chad had been fired but his supervisor never forced him to turn in his ID badge and uniform. Feeling that the company cheated him out of back pay that he was owed, Chad continued to occasionally show up at the Big Blue post-game parties. Wearing his Blue Room uniform and ID badge, no one ever questioned him as he casually slipped in from the back hallways.

While his former co-workers were slammed with serving hundreds of thirsty basketball fans, he snuck in behind the truck, exchanged an empty keg for a full one, and then quietly left. Even the cops that patrolled the loading garage didn't give him a second glance. He continued this for at least another season, maybe two. The only thing that stopped him was the company adopted new uniforms and ID badges.

Checklist Item #4: Officially notify the entire staff of the change.

The message should be simple and politely state that the ex-employee is no longer with the company while introducing the person that will be taking over the ex-employee's responsibilities. This notification process should start the same day the ex-employee is released. The list of recipients should include staff, security, banks/credit card companies, and those on a need-to-know basis such as building custodians/maintenance, vendors, partners, contractors, and customers.

Again, a disgruntled ex-employee with a little motivation is capable of causing all kinds of mayhem in a short period of time. The result is almost always expensive, embarrassing, or both. By making your people aware of these staff changes it greatly reduces the chance of someone becoming an unwitting pawn in an ex-employee's scheme.

Checklist Item #5: Consider changing the locks and security codes.

Some might see steps #4 and #5 as overkill. In many cases, I'd be inclined to agree. It's more of a judgment call that a manager would have to make on a case by case basis. The main reason I included them in this checklist is for risk management considerations. It's better to think about these possibilities and deem them unnecessary instead of leaving them unchecked to potentially be exploited. After being fired or laid off, even the most loyal former employee can become your next nightmare.

Checklist Item #6: Enforce any company policies that pertain to processing the ex-employee's records, emails, and computer files.

This can include processes such as backing up all the ex-employee's files and emails to disc, preparing the computer for a new hire, and etc. If the ex-employee has personal possessions such as photos and coffee mugs around their desk, this would be the time to box them up.

Checklist Item #7: Have all the paperwork ready for the ex-employee to sign during their exit interview.

This is to make sure s/he has paid back any money owed to the company, returned all company property and there are no loose ends with any employee benefits. This has to happen before releasing any reimbursements or final paychecks.

Payroll

▶ Salary through to the last day of employment
▶ Accrued [unused] vacation, sick leave, etc.
▶ Other reimbursements (expense reports, etc.)
▶ Deductions due to any monies owed to the company
▶ Amount of final paycheck

Health / Life Insurance

▶ Insurance companies are notified of employee termination
▶ Date the coverage ends
▶ Insurance information provided to employee (should they decide to take over payment)
▶ Any reimbursement due to the employee for premium(s)

If your company has a Retirement/Pension Plan and the employee bought into it, withdrawal or rollover information should be provided. Last but not least, be sure to get the ex-employee's current contact information and forwarding address.

When handled properly, all this should be settled up in one meeting, typically no more than 30 days after termination. With most SOHO environments, this part of the process usually isn't that involved and can be settled up within a week or less. Because the employee shouldn't receive any money until all the other Checklist items have been satisfied, most of the time this step won't happen until another date. Having the paperwork done is handy because the items in this part of the checklist are important and most of that information will still be fresh, thus lowering the chance of making any mistakes due to oversights. More than likely the ex-employee will be applying for unemployment and should you see the need to contest their claim, even an honest mistake can end up under scrutiny by the employment commission.

Checklist Item #8: Make it quick.

In the previously described morbid martyr scenario, the coordination with their legal department and HR at the main office dragged the situation about two weeks. Mr. H had over half a month to slowly negotiate himself out of a job and hate the world for his mistakes. Jobless depression doesn't take long to fester into a psychotic episode, a sort of living zombie outbreak in its own right. Add a firearm and a death wish and you've got a recipe for something unthinkable to happen—the kind of story CNN loves to cover.

With a plan in place, that manager should have been able to give Mr. H notice that his services were no longer needed, revoke his access to company resources, and escort him out of the office in less than half an hour. A meeting is set up on another date for Mr. H to pick up his belongings, signs off on the exit sheet, and pick up his last paycheck. That's it.

Baron Samedi's Additional Tips:

► Keep a password file.

These days it's nearly impossible to run a company without having at least half a dozen accounts around the web. These are usually set up to manage things like website hosting, payment

processors, paying bills online, and various other services. A key employee (e.g. - an owner, president, head IT person, manager, etc.) should be responsible for maintaining a roster of usernames, passwords, and secret answers along with their websites and functional descriptions. There should be a printed copy (preferably kept in a safe or lockbox), at least two digital copies (e.g. - one on a secure computer and the other copy saved on a USB flash drive), and preferably a third digital copy kept outside the office (e.g. - in a cloud backup like Mozy, Dropbox, iCloud, etc.). Refer to "Password Management" on page 348 for software to manage these accounts.

► Political correctness and avoiding confrontation are overrated.

Both of these drive me up the wall. I'm from the school of thought where if there's a problem, you let it be known. Address it. Go behind closed doors, hash it out, and if it gets messy no one will be the wiser except the cleaning people. When dealing with a problem employee, drawn out resolution processes build tension. The longer the tension builds, the greater the chance something bad will happen if that employee is fired.

Managers that have never done a Risk Assessment of their organization will tend to do things as if those potential problems either don't exist or can't be used against them.

For anyone that doesn't get this point, take a moment to reflect on your teen years. Think about all the stupid risks most of us took during those times. Fortunately we survived, thanks to accumulated lessons learned and some divine intervention. The older we got, the more we became aware of how some of those stunts could have easily landed us in a cellblock or a coffin. As a result, most of us in our adult years will give more thought before we act. We don't approach life with the same youthfully clueless sense of invincibility.

The same kind of thing applies to loss prevention and many small businesses. When managers don't know the vulnerable spots—within themselves or their company—they tend to make decisions as if their business doesn't have any weak spots to be concerned about. Employees, however, have a tendency to make mental notes of every weakness they are made aware of. Some will entertain the idea of exploiting them the minute they feel like they've been wronged. Most people will brush off any destructive notions and refocus on working toward more rational resolutions. Occasionally, there are those few who are disgruntled enough to do damage. They will give the consequences about as much thought as a horny couple thinks about babies or diseases during unprotected sex. Regardless of their status with your company, this is where those people become just as bad as zombies… not-too-bright, frighteningly relentless, and determined to do harm to your company.

Shoot it in The Head—
Safe Data Destruction, Part II (print)

One of the best protections against becoming the victim of a zombie attack, living dead or otherwise, is to cover your tracks. If they cannot see or hear where you've been, they don't know where you are. In the office, this can be seen as referring to the proper disposal of information that is no longer necessary.

"Unnecessary Information" covers a lot of territory. This can be as miniscule as a login and password scribbled on a Post-It note. It can be correspondences with past clients, outdated accounts receivable/payable data, or active user accounts for former employees that are long gone. Whatever it is, when data has outlived its usefulness get rid of it. The more information you have lying around, whether digital or print, the greater the chance that someone—or something—can come along and use that information to take advantage of you. This almost always leads some kind of theft or loss.

Baron Samedi says

"Get the best paper shredder your budget can afford. A business should have at least one business class cross-cut shredder for every copy machine on the premises."

Even with all the advancements in cybercrime tactics, some things are just as exploitable now as they have been since the invention of pen and paper. Like any investigator will tell you, trash often contains all kinds of information about its source—including their secrets. The right garbage in the wrong hands is a dangerous thing.

Dumpster Diving—A Phishing Tale

The air was a soupy 85 degrees by 8 o'clock that evening, another typical summer night in Virginia Beach. During tourist season, since I was the only one in our circle that was old enough to get into the clubs, boredom was a nightly thing most of the time. We all had part-time jobs but, at roughly $3.80 an hour, even in 1990 that didn't go very far. Altogether we had just enough to chip in for gas if we actually had somewhere to go. And as a small crew of hackers with a penchant for pranks, sometimes that's all we needed.

Dumpster diving wasn't illegal back then. It did, however, open up all kinds of possibilities for mischief and petty crimes of opportunity—especially for a crew like ours. When all else failed, this was a good way to pass time and get some low impact excitement. The challenge was to raid each dumpster and leave before someone called the cops. Being on a quest to find <u>anything</u> cool always seemed worth the risk.

Department store and daycare center dumpsters were off limits; the same with any bin that smelled like fresh-cut grass, rotten food or hazardous chemicals. We targeted bins used by companies that dealt with electronic equipment, information technology, and telephony. The hunt was for computer printouts, old manuals, slips of paper or letters with sensitive info (e.g. - usernames/passwords, credit card carbons, calling card numbers, etc.), used equipment, and anything else that could be used to exploit technology one way or another. Even a memo with the right person's name and info on it could lead to a phone call to trick someone within the company into giving us their username and password to access their network.

On that particular evening the hope was to find a prize better than the one from our previous trashing run: a Lown waveform defibrillator. While it was cool for bragging rights, most geeks don't have any practical use for anything that jumpstarts a human heart with a 1000 volt zap. We couldn't sell it to medical professionals, either. A few interested buyers had plans that rivaled something Dr. Frankenstein would do. A local surplus store eventually took it off our hands for $50 bucks.

After a night of finding nothing but rust, cigarette ashes and soggy coffee grinds we were ready to call it quits. At that last bin I glanced inside to see it was empty except for a few dozen white paper bags, all neatly sitting upright. Something struck me as odd—the dumpster was too clean. Anything that was placed, not thrown, into a dumpster must be of value... even for garbage. What I found inside those bags still makes me chuckle to this day.

The dumpster belonged to a McDonald's™ regional office. The bags contained promotional coupons, mostly for the 1990 Summer Blockbuster DICK TRACY. Free Big Macs, free fries, and everything else on the menu was either free or buy-one-get-one-free. Like any sizeable corporation, McDonald's™ has a policy and a process for everything. And thanks to someone disregarding proper policy and disposal procedure, we had stumbled upon a zillion coupons—scratched-off winners that had been cashed in, counted at the regional office, and thrown out. Since they were unmarked, every coupon was still good until their offers expired at the end of the summer.

For weeks we carried around stacks of coupons like cash. We ate McDonald's™ for breakfast, lunch, and/or dinner. Sometimes we got something from McDonald's™ just because we drove by one. And no matter how much we ate or gave away, every time we looked at our coupon stash there seemed to be just as many as before. By early August everyone around us had grown sick of McDonald's™. That's when the seeds of the next idea took root.

Down at the Virginia Beach oceanfront, tucked away amidst the hotels, restaurants, and tourist attractions were places where the homeless, runaways, addicts or other local cliques would hang out. From 1st street to 38th and between the Boardwalk, Atlantic and Pacific avenues, we gave away bundles of coupons at every one of those spots we could think of. We even gave a shoebox of coupons to a lady to take to the nearest battered women's shelter. In exchange for the free food, we only asked on thing of everyone: they all had to show up at the McDonald's™ on 21st and Pacific at 5 o'clock that afternoon. Why 5 o'clock? No reason whatsoever. We just wanted to see how many people would show up.

By the time we arrived at the McDonald's™ the place was already crowded with tourists. As the minutes counted down we began to doubt that anyone would show up... until around 4:57. There were four entrances into the customer area—and they all opened at the same time. People started streaming in. The homeless. Surfers. Skaters. Parking lot attendants. Groups of women and children. Hotel security guards. Drunkards. Even a bunch of beach volleyball pirates showed up. Everyone had coupons in hand. Lines snaked around the building and up the sidewalks. Cars jammed the drive-thru; the four-way intersection had become a seething parking lot. Cashiers frantically did their best to fill orders but they couldn't handle the demand. People just kept coming like hordes of hungry zombies. Enraged at all the free food flying out of her restaurant, the manager started making calls as she instructed her assistant to lock the doors. Refusing to be refused service, this prompted people to try to cram their way in. Tempers started to erupt. When the motorcycle cops arrived we knew it was time to leave.

On the off chance that this book gets into the hands of any McDonald's™ executives, I certainly hope there are no ill feelings. I have utmost respect for the franchise. They are a Fortune 500 corporation with over 400,000 employees spread out across more than 110 countries. They have invested untold billions into anti-theft measures and loss prevention procedures. They are often an excellent role model of how successful companies should handle security. Aside from the fact that the Statute of Limitations has run out, I shared this tale to show how several bored college misfits could pull a prank that took area McDonald's™ locations for thousands of dollars over the course of a summer—and made it happen without a gun, an insider, or stealing a single password. All it took was someone digging in the right dumpster at the right time. If a company like McDonald's™ could still be vulnerable to exploitation by their own trash being used against them, imagine the damage potential if someone with a focused criminal intent used this tactic against the average small business.

Ultimately, the lesson here is data destruction through proper paper disposal—shredding. Most SOHO environments with more than five employees should buy a business-class cross-cut shredder that can handle at least 12 sheets at a time, a duty cycle of 100 to 150 sheets per day, and a container that holds at least seven (7) gallons of waste. The determining factor is how much incoming snail mail and printed paper your office processes on a daily basis. The goal is to have paper shredding become a natural part of your process, as effortless as throwing that same paper away in the garbage can. I personally prefer any shredder large enough to be used in a common area and vicious enough to eat DVDs, paper clips, credit cards, small caliber handguns and anything else I feed it.

Incidentally, it should be noted that McDonald's™ learned from this experience, too. Sometime in September of that same year we returned to their regional office dumpster, hoping for a sequel to our successful summer spree. Padlocks were on each lid. We picked the locks only to discover the bin was empty. For months we returned on occasion; each time the bin was just as empty as before. It was as if that office had stopped throwing out garbage altogether.

ZOMBIE TRIVIA

Q: Who said "...we must stop the killing... or lose the war" and in what George A. Romero film?

(answer on page 384)

Social Engineering—
The Unfixable Flaw in Most Security Standards

NOTE: The information in this chapter might seem like a how-to primer on pulling scams. This wasn't my intent. It's been my experience that once people are aware of these vulnerabilities they have an easier time spotting the scams—and keeping themselves (and their staff) from being exploited.

In the realm of Information Security, Social Engineering is the art and science of an unauthorized person manipulating someone into either providing confidential information or providing services for that person. These skills come in many hues and tints. They are all based on the principle of disguising oneself as an employee, professional, or even a client who is rightfully entitled to something. Such stunts are considered short cons because they are usually brief and part of a more complex plan involving fraud, information theft, reconnaissance, or gaining unauthorized access to something.

Experienced scammers operate with the following in mind:

- ▶ Never forget the premise "You are who you say you are",
- ▶ Always look and sound the part,
- ▶ Be as attractive as possible,
- ▶ Mimicry is your friend,
- ▶ Distraction is your partner,
- ▶ Study your target long before you make first contact,
- ▶ Show extreme trust in the authority of the target being exploited,
- ▶ Figure out the minimum that needs to be said in order to get the target to comply,
- ▶ Whatever you say must be plausible and said with the right amount of conviction.

For example, as a college freshman I was 6'3", weighed around 220 pounds, and in pretty good shape. One of my part-time jobs was being a backstage bouncer at a local concert hall. I could tell strangers the most outrageous tales about backstage weirdness and debauchery and they would have no problem believing me. Since I fit the "big guy bouncer" stereotype, all it took was dropping a famous name and a few buzzwords like 'Green Room', 'Rider' or 'Off Right Wings'; any story short of an alien abduction was accepted as fact. However, anytime I talked with a stranger about computers or computer hacking it wasn't uncommon to receive a different reaction, often ranging from a polite surprise to a hint of skepticism. The technical jargon wasn't the problem; when people don't understand geek-speak they tend to tune it out. Nothing about my physical appearance or demeanor fit the computer nerd stereotype. Even though both of those aspects of my life were true, most strangers accepted my involvement with concert halls much faster and without doubt. People rely on stereotypes far more than they should—and every seasoned scammer uses this to their advantage.

One of the pre-hacking pioneers of social engineering methods is Frank Abagnale, a financial fraud and security consultant that spent most of his young adult life as a con artist and check fraudster. His story was the basis for the book CATCH ME IF YOU CAN and a movie by the same name starring Leonardo DiCaprio and Tom Hanks. As a teen, Abagnale exploited the core social engineering principles well enough to live the high life by impersonating an airline pilot, a doctor, and an attorney... all before he was old enough to vote.

Great social engineering requires the quick adlibbing talents of a Broadway actor, the steely nerves of a trapeze artist, an unshakable will, and just enough practical knowledge of a subject to fool the target audience for at least 5 to 10 minutes at a time. The rest is a loose-knit web of strategic responses, contingencies and a basic escape plan. Anyone that has mastered these techniques has the potential to gain access to (or bypass) virtually any kind of system regardless of platform and security protocols. When performed by a seasoned practitioner, these techniques can seem as effortless and impressive as the Jedi mind trick from STAR WARS™.

For example, back in the 80s there was a car dealership known throughout southeastern Virginia for bragging about selling cars to anyone. Every commercial featured them destroying credit reports by tearing them up, feeding them to a goat, etc. Some digging in their dumpster revealed that their sales reps ran credit checks on almost every adult that came into the showroom. Once or twice a year that dealership received a call that went something like this:

"Good morning, thank you for calling [car dealership]. How may I help you?"

"Good morning, ma'am." I said in my best New Jersey accent. "To whom am I speaking with?"

"Roseanne."

"Hi, Roseanne, my name is Barnabas Collins, senior database engineer with Acme Credit Bureau. How are you doing today?"

"Fine, thank you. And you?"

"[haggard sigh] I'm doing fine, I guess. Hope your day is going better than mine. It'll be better after 5 o'clock. Happy Hour."

"Oh of course", she mused sympathetically.

"Well, ma'am we need your assistance. There's been a bit of a problem; a partial crash of the database containing information for our customers in your zip code. While verifying what we restored from the backups we realized there were some errors with authorization passwords. The access number we have on file for you is [dialup phone number]. Is this correct?"

She checked the number. "Yes, that's right."

"And the login name and password we have on file for your office is [old login and password]. Is this still the password you're using?"

"Well, no it's not. That's the old code."

"Oh my... [shuffled some pages close enough to the phone to be heard] well, ma'am, can I get you to verify your authorization code by reading it back to me slowly?"

"I certainly can," she replied. Carefully, she spelled out each letter as I repeated them aloud, pretending to type them into a database. I had her repeat the entire code twice just for effect.

"Ah yes, there it is. That did it. Okay, we've got you straight, thank you so much for your help, Roseanne. You've just made my day!"

[Rosanne reciprocated the pleasantries as she hung up]

And that was it. With a call that lasted less than five minutes I was given a fresh account password for Acme Credit Bureau—access to pull anyone's credit report. Back then the reports listed complete credit card and bank account numbers, making it easy to weaponize this information or pull off capers that could best be described as FERRIS BUEHLER'S DAY OFF meets OCEAN'S 11. In any case the dealership paid for every credit pull. It was way too much power for a crew of hackers whose average age was 16.

If that example wasn't enough, here are some other antics I pulled off:

▶ Visited a Manhattan-based publishing house by dropping the names of a few editors to get by lobby security, slipping past their cardkey front door security, and wandering around their office unsupervised for almost two hours before they were open for business. I was there to meet with an editor, plus doing reconnaissance for a manuscript I was writing at the time. As of this writing, that publisher still consistently ranks among the top 10 publishers on the planet.

▶ Obtained countless overrides to register for college courses that were closed or denied because I hadn't taken some prerequisite course. In some cases I made this happen by calling over to the other departments while impersonating my academic advisor and then showing up to present the paperwork with his signature on it. This went on for more than two years until I was late declaring my major and my advisor realized he hadn't signed any of my paperwork since I was a freshman. Caught, I ended up confessing. Fortunately he appreciated my industrious enthusiasm for learning.

▶ Gained free access to various trade shows and tech conferences by impersonating a writer on assignment from Associated Press (or some other media outlet). The entry fees were often between $300 and $500 dollars, completely beyond what I could afford as college student at the time. Sometimes I'd bring a friend or classmate along by loaning him my 35mm camera and claiming he was my photographer. After interviewing vendors and presenters, sometimes they would wine and dine us to get favorable coverage in the story. Contrary to the scam-like feel of these stunts, I actually wrote articles about anything I attended, regardless of whether or not it was going into a publication. Eventually I accumulated enough tear sheets and publishing credits to get press passes as a freelancer.

▶ Assisted a classmate as both of us pretended to be Repo Men. He was being paid to retrieve a home entertainment center for a lady whose ex-husband purchased it on a credit card that wasn't closed out during their divorce. The ex defaulted on the payments and the creditors threatened to ruin her credit if she didn't pay. Since she was stuck with the bill she figured she deserved to get the equipment. Unfortunately her ex had already sold it off to support his cocaine habit.

▶ Walked into a ballroom in a 5-star hotel in midtown Manhattan and fixed myself a plate at a buffet full of women who were all attendees at a "Daughters of the American Revolution" convention. I got a real attendee's name from an unclaimed nametag sitting at an empty registration table.

▶ Walked into more than half a dozen companies during business hours pretending to be with the cleaning crew or a telephone repairman, usually as part of a bigger scheme my hacker friends and I had in motion.

▶ Spent time backstage at various Rap, Rock and Reggae concerts in club venues where the club bouncers thought I was with the tour and the tour security guards thought I was a club bouncer. One of my friends, a Rap deejay, was a master at the backstage-without-a-pass trick. He was 6'10, often high on weed, and some would declare him completely insane—all of which contributed to his unshakable belief that he was supposed to be backstage, as if he was part of the tour. Because of his appearance and attitude, security rarely asked to see his pass. His presence backstage seemed so natural he was often bold enough to ask road managers and local radio personalities for extra passes in order to bring in friends who were still outside the gate.

The list goes on…

Why do Social Engineering stunts work? Most of them key into some aspect of evolutionary psychology, others hack into meeting some of Maslow's Hierarchy of Needs (e.g. - Safety, Belonging, Esteem, etc.). In any case it's because of the way the human brain is wired. The following are just a few of the traits and tendencies that social engineering practitioners commonly exploit:

► People tend to try to be consistent with their previous decisions and commitments. Ask someone a series of related questions that elicit an affirmative response and then make the intended request. Sales reps use this often to try to get a customer into the "Yes" frame of mind before making their actual sales pitch.

► People tend to cooperate with people who seem to be in charge, or at least have a commanding grasp of what is going on in a problem situation. The problem could be real, staged, or completely imaginary. This is how my friends and I used to gain access to those credit bureaus.

► People instinctively want to return a favor, to give back. A bartender gives a regular customer a free drink and that customer tends to spend more or give a bigger tip, regardless of the fact that the price of the drinks are marked up so much that the profit margin for a single drink already covered the cost of that free drink.

► People tend to be less suspicious of anyone who looks like they need help. Need to get into an office without a card key? Try this:

Dress to fit the part, carry something bulky like a box of computer equipment and walk a few paces behind a person who is entering that office—more often than not, someone will hold the door open for you.

▶ People feel compelled to mimic the things that people like them say and do. A perfect example of this can be seen with any sitcom. The shows use laugh tracks and applause to evoke viewers to respond by laughing at the right times—even if the scene isn't funny.

▶ People tend to cooperate with those who seem to like them. Flattery will get you everywhere, especially if you're dealing with someone who is in a position where they feel they don't get the recognition they deserve. This is also why the "Good Cop, Bad Cop" tactic often works wonders when trying to get someone to cooperate.

▶ People tend to put a higher value on something that is perceived as scarce or it has been taken away. Lawyers use this trick all the time to influence a jury by asking a witness a loaded question or introducing information that wasn't already approved as evidence. They know the opposition will object and if it is sustained the judge will stop everything and instruct the jurors to disregard what they just heard. Jurors never forget—and those disregarded statements often affect the final verdict.

▶ People are susceptible to a psychological phenomenon called "Inattentional Blindness". We assume we're seeing what we're supposed to see, causing our brains to register what we're looking at to conform to our expectations, regardless of whether or not it is accurate or logical. An infamous example of this occurred with John Dillinger's use of a wooden gun during his legendary escape from Crown Point jail. The gun itself was whittled out of a block of wood, blackened with shoe polish, and Dillinger's reputation did the rest. Once that first guard was overtaken, the crude carving in Dillinger's hand automatically turned into a loaded gun because that is what the guard's brain expected someone like Dillinger to be holding. Had Dillinger been Groucho Marx, the early responses would have been more along the lines of surprise instead of shocking fear. After all, when most people think of Groucho Marx brandishing anything it's probably a cigar and quick-witted innuendo. As a result, it's likely that one of the guards would have noticed the object in hand didn't even look metal, let alone pass for a gun, and things would have taken a turn. Groucho's escape attempt would have landed him in the infirmary. With Dillinger, as he added each guard to the hostage count, the threat became more and more real in their minds... and so did the gun.

▶ Related to Inattentional Blindness, people are also susceptible to something called "Change Blindness". Our attention can be focused on one object and completely miss other things and/or changes happening in plain view. A famous example of this is in the movie THE GODFATHER (1972) during the scene where [Spoiler Alert] Sonny gets whacked in the causeway. The windshield shattered as the attacking gangsters shot up Sonny and the car. As Sonny struggled to escape on the passenger side we see the windshield is almost totally intact. A few seconds later the windshield is gone again. And when Sonny's bodyguards arrive to find everything shot up, the almost-intact-windshield is back in place. The frequency of the magically-reappearing windshield depends on which version of the movie you're watching. In any case, it's called a visual continuity error. Many Godfather fans (including myself) have seen this film numerous times and never caught the mistake. Each time the changes slipped by unnoticed because our attention was focused on Sonny and his violent demise. Pickpockets exploit change blindness all the time by working in teams; one or more players create a distraction as the thief steals the goodies.

▶ People tend to fear loss more than desire gain. Retailers tend to exploit this all the time with "limited time offers" or "exclusive opportunities"

▶ People tend to see something and accept it as real (or true) and then ask questions later. This happens all the time on social media sites like Facebook. How many times has someone forwarded you a hoax or doctored photo because they assumed it was factual although they never bothered to verify its accuracy?

Every one of us has taken advantage of one or more of those human quirks, especially during sales calls, job interviews or first dates. Most of the social engineering stunts my friends and I pulled back then were either pranks or low-level capers of opportunity. Not to wax nostalgic but it was definitely a different time. By today's standards our antics were almost whimsical, like watching the original 1932 film SCARFACE starring Paul Muni and comparing it to the 1983 remake starring Al Pacino. Today, anyone with some basic social engineering skills, a little guile, access to Google and a malicious agenda can do a lot of damage.

Social Engineering and Senior Citizens

Cybercriminals usually work in macro-to-micro mode. They use wide dragnets to capture as many victims as possible. Making use of stolen credit cards or bank account credentials can be done without any contact with the owner. While this is usually good enough for most, some criminals figure out they've got a lead on some identities worth big money and they want to go for it. And the only chance of making this big score happen is by making contact with the mark and employing some social engineering tactics to get the information and/or support necessary. When it comes to potential targets, senior citizens often end up at the top of the list. Here are a few reasons why:

► People who grew up in 1950s (or earlier) were typically raised with polite and trusting dispositions. Call them on the phone and they generally won't react by hanging up immediately. They'll be more courteous. They'll say they're not interested but may be persuaded to reluctantly listen to the pitch. Cybercriminals know this and, in either case, the longer they can keep a senior on the phone the greater the chance they might successfully get the necessary information to pull off a big score.

► Seniors are more likely to have some sort of nest egg: a good credit rating, retirement funds, investments, savings accounts, and own their home. To cybercriminals, this makes them worth their weight in gold... sometimes literally.

► When the elderly have been defrauded, sometimes the crime goes unreported. Sometimes they don't know they've been ripped off or they're ashamed to acknowledge it. Other times they don't know who to contact or they're afraid that their relatives may think they're unfit to handle their own finances.

► Generally speaking, age has an effect on memory. It's not uncommon for the elderly to be problematic witnesses when they report a crime. Cybercriminals depend on this hazy recall to hinder any possible investigation. Many scams and cybercrimes can take up to a few months to be discovered, further adding to the lack of credible timeline information that the mark can provide to investigators.

► Seniors tend to be more susceptible to "home and health" related scams. On the health side this can be anything from discount medication, drugs to improve memory and vigor, miracle cures that the FDA won't approve, and so on. Fraud involving the home might be anything from investment scams, mortgage scams, Medicare fraud, and special "seniors only" programs that are too good to be true.

► For every senior that is reasonably comfortable with computers, there are at least half a dozen or more who are clueless to the point where they either never get online or they cruise the web with reckless abandon. Regardless of their abundant life experience, when it comes to the dangers of cyberspace they can be as naïve as young children.

If you have senior citizens in your life or you ARE a senior that could stand to toughen up your tech game, fret not. There are countless computer classes and tutorials out there, both online and at local sites. A visit to the local library (or its website) will turn up some leads on these classes. NOTE: Most of these classes are either free or charge a nominal fee.

The X-Factor—
How to Protect Yourself When the Ex Turns Zombie

In recent years, the social engineering tactics that were once reserved for hackers and high tech mayhem have made their way into the social media mainstream. I've been getting calls regarding another phenomena has been slowly on the rise. For lack of a better term, I refer to it as The X-Factor. Many of these stories usually begin or end with "Somehow that [expletive] keeps hacking into my [expletive] _____ email!"

Sometimes these are enemies that were once friends or relatives. Sometimes they're stalkers. At other times they're bitter ex-lovers that are scorned or just refuse to let go of the relationship. Whatever the case, they were once close enough to you to know how you think. They know many of your secrets. And now that there's a problem they intend to take out their revenge by exploiting their insider information as much as possible.

Here are some tips to protect your online accounts:

1. Using a free email services such as MSN, Yahoo or Gmail, establish one or more backup email addresses using a pseudonym. Yes, as in do not use your real name. Whether you come up with an anagram of your name or something totally different, make sure it sounds reasonably believable and doesn't resemble your name at all. And make sure the username for the account isn't directly associated with your real name, or new moniker. It's also a good idea to avoid usernames associated with your personality traits, occupation, favorite sports teams, music, or hobbies. For example, if you don't like football, a username like "dcowboys4life" might be a username worth considering. By having that simple reference to the Dallas Cowboys, if your cyberstalker knows you don't care for football, s/he won't easily make the connection that the account is yours. Remember, effective social engineering is all about having just enough knowledge about who you are supposed to be in order to convince the other person that you have legitimate right to whatever you're requesting. Someone like an ex-spouse knows your full name, address, birth date, and

Social Security Number. Armed with that kind of information, a 6th grader could practically track you down in Antarctica.

2.   With the secret questions required to reset passwords, don't use any answers that are directly connected to your immediate life story. For example, if you opt to use the "mother's maiden name" question, use the maiden name of your mother's mother as the answer. Or for the "city where you were born", use the city where a parent or grandparent was born. The reason: when we fall in Love, most of us can't wait to share everything. During the course of the relationship we'll practically tell our life stories several times over. The longer you and your ex were together, the more s/he knows your history—many of the kinds of personal facts that also happen to be used for those secret questions. Most people won't mentally note obscure details as they pertain to their lover's parents.

3.   With any kind of banking, bill-paying or ecommerce websites (e.g. - Amazon.com, Bank of America, JC Penney, etc.), set up your new secret email address(es) to receive notifications and updates from these accounts. Avoid using the email addresses that come with your DSL or cable modem subscription. For example, a fair number of my clients have Verizon DSL and use the email that came with the service. On more than one occasion, using an old copy of the Verizon bill I was able to reset usernames and passwords to the email addresses, add names as an authorized person on the account, request copies of the bill, and even open up additional service on the same account. By using the fake name email addresses with all the obscure information, a problem person won't be able to use social engineering tactics to get access to them.

Just like the technology, the objectives behind social engineering have been taking on new dimensions. Anyone with a halfway decent nose for detective work can dig up all kinds of intel by using Google and poking around on Facebook, LinkedIn and other social media websites.

Facebook and other Social Networks—
The Zombie's Gourmet Buffet

Traditionally, every cybercriminal—from the Script Kiddie wannabe hacker to the hardcore cyberterrorist—thrives on information. In a realm where you are who you say you are, intimate knowledge is literally the raw DNA that will allow you to become whoever you want to be. The rest is just having a plan and the determination to carry it out.

Along with the growth of the Internet, cybercrime was already building momentum like the perfect hurricane. And just as the most dangerous part of a hurricane is the storm surge, here comes social networks. With Facebook alone there are around a billion people who have registered in the same place with their names, partial addresses, school affiliations, jobs, photos, family and friends, hobbies, love interests and their activities. To cybercriminals, predators and voyeurs this was better than Manna from Heaven. Add sites like Linked-In and Twitter and any halfway dedicated criminal will have enough resource material to turn identity theft into a career path.

It should note that these Phishing scams are evolving beyond email and into everything from stealing photos to using social networks—a whole different source of zombie outbreaks that most people aren't ready for.

One of the safety precautions is to make sure your privacy preferences are set. Are they enough? No, but they're a good start. Another safety precaution is to implement the "Do Not Track" plugins (or extensions) for your web browsers. Since this is different for each web browser you'll probably want to visit your web browser's website to inquire for specifics. I tested out a DNT plugin with my Chrome web browser and within the first week of installation it prevented Facebook, another ad network, and several companies from tracking me, blocking somewhere over 1200 tracking attempts.

Baron Samedi says

"With any social network websites, a good safety rule is to never post any more or any less than you would want to see appear in tomorrow's newspaper."

Adversary Targeting— Facebook, Unseen Enemies and You

In between major projects and deadlines, I tend to check out what's happening on Facebook (and other social media sites) at least twice a day. Like any good addiction, I'm not sure why. It seems like anytime I'm on the site I'm being inundated with a steady stream of quaint memes from lovelorn divorcees, angry rants, misinformation, and hoaxes. The assortment of freaks and bizarre video clips are enough to make PT Barnum proud. And even though I'm probably one of the more obscure freaks on the prowl, I always feel like a stranger in a strange land. Why? To sum it up in a word: awareness.

I've worked in web design/development and IT since 1994. And before that, places like Usenet and IRC chat rooms had been my playground since 1989. Facebook is just another marvel of web development, an Emerald City cybermetropolis. It's like Disney World—once you know the mechanics behind the Wizard's curtain you'll be forever jaded by knowing how the magic works.

Since many people don't understand the how or why social media websites exist, there's a prevailing attitude that they're almost like a public service. They treat having access to sites like Facebook, Instagram and Twitter as a right and not a priviledge. Regardless of their origins, they don't exist as part of some altruistic mission to bring the world together. They are not bastions of free speech, owed to its members as part of some amendment to the Bill of Rights. That is all part of the myth.

The reality is that social networks are giant planets of content. Even more ingenious, the developers figured out how to create channels where people could be their own brand and provide their own content; sort of 21st century public access TV meets interactive TV except it is web-based. Their primary objective is to suck us in for hours at a time, providing a captive audience for those companies who pay to advertise their products and services. Generally speaking, the software behind social networks is designed to take every detail related to our individual user experiences—every "like", personal interest, political/religious/social affiliation, sexual preference, gender identification, public/private message, game, and everything we look at—and filter it all through a mind-boggling array of marketing algorithms to determine what product and service ads to show on each page.

Your personal privacy concerns are not the same as the privacy concerns of a social network or its advertising sponsors. In order to have an account on these sites each user must click on a checkbox to agree to some kind of Terms and Conditions of Acceptable Use. By clicking that "I accept" checkbox and the button to continue a user has signed a digital contract giving the corporate owners permission to do whatever they want to do with the information collected on you or about you from the time you've spent on the website. Most people never bother to read those terms before agreeing to them, including the privacy fanatics and Copyright alarmists. Anyone that read the terms would know that most of those Copyright / Privacy Notice posts are an Internet hoax and forwarding them is a waste of time. The truth is simple: social networks provide users with about as much privacy as a stall in a public restroom.

Never before in the history of advertising—or civilization—has this kind of detailed customer profile data been readily available to businesses. This has also brought on a type of transparency that had previously been reserved for celebrities and public figures. Most people aren't prepared to handle this high level of exposure... and they don't know it.

On most social media sites like Facebook, the average person's profile is full of past and present personal data, professional/political/religious affiliations, photos, and insightful clues as to their personality traits. Acquiring this kind of information once required an investigator with the time (and budget) to follow this person and do things like steal their mail or dig through their garbage to compile a dossier. Now, most of that same information can be acquired for free and anonymously with little risk of exposure, making social networks the de facto tool of the trade when it comes to Adversary Targeting.

> **"...Social networks provide users with about as much privacy as a stall in a public restroom."**

Adversary Targeting is what happens when a Mark (i.e. - the person that is the intended subject) posts all kinds of personal information on social network sites and an Entity uses these same sources to collect that information and use it as part of a plan focused on taking advantage of the Mark. The Entity may be a single person, a few people, or a huge organization. The age and profession of the Mark often determines who (or what) the Entity is. Lastly, the Entity's agenda can range from something as simple as curiosity to being as nefariously complex as blackmail or espionage.

For example, if the Mark is Brad, a 14-year old male middle school student, he is more likely to be targeted by an Entity that could be

- ► a shy classmate that has a crush on him,
- ► a bully,
- ► a stalkerish ex, or
- ► a sexual predator.

Or if the Mark is Brad's mother, Brenda, a 40-year old female IT Manager working for a defense contractor, she could be targeted by

- ▶ an interested suitor,
- ▶ an ex-lover,
- ▶ a stalker,
- ▶ a burglar,
- ▶ a scammer / identity thief,
- ▶ a recruiter,
- ▶ a corporate competitor looking to bribe her,
- ▶ a disgruntled former employee with a plan for revenge, or
- ▶ a foreign government agency such as the MSS (the Ministry of State Security, China's equivalent to the CIA) with the intent to steal military secrets.

In the corporate arena, Adversary Targeting happens all the time. A more common variation of this has been around for decades: Target Marketing. Companies compile information on us from various sources—including our credit reports—to send us direct mail promoting their products and services. If most people understood the widespread and invasive nature of Adversary Targeting they would probably never touch another social media website. The following anecdote is one example of how such methods can be applied:

During the summer of 2011, the staff of a New England law firm found itself embroiled in scandal. Their office network had been hacked.

Posing as a courier looking for work, the hacker went to the firm and introduced himself. After talking with the receptionist and one of the paralegals, he was informed that they weren't hiring. Within that brief conversation he gained useful inside knowledge: the names of two employees, both full-figured women. No wedding rings. Physical security and surveillance cameras made physical access to the computers highly improbable. Lastly, the receptionist was using a PC. All of this played a part in the burn.

Armed with this information, the hacker jumped on his laptop and started Googling. After finding Facebook profiles for both the receptionist and the paralegal, he discovered that the paralegal was a 30something divorcee that only logged in occasionally. The receptionist, however, was the typical 20something social network junkie, posting close to a dozen updates daily. Further digging in her Facebook "likes" revealed many things, among them that she was single, a member of the Kappa Kappa Gamma (KKG) sorority, and a fan of musicals.

First, the hacker went online and purchased a USB flash drive with the KKG sorority letters and Coat of Arms. On it, he installed a hidden self-running Trojan horse along with pirated episodes of the first season of "Glee". Next, he had an associate deliver a dozen Madame Delbard roses and a Godiva Chocolate gift basket to the office, addressed to the paralegal from a secret admirer. It caused a stir among the ladies, and in the middle of the hoopla the associate slipped the flash drive onto the receptionist's counter and left.

Later that day the hacker received an email alert from the Trojan. Someone had found the flash drive, plugged it into their computer, and the Trojan delivered its payload—a little remote access tool that bypassed the office firewall and opened up a backdoor. More than likely the receptionist spotted her KKG sorority insignia on the flash drive, asked around if anyone knew who it belonged to, and then plugged it in herself to see what it contained. The Glee episodes were for her benefit, a suitable way to make sure she was distracted long enough for the payload to install. It didn't matter who picked up the flash drive or clicked on an episode; the computer was fully compromised before the first musical number finished.

Within a few days the hacker had full control over every computer on the network. There was a major snag in his objective: there was no sign of what he sought. They weren't anywhere on the visible office network. Aside from the backups, the only places left to check were the attorney laptops and tablets… and they only popped up on the network a few times a day.

An outside IT company maintained the firm's network; a fact that the hacker deduced after finding their invoices in the account's email inbox. In a series of personalized emails supposedly sent from that company, the hacker requested that the staff leave all laptops online overnight for routine maintenance. The real IT person also received a copy of the email request that he supposedly sent. Freaked out by the security breach, he rushed over to the office and notified top management. Taking great care not to alert the hacker, the IT people found the Trojan and set traps on the network. After reviewing the surveillance video they found the flash drive, too, along with seeing the make and model of the delivery driver's car. Within a few days several state investigators raided the hacker's apartment across town.

It turns out the hacker wasn't a curious explorer, identity thief or even a vandal. He was essentially a hired gun. A few months earlier, a wealthy matriarch had passed away, leaving behind a huge estate. Her children, all well into their 30s and older, had grown up enjoying the benefits of her money... until some of them were cut off. As part of contesting the will, the "Haves" and "Have Nots" went to war. Two law firms were brought into the fight—the targetted firm and the one that employed the investigator who hired the hacker. The hacker's mission was to do reconnaissance, retrieving every bit of data related to the plaintiff's case.

Each firm had an impeccable reputation with a roster of big name clients. Neither could afford the bad publicity. As a result, they didn't press charges against the hacker. Damages were paid and the matter never made it to court. Everyone involved was forced to sign a stack of confidentiality agreements; the news media never got wind of the incident. The firm that hired the hacker couldn't afford the public scrutiny associated with employing cybercriminals. And the firm that got hacked didn't want the public embarrassment of having more than 50 years worth of client records get compromised with a bouquet of flowers, a flash drive, and a few episodes of Glee.

The previous scenario isn't an isolated incident. Situations like that happen far more frequently than most corporations will publically admit. Contrary to what we see in the movies, it isn't common for the targets of cyber espionage to be the CEOs, Senators or top nuclear physicists. Those targets are keenly aware of their security clearances to the point of being paranoid. Often they are too difficult to reach. Instead, the best targets are typically minor players—the proverbial nobodies. Because their jobs aren't considered top secret or mission-critical, everything else about their personal lives isn't as prone to be cloaked in high security and secrecy. They are soft targets that can be exploited to get to hard targets.

In the scenario with the dueling law firms, targeting the receptionist was a great strategic move. She was a young, carefree receptionist; her personal life was practically public knowledge on Facebook. Although she might have been considered low person on the totem pole, it was easy to overlook that her work computer was just as important as the CEOs computer on their office network. The hacker used harmless personal information to trick her into helping him crack into her system. Once she took the bait she inadvertently gave him the digital keys to the office.

**Characteristics Common to Most Known
Species of Living Dead (cont'd):**

Eyes: Most zombies have no discernable iris color, leaving their eyes hazed over and jaundiced. They never blink. Reports vary as to the clarity of their vision. NOTE: This is literally one time where it pays to wait till you see the whites of their eyes before you shoot. Of course, zombies in cyberspace have no eyes. They hunt by smell of data.

On networks with more than four employee computers, install an endpoint security package. If you Google "Endpoint Security" or "Endpoint Protection" you'll get quite a selection; most antivirus manufacturers also sell enterprise-level endpoint protection. Writing about all of them is worthy of a publication about the size of the typical issue of TIME magazine. As far as making a recommendation, I've come to the conclusion that the top endpoint protection packages are all great... and they all suck, too. This is because new malware is introduced into the wild by thousands each week. Any new infection may take anywhere from 6 hours to 6 months for anti-malware developers to reverse engineer so their protection software can accurately detect and quarantine it. With that said, none of these packages provide 100% security and their detection success rates go up and down like a barometer. In that King of the Hill game no one stays on top for very long.

Ultimately, what seems to work best is to test drive several endpoint packages (each one over a month or so) and see which one is best suits your office environment. If an endpoint package interferes with daily workflow of the employees they are prone to try to leave it disabled, rendering it useless. Think of endpoint protection a bit like an umbrella—it's not complete protection against getting wet in the rain and if it's too big or too small it probably won't get used at all.

Remote Access to your Small Business Network

Remote Access

Once upon a time, having remote access to files on a computer within your small business network was about as elite as having a car phone in the 80s—a brag sake to those who had it and an unfulfilled wish to those who couldn't afford it. Now, many of the solutions are much cheaper, some are even free. In today's competitive business climate, key employees at every company should have some form of remote access in order to be more productive. And while this topic is worthy of its own book, I'm including this summary both as an introduction to different types of remote access and to address the security concerns with each one. I should also note that many of these remote access solutions are also PC, Mac and/or Linux compatible.

Baron Samedi says

"If you're not familiar with what a port-forwarding rule is, do yourself a favor—read this section, figure out the type of remote access that sounds like it would best serve your needs, and then talk to an IT professional about making it happen."

Each of the following remote access types requires being comfortable with basic networking. Minor changes need to be made with your firewall or router, specifically opening a TCP port and directing them to your desktop computer or server. This is to allow for connecting to the remote control program (or feature) from outside the network. And although adding a port-forwarding rule to your firewall/router isn't difficult, doing so incorrectly can make things get a little squirrely, especially as the rules add up—which is why it's best to only make these changes if you're comfortable with basic computer networking.

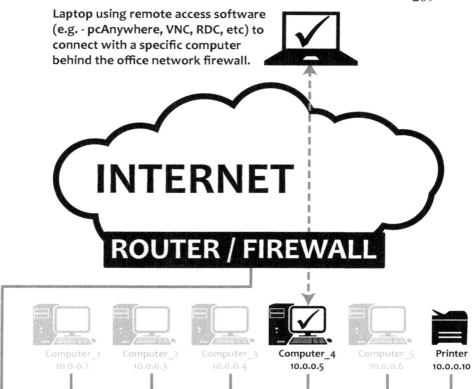

Laptop using remote access software (e.g. - pcAnywhere, VNC, RDC, etc) to connect with a specific computer behind the office network firewall.

INTERNET

ROUTER / FIREWALL

| Computer_1 | Computer_2 | Computer_3 | Computer_4 | Computer_5 | Printer |
| 10.0.0.2 | 10.0.0.3 | 10.0.0.4 | 10.0.0.5 | 10.0.0.6 | 10.0.0.10 |

Office Network

Remote Access Software (Free-n-Cheap)

Among the most notable Free-n-Cheap remote access utilities are VNC (Virtual Network Computing) and Microsoft Remote Desktop Connection. Fortunately the price of these solutions is no reflection of a lack of quality.

VNC is platform-independent, meaning you can do things like be at home on a Mac and use it to take control a PC at your office. There are a number of VNC-based utilities that are available, including UltraVNC and TightVNC. Some are free, some are commercial, and they all include both server and client components that can be installed on any Windows

PC. For Mac users, VNC is built into OS X (10.5 and later), plus VNC is readily available for other flavors of Linux and BSD. I've personally used VNC for more than a decade for tasks like managing low-risk web servers located in San Diego, California, while living in Virginia. I also use it to do things on the headless Linux servers on my own network instead of having a KVM or separate monitors for each machine. As long as you're using a typical high speed connection to access, you can do pretty much everything through VNC that you could if you were physically at that computer—except audio isn't supported and the frame rate isn't fast enough to handle animation or video smoothly.

Remote Desktop Connection (RDC, also called Remote Desktop, formerly known as Microsoft Terminal Services Client) works similar to VNC except it is a Microsoft component that was built into several versions of Windows, particularly XP, Vista, 7 and 8. It should also be noted that, as of this writing, only the professional versions of Windows XP, Vista, 7 and 8 have desktops that can be controlled from remote using RDC. For those who are using the home or student editions of Microsoft Windows, fret not—unlike Remote Desktop, VNC doesn't discriminate.

On the security side, these utilities are pretty straight forward. With the VNC server (i.e. - the part of VNC that resides on the computer you're accessing from remote), you have the option to turn on encryption. When accessing your computer from remote, data has to be constantly passed back and forth. Encrypting that data will add a much stronger layer of protection. Although it may have a slight affect on the speed of your connection, if you want to make sure your system stays secure, it's worth the little extra overhead. Last but not least, keep your operating system current, make sure that anti-virus software is installed on that computer, and be sure it stays up to date, too.

Whether using VNC or Remote Desktop, these types of remote access require forwarding a port number to a specific computer on the network that the user wishes to control from remote. Another way to look at it is as if you lived in a house on 2600 Main Street with thousands of neighbors and thousands of deliveries were made daily by UPS, FedEx, and USPS; any packages marked for 2600 will be directed to your house, regardless of the source or the carrier. This is why these kinds of remote access solutions tend to be free or pretty inexpensive—they're great, but best suited for a single user. On a business network, for every additional user that wants this kind of remote access to their computer, another alternate port needs to be opened up on the firewall/router and pointed to that machine. Setting up any more than five users with this kind of access will fast become a nightmarish administrative headache.

Remote Access Software (Commercial)

Similar to VNC and Remote Desktop are the commercial remote access software packages. They usually have a host/server component and a client/remote program that allows for access to the PC. One of the oldest and most respected in this category is Symantec's pcAnywhere. And while VNC and Remote Desktop seem to work the same on the surface, they're nowhere near as feature-rich as their commercial counterparts, including compatibility with the major platforms (PC, Max, and Linux).

Although commercial packages like pcAnywhere do cost more, they have far more features than their free counterparts. Their remote control experiences are much smoother, to the point where they feel like you're sitting at that machine. And lastly, users have access to better technical support.

On the downside, commercial packages like pcAnywhere require the same port-forwarding through your firewall/router like with VNC and Remote Desktop. This also means they are prone to the same administrative headaches for anyone who tries to set up more than a handful of users this way.

NOTE: Should you decide to use pcAnywhere, be sure to install version 12.5 SP4 (or Solution 12.6.7) or later. In January 2012, Symantec confirmed reports that the source code for pcAnywhere had been stolen by hackers and leaked into cyberspace. Symantec has since fixed the problem but, in the interest of security, all versions older than 12.5 SP4 should be treated as unsafe.

Cloud-Based Remote Access Services

Second to cloud-based storage and backup services, this type of remote access service has gained a lot of popularity. Well-known packages include LogMeIn, GoToMyPc, and TeamViewer. Each one of these programs has both a Windows and a Mac version, and all but TeamViewer use a web browser to make the connection. This type of remote access service opens up a "window" into whatever computer you've installed it on so you can work with it as if you're sitting right in front of it. The way it works is pretty simple: you install a program on both your office computer and your laptop. The program on the office computer stays connected with the web-based service. Whenever you want to access your office computer you run the program on your laptop, log into the same web-based service and Cha-Ching! You're connected.

When it comes to remote access to desktops using mobile devices, as of this writing the Splashtop Pro package is among the leaders of the pack. So far, versions of Splashtop Streamer are avaiable for Microsoft Windows XP on up to Windows 8 (including the Home Premium versions, which do not support RDP), Mac OS X 10.6 (Snow Leopard) on up. The remote desktop client for Splashtop is also available for Apple devices (iPhone, iPad, iPod Touch), Android, and various other tablets and high-end eReaders (Blackberry Playbook, HP Touchpad, NOOK, and Kindle Fire) as well as Windows and Mac. Unlike other packages, Splashtop uses its own protocol to support real-time video and audio.

A huge benefit to this kind of remote access is that it doesn't require changes to a firewall to work. No need to set up port-forwarding and all the hardcore IT nerd stuff. Unlike Remote Desktop, pcanywhere and VNC, this solution scales well with a bunch of other computers on the network. Although they use a separate hosting website, these clients don't consume a lot of resources.

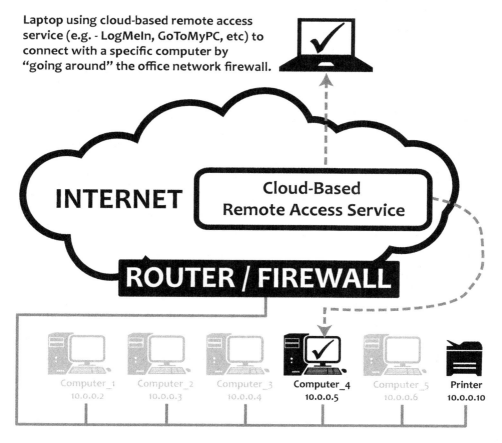

Laptop using cloud-based remote access service (e.g. - LogMeIn, GoToMyPC, etc) to connect with a specific computer by "going around" the office network firewall.

INTERNET

Cloud-Based Remote Access Service

ROUTER / FIREWALL

Computer_1 10.0.0.2   Computer_2 10.0.0.3   Computer_3 10.0.0.4   **Computer_4 10.0.0.5**   Computer_5 10.0.0.6   **Printer 10.0.0.10**

Office Network

When it comes to hosted remote access, the biggest downside is most of them charge a monthly or annual fee for commercial use. Although it is possible to set up your own private-cloud remote access service, they have not been included in this chapter. Most SOHO environments cannot justify the added expense, plus they should be set up by an IT professional.

NOTE: For noncommercial use, some services like Teamviewer and LogMeIn have free accounts. All the services have trial periods that are worth test driving.

Remote Access over a VPN

A VPN (Virtual Private Network) allows you to connect your computer to your private home or office network. It can also be used to securely connect one or more computers and networks together over the Internet. VPNs come in one of two main types: site-to-site (e.g. - making a bridge between two separate office networks) or remote-access (e.g. - connecting an individual computer to an office network). For the purposes of this chapter, we're focusing on personal remote access. The VPN creates a secure tunnel between wherever you are and a remote network, giving you access to all the resources on that network (e.g. - printers, shared folders, file servers, etc.). Simply put, it makes your computer connect as a full member of the office network, no different than if your computer was in the office like all the others. Variations of the VPN are how many businesses have kept their branch offices and home offices connected with the main office network, regardless of physical locations.

There are some pros and cons to this solution. To put them into perspective, a basic technical overview of VPN is required. Everything connected to the network is assigned what is called an Internet Protocol (IP) addressed. In many ways, an IP address is the Internet equivalent of a phone number, and for the purposes of this chapter we'll stick with the more commonly used IPv4 address format (e.g. - 192.168.1.1). Every network has a unique IP address (or range of addresses), all separated by firewalls that prevent anyone on one network from accessing another. Creating a VPN requires (1) either a VPN-capable firewall on the destination network or a VPN server, and (2) VPN software on the computer that will be connecting from remote. For example, let's say you're at the airport in Los Angeles waiting on a flight, on your way back to your home office in Virginia Beach. Establishing a VPN connection from your laptop to your office network will make your laptop act as if it is still physically on the Virginia Beach office network and not 3000 miles away.

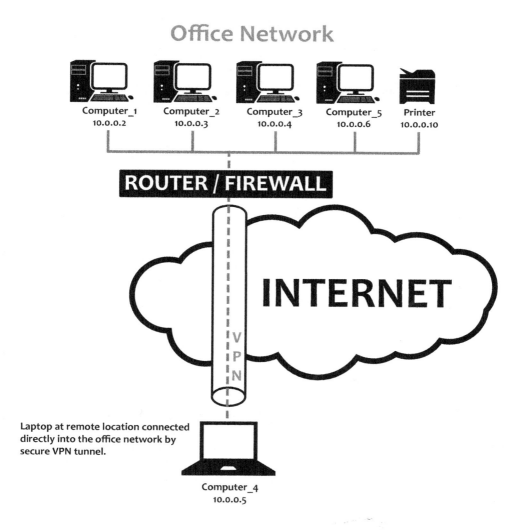

Office Network

Computer_1
10.0.0.2

Computer_2
10.0.0.3

Computer_3
10.0.0.4

Computer_5
10.0.0.6

Printer
10.0.0.10

ROUTER / FIREWALL

INTERNET

V
P
N

Laptop at remote location connected directly into the office network by secure VPN tunnel.

Computer_4
10.0.0.5

For the typical SOHO environment, the downside is that this kind of remote access requires routers that cost a little more and some IT experience to setup. The typical DD-WRT compatible wireless routers (e.g. - Netgear, Linksys, etc.) with built-in VPN support start at around $160 dollars USD. A growing number of them also support OpenVPN, a free open-source VPN solution that provides an alternative to other protocols like IPsec. Setting up a VPN connection gets into a maddening assortment of encryption strengths, certificates, NATs and other stuff that is best left to an experienced IT consultant. The upside to these higher upfront costs is that the VPN provides a more secure "on the office network" experience, plus the tunnel can be used to provide added security for other remote access solutions mentioned in this chapter.

SSL VPN

An SSL VPN (Secure Sockets Layer virtual private network) is form of VPN that uses your web browser to establish a secure connection between a remote desktop/laptop and an office network. Even better, it doesn't require any special client software installed on your computer. The office network, however, requires a special appliance to handle the incoming remote connections. SSL VPNs allow for direct access to file servers, web servers, email, etc. Some also provide network access to desktops and other internal servers. Contrary to other VPNs, the SSL VPN allows the network administrator to have greater control over who can access what resource on the network. Since SSL encryption is built into every web browser, there's no special software to maintain.

As of this writing, one of the most popular SSL VPN solutions is OpenVPN. The main advantages of OpenVPN are that it's easier to configure than IPsec, compatible with networks that are dynamic (using DHCP) versus just a static IP address, and cheaper than other VPN solutions. It's available as both a client/software solution you can download and install (**http://www.openvpn.com**) as well as provided by some VPN services out there (e.g. - AlwaysVPN, SunVPN, Hidemyass, etc.).

SSL VPN and IPsec/L2TP both have their advantages and drawbacks. Because of the ever-changing nature of these technologies, it's best to work with an IT professional to carefully weigh the pros and cons to figure out what will be serve your needs.

Server-Based Remote Access

One last form of secure remote access comes built around Microsoft Windows Server Essentials, also known as Windows Small Business Server or SBS in versions prior to 2012. For the sake of this chapter, I'll refer to this collectively as SBS. Regardless of the name changes, SBS is a suite of heavy-duty Microsoft applications geared toward small businesses with less than 75 users. It also comes with Remote Web Workplace, an SSL-secured portal that allows you to read your email through a web-based version of Outlook, access your company intranet, or connect directly to your office PC.

Remote Web Workplace allows you to use Internet Explorer to connect with any desktop computer or server on your office network. Similar to SSL-VPN, there is a little set up required (e.g. - opening ports on firewall, install SSL certificates, etc.). Once in use it will feel much like Remote Desktop, system chimes and all. The downside with SBS is that your network has to be built around it. Since this server has to be first, if you've already got a network set up with it's own domain then adding SBS could possibly be problematic. If you don't have an Active Directory-based network then this investment could be well worth it.

As a small business owner, once you experience the benefits of remote access it becomes both a time saver and a lifesaver. It's worth the time and effort to explore the options that work best for you. There's nothing like being able to access your files in a pinch or sit in a restaurant and get your work done. A very comprehensive list of remote access software packages can be found here:

http://en.wikipedia.org/wiki/Comparison_of_remote_desktop_software

THE LAST MAN ON EARTH (1964)

The Cloud:
Sanctuary or Sacrificial Altar?

Unlike the other forms of remote access, the Cloud needs special attention. As of this writing, none of the others have the same buzz among small business managers and owners. I believe we will come to see the cloud as a mixed bag, which I'll address shortly.

On the surface, the cloud refers to any computer network that allows you to access and share data across Internet-connected devices. Beyond that basic definition, a cloud is one or more servers that a company owns, allowing its users to manage their own files and information. The term "cloud" came from the tendency for people to use a cloud when creating diagrams to illustrate the Internet. In the early days of the Internet, many geeks used the magic cloud analogy the help people understand that you could put a file into it at one location and someone else could retrieve that file from another location.

With cloud services, you can log in, store information and files, and then conveniently retrieve them from anywhere else using any networked device. Cloud computing allows you to subscribe to computer resources and online storage space at a much lower cost than if you purchased all the hardware and software and set up the network yourself. Most people have already been exposed to this concept with online email providers like Hotmail, Gmail and Yahoo, giving us the ability to send and receive emails from anywhere with an Internet connection.

Types of Clouds

Depending on your needs, there are different types of clouds available.

As a home user, there are plenty of free cloud services out there to choose from. Among my top picks would be iCloud, Google Drive, SkyDrive and Dropbox, all of which have a ton of space.

As a small business manager, you are likely to start out with a using a Public Cloud and eventually graduate to a Hybrid Cloud (some Public Cloud applications and a Private Cloud connected to your internal IT infrastructure).

1. **Private Cloud** - belongs to an organization or company and limits access to their people only.
2. **Public Cloud** - can be accessed by anyone with an Internet connection that has subscribed to that cloud.
3. **Community Cloud** - similar to a private cloud except it is shared among two or more organizations or companies that have similar needs.
4. **Hybrid Cloud** - essentially a combination of at least two of the previously mentioned cloud types.

Currently, the most common use of the cloud is for some kind of storage. A well-known example of this kind of service is Apple's iCloud. It allows a user to store photos, documents, contacts, email, to-do lists, schedules and other data in an online space, making them accessible from anywhere using another mobile device, smartphone, or computer. Similar examples include DropBox, Google Drive, Box, and Microsoft SkyDrive. All of these have free and commercial service offerings.

There are three main types of Cloud Providers:

► **Infrastructure as a Service (IaaS)** - rather than buying everything necessary for a network infrastructure (e.g. - servers, software, network equipment, and etc.), you pay a vendor for these services and they bill you based on the amount of resources you use.
► **Platform as a Service (PaaS)** - you pay a vendor to provide and manage an operating system and everything else required to run certain platforms.
► **Software as a Service (SaaS)** - instead of you purchasing a software license and installing it on your own computer(s), you pay subscription fee to a vendor to access the software over the Internet and use it. Usually the vendor manages the hardware, software and all updates.

With each environment from IaaS to SaaS, the cloud provider has more control and the subscriber has less control over what they can do within that cloud. What this means is that you, as the subscriber, can choose the level of control you need over your services and the information you're managing.

For example, let's say you're a solo programmer that has developed some software with a new approach to music distribution and intend to compete with iTunes. Once upon a time this idea would be almost unheard of unless you had a minimum investment of $250,000 to put into leasing an office space, setting up a robust network with a broadband connection, and configuring the servers where your software will reside; closer to $1 million if you include the salaries of the staff necessary to run it. By subscribing to an IaaS cloud provider, the good news is that you can get access to the all the infrastructure you need to compete with iTunes for a fraction of that minimum investment. The not-so-good news is that cloud computing a bit like a marriage—a commitment that may seem easy to make but it can be hell to separate from down the road. Even with subscribing to a SaaS provider, such moves shouldn't be taken lightly.

The Bright Side of Cloud Computing

As of this writing, we're in the early Gospel era of cloud computing where some of the positive benefits exist and others are closer to the promise that many cloud providers hope will lead them to untold riches.

1. **Convenience** - Nuff said.
2. **Collaboration** - this is almost a no-brainer, too. Since the cloud can be accessed anytime from any computer, it's easy for employees to collaborate and exchange information regardless of time or location. Files can be exchanged with customers, too, especially the kinds that are too big for email attachments.
3. **Reduced overhead** - cloud computing promises to lower operating costs, particularly with how much a company has to spend on hardware, software and the IT resources to manage them.
4. **Scalability** - Some cloud computing services charge their clients

based on how much they use, similar to an electric bill. As your business needs grow, cloud services can easily accommodate for that with a minimum of effort and expense. As of this writing, with most working cloud computing sites this is more of the promise and not a reflection of today's reality.

5. **Better technology, lower prices** - Small businesses can subscribe to cloud services, giving them access to software and/or hardware that they ordinarily wouldn't be able to afford if they had to fulfill those needs in-house. Again, this is generally more of the promise of "the cloud to come" versus what is already here.

6. **Lower technology investment** - subscribing to cloud services will eliminate the need for a company to purchase high end servers and software licenses. More promise, far less proof of concept.

Titanium or Tulips— The Realities of Cloud Computing

There are a couple of metaphorical realities that businesses can expect with cloud computing.

The first is Titanium. Discovered in the late 1700s, it didn't take long to figure out this element has value. Year after year, everyone who was made aware of this metal saw the potential (and the dollar signs) but couldn't figure out how to work with it. Industries didn't figure out how to efficiently process Titanium until the 1930s. Today, after years of refinement, Titanium is used in everything from aerospace engineering to jewelry. For many purposes, it's worth more than its weight in Gold.

The second is the Tulip. No, not some obscure clandestine technology; a tulip, as in the garden perennial that blooms every spring. In Amsterdam during the 1600s tulips were luxury items that were bought and sold much like commodities on today's stock market. Tulip merchants started selling the rights to next year's tulips harvest. Once commoners got rich off of buying and selling tulip futures, Holland found itself swept up in Tulip Mania. Prices soared. Tulips sold many times their weight in gold.

One day the tulips stopped selling; investors panicked and rushed to sell. Shares that once sold for as much as 500 guilders (over $8000 dollars in today's US market) were now worthless. Those that didn't sell in time lost fortunes. By many accounts that was the first stock market Boom and Bust in history.

In both scenarios, the strong perception of value was there. With Titanium, the value was realized early but no one could have predicted how long it would take for the technology to catch up to the demand. Countless people who tried to cash in wasted a lot of time and effort. With Tulips, the market made the value increase until someone said "What are we thinking? These are just fancy flowers". Both show the kind of eventual reality that we can expect of the cloud. My guess is that it will turn out to be a combination of Titanium and Tulips with one scenario prevailing as the norm.

And, yes, there is value in the cloud, just like before. Many of the cloud services of today would have been referred to as Application Service Providers (ASP) if they existed back in the 90s. The problem is that for every genuinely brilliant development team there were easily half a dozen Tech-Savvy Snake Oil salesmen on the prowl, pushing the hype to make quick money.

My apprehension comes from first hand experience. I was co-founder of an early Internet Service Provider (ISP) and ASP that started in 1994, back before most people had ever heard of the Internet. Almost all the current cloud hype I've seen or used before, throughout the dot-com rush of the mid-to-later 90s. Cloud computing is mostly a rebranding of old concepts and components with a combination of newer programming languages, smarter interface designs, and a more mature implementation—and the competition is more ferocious than ever.

By the summer of 2000, when we began to feel the effects of the dot-com bubble bust, many ASPs that didn't have a solid business model (or a healthy war chest in the bank) started to either crash or implode. While we had a solid business plan, unfortunately our unsinkable ship had already hit the iceberg, thanks to a bad merger with some of those High-Tech Snake Oil salesmen. Like with Tulip Mania, the only people who raked up were those who got in and sold out before the crash. Anyone that invested in companies with flimsy business models lost a ton of money. Most of those that invested sweat equity watched their companies, their dreams, and their jobs virtually explode overhead like the Space Shuttle Challenger. Bankruptcy attorneys were as happy as vampires in a blood bank as they marauded through the failed ventures. Auctioneers slapped price tags and lot numbers on anything bigger than a thumbtack.

The onslaught didn't end with the dot-com industry, either. When those ASPs went belly up, bankruptcy attorneys confiscated all their web servers along with everything else. Numerous startup companies—who had based their businesses on custom websites and applications they paid the ASPs to develop and host—found themselves victims of the collateral damage. The feeding frenzy that came with liquidating fallen ASPs meant that anything stored on their web servers was lost, destroyed or unknowingly sold to the highest bidder. Many of those startups found themselves without their websites and applications, without all the business information stored in those apps, and absolutely no way to track down the physical web servers that contained their data. It was the virtual equivalent of having their offices destroyed in a hurricane, forcing them to find another ASP and spend thousands to recreate those applications. Anyone that couldn't afford to rebuild lost everything and went out of business.

Doom and gloom aside, I'm more or less a fan of what the cloud can do for a small business. At the same time, I don't think it's wise to hail it as an end-all-be-all replacement for having your own software on your own platforms within your own IT infrastructure. As of this writing, there are too many minefields of headaches and unresolved issues. Here are a few:

1. **Privacy**—No matter what, the cloud service provider you're paying has access to all of your data. They know your business. Anyone that works in their company potentially has access to your data, too. And depending on the terms of your service agreement, there's no telling how much data they might collect based on your activities and how they might use (or sell) that information.

2. **Local Availability**—if your Internet connection goes down or your cloud service provider goes offline, your business is down, leaving you without access to your information until the service provider is accessible again. And since most cloud services are subscription-based, God forbid if money gets tight and you can't pay your bill. Look into Cloud Insurance.

3. **Cloud Access during a Disaster**—Not all cloud services are created equal. How fault tolerant is your cloud service provider? All it takes is a prolonged blackout, network outage, or even a simple unpaid Internet bill and any cloud-dependent part of your business might as well be buried on the dark side of Moon. Look into Cloud Insurance.

4. **Control over your data**—if you decide to cancel the cloud service, there are all kinds of issues to contend with regarding your data. How much of it can you get back? Will you be able to get your data back and, if so, can you import it into something (or somewhere) else to resume business? And since you've decided to go in another direction, how can you be sure that the service provider has destroyed your data? Read the fine print of your contract and weigh the costs BEFORE you even think about entering into a long term cloud solution for your business. Look into Cloud Insurance.

5. **Data security**—some types of cloud service providers have become a magnet for attacks from cybercriminals and Botnets all over the world. For example, back in 2009 there was an incident where cybercriminals had exploited Google's AppEngine and used it to house a Botnet command center that controlled legions of zombie computers. These kinds of incidences aren't isolated; they happen about as often as extremist attacks in the Middle East. Their stories aren't sensational enough to make it to the nightly news. Look into Cloud Insurance.

6. **Marketing hype versus proven substance**—Titanium or Tulips? Nuff said.

It should also be noted that many industry-specific laws and regulations are still rooted in business principles based on 20th century technologies. They don't take into consideration things like the use of third party cloud computing services as part of a core business model. Let's say if you're using a SaaS accounting cloud for your business and your data gets destroyed, would their insurance compensate you for your loss? Could you sue for damages even though there was probably an indemnity clause in your service agreement when you started using their service? And whose laws apply—the laws where you live, the laws where the SaaS company is registered, or the laws wherever your data is physically located? Until those kinds of challenges are resolved, it would be prudent for most small businesses not to rush to jump totally into the cloud. Most companies will probably continue to have a hybrid environment, taking advantage of some cloud services while maintaining most (or all) of their IT infrastructure in-house.

While there are free cloud services offered through providers like Google, the terms of service and privacy policies that they currently have don't always clearly define what they will and won't do with your data. Besides, from a business perspective, using those offsite freebie cloud services as part of your business workflow is a little like building a room addition onto a house that you're renting and can never own—you'll become dependent on it although you have little or no contractual control and the landlord ultimately holds all the cards.

The Rookie Mistake—First Burn in the Cloud

With the typical small business, the first big "Look before you Leap" lesson regarding cloud services will often involve something that most managers never associate with the cloud: their company website. More specifically, how (and where) the company website is set up on the Internet. And just like every zombie story starts with someone who goes into a situation without a clue as to what they're doing, the same kind of mayhem applies.

Aside from establishing the need for a website, usually the next immediate issue is that no one in the office has any professional web design experience. The task commonly ends up in the hands of whoever is perceived as the most tech-savvy person in the office. Most of the time the extent of this person's web design knowledge comes from a class project back in school, a few tech magazine articles, or a little Google research. Any spirited enthusiasm is often fueled by infomercials that make building websites look easy. With the pressure on and anxious to impress the boss, they'll explore any and all options to get the company website built. And just like fear leads to anger, anger leads to hate, and hate leads to suffering, these folks will often jump on the first few offerings that are too good to be true—without any clue about the possible consequences. While working on this book, one of my clients made such a mistake.

A quick dot-com flashback is required here. From the mid-90s to early-00s, running an Internet Service Provider company was like giving computer geeks and tech entrepreneurs a license to print money. Businesses were paying tens of thousands for a modest company website and between $200 and $3000 a month to host them online. Since the web design game was full of startups, many began undercutting and cherry-picking clients from each other. Brand loyalty had dwindled to nothing. It wasn't uncommon for businesses to try to sneak out of their year long contracts by moving their websites to any hosting service that had made a better offer.

Today, the average small business website costs less than $1000 USD to create AND host for a year. Web design companies that also provided hosting had to come up with new practices to attract and retain their web clients, some of which are best described as insidious because they seek to exploit those that don't know any better. The politically correct term for this is "vendor lock-in".

The problem with most bad hosting deals isn't a legal one. With most vendor lock-in tactics there wasn't a need to break any laws. Instead, they play into the egos of business managers that know just enough about the Internet to be dangerous, providing all the shiny chains and handcuffs necessary to happily lock themselves to the deal. I also call these types of web hosts Roach Motels because, like the insect trap, they're super easy to get into and getting out feels damn near impossible. In this case, the motel was Acme Web Hosting.

Sometime before I came into the picture, my client hosted their website in-house. Due to billing oversight with a domain registrar they thought it was a good idea to outsource it. Hastily my client signed into a deal with Acme Web Hosting; all it took was a phone call and a credit card. Sometime after I started managing their network they changed their minds and wanted to bring their website back in-house again. Getting them out of the Acme deal proved to be harder than planning a casino robbery.

To start, my client had given Acme full administrative control over their domain name, client-company.com—a mistake potentially as dangerous as signing over power of attorney. Even worse, once Acme had client-company.com transferred to another domain registrar and they didn't provide any of the authorization credentials. As far as the registrar was concerned, they owned the client-company.com domain. At that point if they wanted to make my client's entire Internet presence disappear (email addresses, website, etc.) there wouldn't have been anything we could do about it.

The other part of Acme's deal was to rework all their hosted websites to use a Content Management System (CMS) they had developed in-house. The selling point was that the CMS allowed hosting customers to easily make changes to their web pages. And while this was true, the drawback (hidden in the fine print) was that once the client-company.com website was fitted into the CMS framework, there was no going back to its original state. If the reworked website wasn't running on an Acme web server with Acme's CMS it wouldn't work anywhere else—period. The choice to cancel Acme's hosting services came with one of three options:

1. move to another hosting service and use a version of the client-company.com website they had online before switching to Acme (usually very outdated files, if available at all),

2.　move to another hosting service and pay someone to build a new client-company.com website, or

3.　stay with Acme.

Since options #1 and #2 required an unexpected-yet-significant investment of time and money, I suspect most non-tech savvy customers chose #3.

Over the course of a few days it took a string of phone calls and emails to clueless helpdesk techs to finally get ownership of the client-company.com domain name restored to my client. A few days after that I had a new web server set up, followed by working with their marketing director to get a new website online. *My client's unplanned (and ill-researched) decision to jump into a cloud arrangement took less than 20 minutes to get into and cost their company about two weeks and several thousand dollars to get out of.*

Venturing into the Cloud—The Top 7 Considerations

Before subscribing with any Cloud Service Provider, evaluate the following:

1.　The level of control you need to have,

2.　The resources you'll gain with this new cloud service compared to what you already have at your disposal in-house,

3.　A clear understanding of all your mission critical application / data dependencies,

4.　A general idea of your company's growth path,

5.　The provider adheres to industry standards such as the OpenStack Initiative or CDMI (Cloud Data Management Interface). By dealing with a provider that works with one or more of these standards it'll be easier to find applications to help you move your data from one cloud to another.

6.   Review every aspect of the Cloud Provider's actual resources (bandwidth, network, servers, staffing, their level of redundancy, talk to customers to get verbal testimonials about quality of service, etc.). I can't stress how necessary this is, primarily because many service providers oversell their services, banking on the fact that not all of their customers will be accessing their cloud at the same time. If all their customers had to access their cloud at the same time, someone isn't going to get in. It happens all the time with phone companies during situations that cause high volume usage (e.g. -disasters, huge gatherings, etc.) and we get "All circuits are busy" or "Your call cannot be completed at this time" messages.

7.   The legal recourses at your disposal in case the cloud service is discontinued (e.g. - cancelled, unpaid bill, etc.), changes ownership, or their outage causes you to lose time and/or money. READ THE FINE PRINT of your contract.

If you aren't able to fully qualify your answers for any one of those six points, consider yourself NOT ready to put part of your business (and your money) into a Cloud Service Provider. Out of the companies I've worked with who have entered into a cloud service agreement, every one of them that jumped right into it without doing their homework later discovered they made at least one major oversight—and I had to correct all the problems that followed. Those mistakes were expensive and avoidable. Admittedly, I could only complain but so much because I was well paid for my time.

Private Cloud

Any company that wants to experiment with the benefits of incorporating cloud storage into its workflow should start by doing so in-house. My recommendation is to begin with a Free Open Source private cloud solution. My personal and professional preference is OwnCloud (**www.owncloud.org**). As of this writing it's free, commercial quality, and has optional enterprise-level support packages. I was able to take a four year old PC, install Linux and OwnCloud on it, drop in onto their network, and have them set up with their own private cloud storage online within an hour. With this approach, your storage space is only limited by the amount of free space on that server's hard drive. You can also set up accounts for employees and clients, enabling them to use your cloud to share files instead of subscribing to services like DropBox.com.

Baron Samedi says

"When it comes to the Cloud, I'm reminded of a Billie Holliday song:

*Them that's got shall get
Them that's not shall lose
So the Bible said and it still is news
Mama may have, Papa may have
But God bless the child that's got his own
That's got his own."*

Disaster Recovery and Backups for Home and Office

Disaster Recovery—The Plan

According to the SANS Institute, disaster is defined as "a sudden, unplanned catastrophic event that renders the organizations ability to perform mission-critical and critical processes, including the ability to do normal production processing of systems that support critical business processes. A disaster could be the result of significant damage to a portion of the operations, a total loss of a facility, or the inability of the employees to access that facility." Simply put, it could be anything that puts you out of business temporarily or permanently. Fire. Stolen or destroyed equipment. Biblical locusts. You name it.

A Disaster Recovery Plan (DRP) deals with restoring your business facilities to normal after a disaster. A Business Continuity Plan (BRP) deals with keeping your business operations running after a disaster. For most small businesses, together they are like flood insurance—people have an idea how important it is, few bother to take it seriously enough to get it, and those that have it often neglect it… but the minute a flood hits it will be hailed as a life saver.

Disaster Recovery and Business Continuity plans are each worthy of their own college courses. Think of them as being separate yet equally as important, like the two sides of a dollar bill. They exist for one reason: S**t happens. After considerable thought, Business Continuity was largely omitted from this book. Although I have seen plenty of BCP templates onn the Internet, I've yet to see one that is generic enough to be adequate for most small businesses. Since Disaster Recovery focuses more on the technology side of things like backups it was more important to address the basics of a DRP. While it should be noted that coverage in this book is no substitute for working with a professional team to come up with your BCP and DRP, these exercises should help you understand the gravity of this need. Misfortunes happen. Things have a tendency to go sideways quickly when there's no plan in place. Even a rudimentary DRP will provide enough of a blueprint to get your business back up and running as soon as possible.

Prior to the 1990s, BCPs and DRPs were much closer to being one in the same. Disaster Recovery Plans were often treated as something reserved for huge companies with mainframe computers that took up half a room; the plans were put together to satisfy auditors and policy pushers. By 2010 all that had changed. The power of those monolithic old mainframes was now sitting on the average person's desk in a tower or a laptop. Companies once spent thousands of dollars a month for an Internet connection that was a fraction of the speed that today's home user enjoys. Once the costs associated with computing and connectivity came down, the capabilities once reserved for big players were now available to the SOHO environments. For many small offices, this newfound power also introduced a new set of problems and demands.

The attacks of September 11th, Hurricane Katrina, and the ever-present threat of cyberattacks are just a few examples of just much how times have changed. These days, having a Disaster Recovery Plan is almost as much of a necessity for the SOHO environment as they are for large corporations. And the DRP has to be well-documented because even small office networks can get pretty intricate. Most important of all, the recovery process has to be fast. Downtime can cost thousands of dollars a day in wasted employee time, lost revenue, long-term loss of customers, and even lawsuits for failing to meet client (or investor) obligations due to the outage. Lacking a DRP is worse than the Zombie Apocalypse because business disasters happen every day.

Baron Samedi says

"Spending up to 25% of your company's annual IT budget on the network side of your disaster recovery plan is a smart move. This is also a great way to audit your internal business processes and find spots that need improvement."

Developing a DRP can be done in-house by hand, prepared using DRP software, or subbed out to a company that specializes in disaster recovery. Regardless of the approach, always keep in mind that drafting a DRP should always be approached as an exercise in common sense. There's no right and wrong way to start drafting this document. With that in mind, the following factors should always be taken into consideration during the planning process:

▶ **People—in particular, employee safety and well-being.** The plan has to include alternate locations where the staff can go if the office is unavailable. There should also be some kind of incident notification (e.g. - everyone receives an SMS text and/or a phone call) as well as further instructions as to what to do if the situation escalates. Disasters are chaotic enough. By making sure everyone knows what to do in these situations, it lets everyone know that they still have paychecks coming, making it that much easier to get back to business as usual.

▶ **This is an all-inclusive project.** To make sure you've covered all the bases, you and your DRP planning team should include IT, management, human resources, sales & marketing, production, and even outside consultants (particularly for Information Security and Building Security). Although most SOHO environments don't have corporate divisions, the other reason to get all this input is to spot and eliminate possible conflicts between departments. This especially applies to situations where available resources might somehow be limited and have to be prioritized in order to speed up the recovery process. For example, let's say there was a small fire that did mostly smoke damage and the first phase of the recovery was to have IT check out all the computers. To make things go smoothly, everyone else would need to know to stay out of the office until IT was finished getting the network back online to avoid interfering with them.

▶ **Understand the impact.** In order to fully understand how detailed your DRP must be you need to have an accurate assessment of what is at stake—the consequences and financial impact of what you stand to lose if some part of the company isn't covered by the plan. This should also include a thorough understanding of how each part of the company may affect the others. This will help determine the order in which the recovery process has to follow, the expected timetables to completion, and prioritize the spending. For example, at first glance at an architecture firm, most would tend to think that fire or water damage would be their biggest threat due to the paper and printed plans we traditionally associate with architecture. Back when a majority of architecture was done by hand with pencils and drawing tables, that would make the case for a majority of disaster prevention spending to focus on things like fire extinguishing sprinkler systems, possibly offsite paper storage, and/or other document solutions. Today, all professional architecture is done using computers, the dangers of fire and water are a distant second and third compared to keeping their production network fast, safe, and well archived. An architectural firm is practically dead if their CAD production environment and all their files (i.e. - drawings and spec documents) aren't intact. As a result, a larger portion of their disaster prevention budget will be spent on Uninterruptible Power Supplies, high-end backup solutions, some kind of offsite backup, and network security.

► **Always keep in mind that security goes hand in hand with redundancy.** For example, an insurance broker shared with me that one of his clients, a major restaurant chain, requires that if a cash register at one of their locations gets stolen or destroyed, the remaining cash registers at that location have to be destroyed (or recycled?) and they all have to be replaced. At first glace this might seem like a huge waste. However, from a security perspective, it only made sense. The cash registers are all essentially a hive mind: networked PCs that were specifically configured to work together as one unit and send the data back to a regional office. If one fell into the wrong hands, the information on it could be used to compromise the others. Plus, the cost to replace all the machines pales in comparison to the potential losses from having the remaining units hacked, not to mention the open-ended threat against the regional office's servers.

► **A smart approach to disaster recovery planning is to figure out how to tie it into your overall business growth and marketing goals.** For example, let's say you're a startup accounting firm that uses a renowned online backup solution that archives your computers every night. You can take advantage of it by incorporating their brand into your business profile as one of your partners, lending further credibility to your name. Anything that helps you stay in business should also be a competitive advantage.

► **Your DRP should be revisited at least once a year, maybe sooner depending on how fast your business grows or changes.** Put it on your calendar on a date that's easy to remember (e.g. - the first day of Q4, your company's anniversary, etc.). This is also a good time to make sure that all aspects of your plan—and your business—comply with applicable local, state, federal and industry codes and standards.

Like a Business Plan, your DRP should be considered a living document. It should grow and change along with your business. This plan should be tested at least once a year, preferably after you've reviewed it or made updates. Without any tests it will be more difficult to spot areas that don't work or need improvement.

And once your plan has come together, here are a few major points to always keep in mind:

1. **Keep one or more copies of your DRP offsite.** If you've got an office, keep a copy of the plan at home. If you've got a home office, give a copy to a trusted friend or put it in a safety deposit box. Maybe save a copy on a USB flash drive and hide it in your car or stash a PDF copy inside your smartphone.

2. **A working DRP is something to take pride in.** Be proud of it. Own it. And make sure everyone else in the office believes in it, too.

3. **An untested plan is a useless plan.** I can't stress this enough.

For most small businesses that need a jumpstart with the Disaster Recovery Planning process, the SANS Institute has an awesome starter document. You can download it here:

http://www.sans.org/reading_room/whitepapers/recovery/ disaster-recovery-plan_1164

Disaster Recovery—Backups

Baron Samedi says

"For the typical SOHO environment with less than 10 employees, get an external hard drive for each computer on the network. Each external drive should have at least double the storage capacity of that computer's hard drive. So, for example, if you have a desktop with 500 GB storage, get an external with at least 1 terabyte (TB). AND be sure to test your backups (the software and the media itself) at least once a quarter."

Since the average business relies heavily on computers for production and administration, backups are at the core of any Disaster Recovery Plan. Although DRPs are the road map to return you to the Promised Land, the part of the plan you'll probably depend on the most is the backup solution. And just like the importance of DRPs are commonly disregarded, so are backup solutions. Like car insurance, everyone should have it, not everyone does, and the minute you're caught in a situation without it you <u>will</u> be singin' the Blues.

In a survey about backups performed by Kabooza, a Swedish web technology company, out of 4257 respondents in 129 countries, 82% didn't do regular backups of their home computers. 66% had experienced critical data loss on their computers due to viruses, hard drive crashes, physical damage or theft, and of those respondents 42% had experienced the loss within that past year. That survey was conducted between December 2008 and January 2009. Based on trends since then, more than likely those numbers have only increased.

On the business side of that equation, my information is a bit more empirical. When it comes to the subject of Backups and Disaster Recovery, I'll use a sampling of 10 companies I've worked with to paint the picture:

- ► When asked to produce a Disaster Recovery Plan of any kind, none of them could.
- ► 5 of the 10 had no scheduled backup solution.
- ► Of those 5 with a backup solution, 2 of them only backed up key computers on their network (production server, mail server, database server, etc.).
- ► Of those 5 that didn't have a scheduled backup solution, 2 of them occasionally backed up certain data files by hand to an external hard drive or a USB flash drive (e.g. - QuickBooks files, My Documents folder, etc.).
- ► Of those 5 with a backup solution, 2 had some kind of scheduled partial backups where the data would physically end up offsite.
- ► Of all 10 companies, none of them had an enterprise-wide backup solution that covers the employee desktops and laptops as well as their larger servers.
- ► Of all 10 companies, only 2 had anti-virus solutions that protected every computer on their network. All the rest used "whatever came on the computer" when they bought it.
- ► None of them saw the cost benefit of investing in an enterprise-wide backup solution.

Different types of backups

If you Google "backup software", about 1.6 million exact matches will come up - over 54 million if you don't put those keywords in quotes. Choosing a backup solution can be just as confusing. The subject itself is worthy of its own book. For the purposes of this section, I've focused only on the concepts that would matter to the typical SOHO.

From a business continuity / disaster recovery perspective, availability is the first consideration for a backup solution. Availability refers the amount of downtime your business systems will (or will not) experience in the unplanned event of a computer (or network) becoming unavailable, whether due to a crash, theft or some kind of catastrophe. Any given backup solution will either be classified as High Availability, Remote Availability, or some combination that leans more towards one or the other.

A High Availability (HA) backup solution gives you the ability to get back up and running after a disaster with the least amount of downtime. The typical HA solution would be connected to one or more of the computers on your network, performs a backup at the same time every day, and will alert you if the scheduled backup doesn't happen. High end systems may even include complex failovers, meaning if one computer dies there is a standby computer that can instantly take over, data and all. Although this kind of "no downtime" solution is the ultimate for a business of any size, they generally cost more than what most small companies have invested in their entire network. With HA solutions, generally the faster the recovery time you need, the more you're going to spend, but the benefit is that a full system restoration can happen with little or no preliminary configuration work on your part.

The Remote Availability (RA) solutions take the ability of HA and expand it to include other physical locations, usually over the Internet. Most RA solutions are "set it and forget it"; once you're satisfied that it's configured properly you just go about your business and it'll do the rest. Along with the conveniences there are some major drawbacks. Unlike with an HA solution, doing a full system restore will take longer because you'll have to partially get the computer back to a point where it can run the RA software. Along with that, the backup/restoration process is at the mercy of your Internet speed; peak traffic hours will make for slower transfer times between your office and the remote location. Backups won't be accessible unless those computers are on the Internet. For most small businesses, RA solutions will mean subscribing to an online backup service like Mozy or Carbonite, making for a much lower upfront cost than HA solutions. The biggest benefit that dwarfs all the drawbacks is the fact that an RA backup gives your important business data the ability to survive a fire, flood, or natural disaster—any major catastrophe that destroys your entire office. The peace of mind alone is worth the extra work and headaches.

Full, Incremental, and Differential

Full Backup

A full backup is just as the name implies—a full copy of everything on a computer's hard drive. The upside is that it is a complete copy of all your files, making it easy to find anything you're looking for on that computer. The downside is that this type of backup takes the longest to perform, requires the most space on the backup media, and it is redundant because most of the files on your hard drive don't change from day to day. From a practical sense, it's a bit overkill to backup your entire computer every day.

Incremental Backup

An incremental backup searches for any files that have changed since the last backup. The upside is that it's fast, it requires the least amount of storage space, and it allows for backing up multiple versions of the same file. The downside is that if you have to do a full system recovery you'll need to start by reinstalling the last full backup, followed by restoring each incremental backup in their correct order. In some situations this can make it difficult to find a particular file in the backup set.

Differential Backup

Similar to the incremental backup, a differential backup archives any files that have changed since the last FULL backup. Since these backups are usually performed at regular intervals, the upside is that it takes less time and space than a full backup while also providing a more efficient restoration process than the incremental backups. Each backup stores most of the same data along with anything added since the last full backup. The downside is that each successive backup takes longer as more files are updated or changed.

To put this into perspective, let's say your office computer is your current mode of transportation, a Ford F-150 pickup truck. And let's say someone crashed into your truck.

A high availability full backup would be the equivalent of having a spare F-150 pickup truck that is the exactly like yours—make, model and year—sitting out in the parking lot. Getting back on the road would require little more than the effort it takes to move equipment from the crashed truck to the spare truck. This truck becomes the main truck until the other truck has been repaired.

A remote availability full backup would be the equivalent of having a spare F-150 pickup truck that is the exactly like yours—make, model and year—sitting in a storage unit across town. Getting back on the road would require little more than making a call and waiting for someone to bring the truck to you. Once the spare truck is there you move equipment from the crashed truck to the spare truck.

The incremental backup would loosely be like renting a different F-150 each week. The rental would be the same make and model as your current truck but older. The effort required would be the time it takes to go to the rental place at the end of each week to swap trucks, continued until you're able to get your current truck back on the road.

And the differential backup would be like having the last five F-150 trucks you owned sitting out in the parking lot—but each one is not up to 100% working condition. You would swap from one truck to the next in order, as necessary, until your current F-150 truck is road worthy again.

The Difference between Backup Software and Imaging Software

Although you'll hear some people refer to "Backup software" and "Imaging software" interchangeably, they're not the same. In order to understand which will suit your needs best, you have to know the difference. To put this into perspective let's forget about computers for a minute. Let's say you're starting a magazine and you've just finished putting together the first issue. You've got two different programs, **Backup** and **Image** both designed to keep a copy of the magazine.

▶ **Backup:** would make a copy of every article in the magazine along with a notation of what page each article is on. The upside is that this process is faster than making an Image copy, plus if you lose any article in the magazine you can click restore and retrieve just that article. The downside is that if you happen to lose the entire magazine, you'll have to remake the basic magazine layout from scratch in—design the cover, table of contents, and etc—in order to have the pages where you can drop the articles back in place.

▶ **Image:** would make a copy of the entire magazine from cover to cover. The upside is that if you lose the magazine, you can click restore and have the whole magazine intact, exactly like the original. The downside is that this process takes longer and you can't pick out any particular article to recover; anytime you use this program you'll restore a copy of the entire magazine.

In reference to computers, backup software generally just copies your data (files and the folders where they are stored). Imaging software makes a full, exact duplicate of your hard drive—an exact clone of the operating system, all software, your data (files), and your preference settings.

Backups for Business

Backup software is great for anyone who is mostly concerned about data loss. Power users inclined to use backups more often because of the amount of data they produce on a regular basis. They're generally not as concerned about the reinstallation process, especially if they're prone to upgrade computers every few years.

The other issue is TIME. Imaging an entire hard drive takes a lot longer than backing up files. Also, with more and more companies using cloud backup services that charge by the amount of data stored, it's only cost-effective to use them to backup your important data, the files you can't replace. Everything else, such as the operating system and software, can be reinstalled locally from CDs and DVDs.

If you're only using backup software to backup your files, it means if your system gets messed up you'll have to take the time to reinstall the operating system (e.g. - Microsoft Windows, Mac OS X, or Linux), reinstall all the software, and then restore your data from your backup. After that you'll need to redo all your settings, too. Getting your computer back to the way it was can take anywhere from several hours to more than a day.

Images for Business:

The use of imaging software to clone a hard drive is a great way to cut IT maintenance costs for the following reasons:

► **Hard drives fail:** The average hard drive (IDE, SATA, SCSI) is rated to have a life expectancy of about 3 to 5 years, depending on the manufacturer and amount of use. I've seen some hard drives last more than 10 years and others barely make it past 3 years. By creating an image of an old hard drive to a new hard drive, you'll prevent the downtime that comes with rebuilding the system by reinstalling the operating system (e.g. - Microsoft Windows, Mac OS X, etc.) and all the software (e.g. - Microsoft Office, Adobe Creative Suite, your favorite games, etc.). Between reinstalling the operating system, the system updates, and all the software, it can take anywhere from 6 to 16 hours to get a typical business workstation back to being ready for daily use.

► **(Nearly) Immediate Recovery:** If you make images of your hard drive on a regular basis, if you computer experiences a major crash (e.g. - virus or similar catastrophe), you can just restore from the image and you're good to go. When it comes to recovering a computer from major disaster, this is about the closest most of us will have to an immediate fix. Your workstation will have all its software, all the data and you won't have to spend hours rebuilding your system. As of this writing, a 1TB hard drive might take up to a little over 6 hours to restore, depending on the speed of the hard drive and computer.

Quickie Overview of the Backup Process

With most of the SOHO networks that I've seen, if they've got any kind of backup solution it's typically tape based. Most data backup systems these days that can handle small businesses will have two main parts: "central control" and "agent". The agent program is installed on every computer you need to backup. Central control is set on a stand-alone computer where the backups are stored. The backup process is set to run on a schedule, usually once a day. Since it can take several hours to back up a computer, most IT admins set their backups to run when there's the least amount of activity, usually in the middle of the night. By the start of the business day, the backup is finished. An employee then takes that day's backup tape out, puts it in a safe place, and inserts the next backup tape.

What backup solution works best for you?

In many ways, small business backup solutions are much like hairstyles; the more sophisticated they are, the more they need professional assistance to create and maintain them. All the hardware and software for any backup solution should fit the company. This is especially true with small businesses because every penny counts. Coming up with a general purpose tape-based or disk-based backup solution to include in this section was a problem because there are too many variables to consider. For that, I would recommend you consult with a knowledgeable IT professional.

For a SOHO environment with fewer than five computers in use, an inexpensive yet highly effective backup solution would require the following:

1. **Disk Imaging (Cloning) software—Nova, Acronis, Norton Ghost, Clonezilla, etc.** This software will clone your main computer hard drive to a hard drive in an external case.

2. **A hard drive in an external case.** This external hard drive should match the one inside your computer in type (e.g. - IDE, SATA, SCSI, SSD, etc.), dimensions (2.5", 3.5", etc.) and storage (e.g. - if your main computer hard drive has 500 GB of space, the external hard drive should have a capacity of 500 GB or more). NOTE: The hard drive and external case are purchased as separate items; they are NOT the same as just buying an external hard drive. The intent is to be able to either (A) use the backup hard drive in the external case as a source to restore the hard drive inside the computer after a disaster (e.g. - recovering from a virus attack or major system crash) or (B) completely remove the hard drive from inside the computer and replace it with the backup hard drive from the external case.

3. **Subscription to an online backup service.** The online backup service is solely for taking a snapshot of your business data on a daily basis; all the kind of day-to-day files that usually ends up in your "My Documents" folder. The disk cloning system is to make a snapshot of your hard drive to capture your entire production environment on that particular computer. This approach is almost like coming up with your own custom "System Restore" feature; you basically click a button and your hard drive gets restored to the point where it was when you did the last clone. And since all your day to day files are backed up nightly using the online service, you can click and have them restored, too. When set up properly, in the event of a major system crash you can have that computer back online within a few hours and lose less than a day's worth of work.

NOTE FOR MAC USERS: Mac OS X comes with a pretty robust backup solution: Time Machine. From the description in the instructions posted on the Apple website, Time Machine is "the built-in backup that works with your Mac and an external drive (sold separately) or Time Capsule. Connect the drive, assign it to Time Machine, and start enjoying some peace of mind. Time Machine automatically backs up your entire Mac, including system files, applications, accounts, preferences, music, photos, movies, and documents. But what makes Time Machine different from other backup applications is that it not only keeps a spare copy of every file, it remembers how your system looked on any given day-so you can revisit your Mac as it appeared in the past." Source: **http://support.apple.com/kb/HT1427**

Inexpensive SOHO and Home Backups

When it comes to backup solutions for any given budget range, there are enough alternatives to fill a book of their own. For the SOHO and Home computing environments, consider a blended approach to backups. Because this book is meant to be general purpose for PC, Mac and Linux, the following steps are meant to be more of a guideline to the process:

1. Purchase an external hard drive for each computer. Each external should have at least double the storage space that came with the computer's hard drive (e.g. - for a computer with a 500 GB hard drive buy a 1 TB external hard drive.

2. Use a regular data backup to handle all the files you'd typically store in folders like "My Documents" or "My Pictures". This would also be a good reason to use a cloud-based backup solution like one of the following:

   ► Mozy:_
     http://mozy.com/

   ► Carbonite:
     http://www.carbonite.com/

► Barracuda Backup Services:
https://www.barracudanetworks.com/products/backupservice

NOTE: One of the benefits of the cloud-based backup solutions is that they can be scheduled to automatically back up your designated folders on a daily basis.

3. Prepare your computer by doing the following:

- use your anti-virus and anti-malware software to scan the computer and make sure it's virus-free,
- make sure your operating system is fully updated,
- make sure you've got all your productivity software installed (basically anything you use on that computer for day-to-day work),
- make sure you've got your data backup software installed and configured, especially if you're using an online cloud backup service.
- make sure you've got your computer set up just the way you like it (e.g. - desktop icons, wallpaper, etc.).

4. Use your imaging software, create a disc image of the computer's entire hard drive (as the source) and store it on the external hard drive (as the destination).

5. Once you've finished creating the disc image, unplug the external hard drive and put it in a safe place. My recommendation is to store it in a fire-safe waterproof document and media chest. The Sentry Safe F2300 is a good choice because it's low-cost, doesn't take up much space, fireproof for up to an hour (UL classified) and ETL verified waterproof.

In the event of a major system crash (e.g. - damage from a virus, a hard drive crash, computer won't boot, etc.), you simply reverse the steps in this process:

1.   Pull out the external hard drive for the crashed computer and plug it into the machine's USB port.

2.   Run the image software and choose the "Restore" option. Follow the steps to restore your computer's hard drive from the stored image on the external. This will bring your system back to the way you like it with all your programs installed.

3.   Use your online data backup source (e.g. – Mozy, Carbonite, etc.) to restore your files (e.g. – "My Documents", "My Music", etc.). By using both backup methods, you'll probably have that computer back online in less than 3 hours with less than a workday's worth of work lost. This is far better than the 6 to 16 hours it can easily take to manually reinstall and reconfigure everything on your computer… and this doesn't include any lost work.

The choice between imaging and backup software depends on your needs. If you want to avoid reinstalls, imaging is the way to go. If you just want to copy data, backup is top choice. Fortunately, several top backup software programs offer full imaging as an option, and many imaging programs allow you to backup only specific files if you wish. If you choose a package that excels at both tasks, you can't lose.

When Plan B Fails— A Final Caution about Backup Solutions

Baron Samedi says:

"Always double-check your backup settings (i.e. - what files and/or system configurations are included). Test the backup once every 3 to 4 months to make sure it's still good."

Regardless of your choice of backup solution, you'll eventually take it for granted. We see the same thing happen with fire prevention. U.S. building code standards are the strictest they've ever been. Smoke alarms and fire extinguishers have been widely available since the mid 60s. Most people reading this book can't remember a time when schools and office buildings didn't have mandatory fire drills. Even with all these preventative measures, roughly every 30 minutes in the U.S. someone is injured in a fire—and every 169 minutes someone dies (CDC). Why? Regardless of all the technological advances and precautions we take, fires happen. They are a natural part of the physical universe we live in.

While writing this book I had to re-learn the lesson about double-checking backup settings. The disaster happened with my diagnostics laptop. Since I took it with me on all my IT service calls, I used it to do everything from testing networks to documenting my work. Those client notes were the basis of my billing. Several months earlier, I had switched backup programs. Once I setup and successfully ran a full backup, I put it on a schedule and didn't give it a second thought.

One weekend something went wrong during a system update, causing the laptop to repeatedly crash. Trying to undo whatever the update did would have taken hours. I decided to start fresh by erasing the hard drive and restoring the laptop from the most recent backup.

At first it appeared that the restore worked fine. Figuring everything was back in place, I went to open my time tracker and it was blank. I went to check the hidden folder where the tracker stored my notes to find the hidden folder was missing—along with all the hidden folders. Griped with fear and loathing, I had to go stretch out on my bed, flushed with the inevitable truth: For months my backups for the laptop had been incomplete. Under the assumption that I would get all my files once I finished the restore process, I had erased my laptop hard drive—including the hidden folders with more than a year's worth of client notes—and then wrote over it with incomplete data from the backup.

This was catastrophic for me and my business. The damage was incalculable. While setting up which folders to backup I overlooked a default setting that ignored certain folders. As a result, 99% of the backup was fine. The 1% that was left out included hidden folders, one of which contained all the notes and billing information for my clients. Thousands of hours worth of work. I might as well have been a PhD student that finished my doctoral thesis only to toss the only copy into a fire right before turning it in so I could graduate.

To get my files back I loaded up some data recovery software and spent the next 76 hours hackin' and slashin' through more than 3 billion sectors to retrieve a little over 1 million pieces of textural data. Within those million pieces I managed to reassemble the fragments that made up my client notes. Aside from the miracle of getting my notes back, I found segments of source code, evidence of websites I had visited weeks earlier, sensitive client passwords, deleted emails, pieces of chat conversations, etc. This was a shocking reminder that data may get discarded or lost inside a computer but it takes extreme measures to truly get rid of it.

Lessons to remember for any Disaster Recovery scenario:

- ▶ Don't panic—it clouds your judgment.
- ▶ Don't ever discount the power of Faith.
- ▶ Almost any lost files can be recovered depending on the time, resources and determination you can put into the effort.
- ▶ Double check your backup settings before you use it for the first time. Make sure you have selected all file types, folders, and everything else on your system that you want protected by your backup software. Nothing hurts worse than doing a restore from a backup then discovering it doesn't have the files you need.
- ▶ Make a separate routine backup of your business data that is kept outside the office. Whether it happens once a month or once every six months depends on the nature of your business. Consider this offsite backup an added insurance policy for your business.
- ▶ Test your backup at least once every 3 to 6 months to make sure it is good. How you do this depends on your backup software so refer to the documentation.

Protecting your Investment—The Happy Audit

Whether you're a Survivalist, Doomsday Prepper, or you're expecting World War Z to break out any day now, keeping good track of your inventory is a key survival skill. On a daily routine it's more important than knowing how to use a gun. When considering any Apocalyptic scenario, the last thing most people think about is the word "Audit". This will be one of the few times in your life where that word will actually save you from an immeasurable amount of stress. In this case, audits are another layer of protection for your business network. After a major catastrophe you're faced with having lost everything. The results of a good set of audits will help make sure you know everything that needs to be replaced.

Some audits are simple, only consisting of a basic list of every computer, printer, and device plugged into your network. Other audits go more in-depth with all the computers, including a roster of all software installed on each computer. And still, there are even deeper audits that have all of the above and then include an assessment of security of each computer and the network as a whole.

For most SOHOs a middle of the road approach will suffice: list everything on the network (all computers, printers, routers, miscellaneous devices, etc.) and a roster of all the software installed on each computer.

At home or in your office, the computers you use are the culmination of a series of investments. It takes money, time and effort to get just one computer the way you need it. Multiply that times the number of computers you own or manage and that investment adds up. And after a few instances of having to rebuild everything from scratch, it will become evident why there has to be a better way to protect the time you've put in, or at least streamline the process of getting it all back if you lose it. By doing an audit to inventory of your equipment, software licenses, security configurations, and network settings, you'll be doing yourself a huge favor. Consider it part of putting insurance on every computer and mobile device you own.

The following are a few free audit packages to get you started:

► **JDisc**
   http://www.jdisc.com/en/
   JDisc Discovery automatically documents your network and
   detects detailed hardware and software inventory for all major
   operating systems (including HP-UX, Solaris, and AIX). All
   information is available through a fast and easy to use user
   interface.

► **WinAudit Freeware v3.0.8**
   http://winaudit.zymichost.com/
   This is a stand-alone package, an excellent choice for anyone
   with less than 10 computers and devices on their network.

► **PC and Network inventory system**
   http://www.spiceworks.com/free-pc-network-inventory-software/
   This inventory system is part of Spiceworks, a free
   ad-supported IT systems management and helpdesk package.

► **OCS Inventory NG** (Windows, Mac OS X, Linux)
   http://www.ocsinventory-ng.org/en/
   NOTE: This package allows for managing assets on your
   network using a web-based interface. Although it is free, it
   requires a web server to run.

► **Open-AudIT**
   http://www.open-audit.org/
   Taken from the Open-AudIT website: "Open-AudIT is an
   application to tell you exactly what is on your network, how it
   is configured and when it changes. Open-AudIT will run on
   Windows and Linux systems. Essentially, Open-AudIT
   is a database of information, that can be queried via a
   web interface."

License Key Finders

Software Asset Management is the practice of managing every aspect of the software used within your company from the day it was purchased to the day you replace it with another package. In the SOHO environment, most small business owners and managers can't remember the last time we used those three words side-by-side in a sentence. License key finders are a big part of that practice and in a perfect world they wouldn't be necessary. The main reason we need license key finders is simple: Real Life is messy—and so are people.

For every computer owner who keeps all their software and manuals in a safe place there are half a dozen others who lose track of the physical media after it has been installed. No one gives it any thought until there's a catastrophe of some kind and its time to reload all their programs. This is especially the case in the aftermath of natural disasters such as hurricanes, tornadoes and floods. Some software vendors have been known to refuse to replace software or honor updates because the owner couldn't show proof of ownership by providing the license key number.

Anyone that has ever installed software knows that license keys accumulate like keys in the real world. Just purchased another car? Expect a new set of keys (or key devices). Just bought a new mountain bike? Keys for the bicycle lock. Need to put stuff in a storage unit? Expect a set of keys for the lock that goes on the door. The list goes on.

> "...vendors have been known to refuse to replace software or honor updates because the owner couldn't show proof of ownership by providing the license key number."

For those that aren't familiar with license keys, they are also called product keys, CD keys, serial numbers, or key codes. These keys are often an alphanumeric code of any length required by many software programs during installation. Each license key is unique and assigned to that specific purchase of the software package. Their main purpose is to combat software piracy, preventing people from buying a copy of the program and then spreading around many unauthorized copies. With packages like Microsoft Office retailing new for around $250 USD and some business software packages costing into the thousands, it's not uncommon for the software on a computer to cost more than the current value of the computer itself.

In a time when zombies are afoot, contagions can cause damage to installed software just as easily as your data or the operating system. Keeping up with your programs and their licenses is just as important as keeping up your car along with a valid driver's license and license plates. This is where the license key finder comes into play.

A license key finder is a program that will dive into the depths of your computer and retrieve as many license keys as possible. These serial numbers are often encoded or well hidden, earning the license key finders the label of not being an exact science. Whether you're just a highly organized person who wants to keep all your software keys in one file or you're that person who has misplaced the license info for half your programs, getting a license key finder is a good idea. Although the following examples are free, the commercial license key finders aren't that expensive and generally worth every penny.

- ▶ **The Magical Jelly Bean Keyfinder**—this program is a free utility that retrieves product keys from the registry. It also has the ability to find product keys for many Microsoft Office programs, along with product keys from other non-Microsoft programs. **http://www.magicaljellybean.com/keyfinder/**

- ▶ **LicenseCrawler**—differs from other key finder programs in its almost full-text interface, which I like. I found LicenseCrawler to be very effective at finding serial numbers for the many programs on my PC. It finds keys for many Microsoft products such as versions of Windows and Office, Adobe products, and many more. **http://www.klinzmann.name/licensecrawler.htm**

▶ **ProduKey**—is a small utility that displays the ProductID and the CD-Key of Microsoft Office (Microsoft Office 2003, Microsoft Office 2007, probably up to 2010), Windows XP, Vista, 7 and 8, Exchange Server, and SQL Server installed on your computer. This utility can be useful if you lost the product key of your Windows/Office, and you want to reinstall it on your computer. **http://www.nirsoft.net/utils/product_cd_key_viewer.html**

▶ **Mac Product Key Finder** 1.0—Same game, different name, just for Mac OS X. **http://mac-product-key-finder.com/**

14 Free Product Key finders— **http://pcsupport.about.com/od/productkeysactivation/tp/ topkeyfinder.htm**

NOTE: As the years go on, more and more packages have begun encrypting their license keys. If this trend continues, license key finders may become obsolete. After you acquire new software, always store your keys somewhere safe and reliable.

Home Backup Solutions

Out of the countless residential computers I've serviced—new and old, PC or Mac, desktop or laptop—three things have always been true more than 99% of the time: (1) No one ever uses the backup feature that came with their computer. (2) No one ever buys third party backup software. (3) Even after losing files to a major crash, most people will continue to work without routine backups. The closest to a regular backup routine I've seen is that some people copy important files to a USB flash drive, external hard drive, or disc media.

The average household computer runs the risk of having a major crash at least once every 2 to 5 years—even with current anti-virus software. When this occurs (especially after year 5), many will use this as a reason to buy a new computer and discard the old one. Others will pay to have their current computer cleaned up and the software reinstalled. In either case, all the irreplaceable data like documents, family photos and video clips are often lost forever—needlessly because this could have been prevented.

Backup Software

Online backup services work much like traditional backup software. With an online backup service, however, your important files are securely uploaded to a professional data center somewhere on the Internet. For home there are quite a few inexpensive solutions to choose from. The following selections were chosen because they all have free starter packages and they're all secure. With these free plans the amount of space may not be enough to backup all your photos, music, and everything on your computer but enough to back up the average My Documents folder—perfect for protecting all your important documents such as wills, contracts, research papers, financial information, etc.

- ► **Symform**—up to 10 GB online storage. Also provides the ability to synchronize your files across all your devices. **http://www.symform.com/**

- ► **Cyphertite**—up to 8 Gb online storage. **https://www.cyphertite.com/**

- ► **Mimedia**—up to 7 GB online storage. **https://online.mimedia.com/**

NOTE: Each backup solution uses some form of encryption. This provides a fantastic layer of protection for your files by keying everything to a long password or passphrase. While this is a good thing, you must remember to write down your passphrase and keep it in a safe place. Without your passphrase you risk completely losing access to your files.

Imaging software

The typical household with at least one computer will find the following benefits to using imaging software:

► **Family memories**—Most home computers end up having personalized accounts for each family member. Each account has its own contacts/address book along with some documents, bookmarks, playlists of music, and collections photos and video clips. With the exception of some minor updates and a few new files, most of this data doesn't change once it is on the computer.

► **Children**—I love children, but I have to make this fact perfectly clear: children will click on anything and deny it faster than a cheating politician. Out of the countless infected residential computers I've disinfected and/or rebuilt, more than 80% of them had software (e.g. - Limewire, Bearshare, etc.) that are known sources of zombie contagions through infected files—and generally those programs weren't installed by an adult.

By creating a disc image of your computer's hard drive at least every 3 to 6 months you'll be saving yourself money in the long run. Just like a PC or Mac comes with a System Restore, think of this as a restore that resets everything to the way you like it—including all those awesome irreplacable photos and other personal file. Although the process may tie up your computer for a few hours it is worth every second of it. As of this writing, the cost of data recovery due to a computer crash starts at around $300 dollars and goes up from there. That crash could be brought on by a virus, hard drive crash, or some other form of file corruption (accidental/unintentional/deliberate). The other obvious benefit is the peace of mind knowing that those great memories from Christmas' past or that Hawaiian vacation aren't an unexpected virus away from being lost forever.

There are numerous disc imaging packages on the market. If you don't already have one, an excellent package to start with is Clonezilla. Similar to True Image® or Norton Ghost®, Clonezilla is a partition and disk imaging/cloning program. It helps you to do system deployment, bare metal backup and recovery. Best of all, it's free. **http://www.clonezilla.org/**

Baron Samedi says

"Doing an image snapshot of your computer hard drive once a month can save you hundreds of dollars in IT repair costs—especially in households where children and young adults regularly use the computer."

and

"Even if you don't bother to backup anything else on your computer, protect yourself by protecting your important documents."

Apocalyptic Emergency Identity Recovery Kit

In these times, a news day doesn't go by without a story of some runaway fire or natural disaster that destroys everything in its path, leaving its victims with nothing. We've become so desensitized to these events that we often take them for granted—until disaster robs us of everything we own. When that happens, there are no quick happy endings like the movies.

Even though your digital identity is just as important as your physical presence, the paper trail that connects the two is more important than ever before. If you want to test it, try getting a replacement Driver's License without a state-issued Birth Certificate and valid proof of residence. Or try getting a job at McDonald's without at least a valid Social Security Card. You'd have a better chance at successfully robbing a bank.

Whether the disaster is Hurricane Katrina or a common house fire, survivors all have stories about how bureaucracies and insurance companies are often unsympathetic to people who have lost everything. It's a sad commentary about how a simple twist of fate can destroy our homes and knock us back to financial childhood. Once you've hit that bottom it can take years to get some semblance of your life back.

Fortunately, there is a solution. Compared to the consequences, it is very inexpensive and simple enough that most of it can be handled by the average 6th grader. Best of all, it can fit in the palm of your hand.

To make this happen you'll need the following:

- ► A computer (preferably yours)
- ► At least one USB Flash drive (also known as a thumb drive, jump drive, pen drive, or memory stick—needs 8GB or more free space)
- ► Any standard flatbed scanner (or All-In-One printer)
- ► Fire-Safe Waterproof Document and Media Chest (optional)
- ► One or more Jumbo Ziplock bags and a piece corrugated cardboard per bag (optional)

The following is a list of the types of important documents you'll want to include in your kit, listed here in no particular order:

- ► All Birth Certificates and/or Adoption papers
- ► All forms of identification (Driver's License, Passport, Social Security Card, Military ID, Employer ID card, Health Insurance ID, Voter Registration ID, etc.)
- ► Professional licenses and certifications (Business, Trade, etc.)
- ► Immigration-related documentation (Green card, Naturalization, Work Visa, etc.)
- ► Insurance documents (Property, Auto, Rental, Life, Health / Dental, etc.)
- ► Pay stubs (at least one per current employer)
- ► Will (or Living Will)

- ► Trust / Inheritance / Heir Property documentation
- ► Marriage License (and/or Divorce papers)
- ► Power of Attorney documents (Property and Personal)
- ► Vehicle titles (Vehicle Registration / Ownership)
- ► Real Estate documents (Deed of Trust, Mortgage, etc.)
- ► Lease agreements (and at least one billing statement)
- ► Storage contracts (and at least one billing statement)
- ► Bank/Credit Union statements (at least one for each account)
- ► Credit Card statements (at least one for each account)
- ► Utility statements (at least one for electric, water, gas, etc.)
- ► Income statements (Child support, Alimony, Palimony, etc.)
- ► Payment statements (Child support, Alimony, Palimony, etc.)
- ► Retirement accounts (IRA, 401K, etc.)
- ► Government Benefits (Social Security, Veterans, Disability, etc.)
- ► Veteran Discharge (DD Form 214)
- ► Investment accounts (Bonds, Stocks, Mutual Funds, etc.)
- ► Corporate contracts (particularly anything you have ownership in)
- ► Job-related agreements
- ► Recent tax return (local, state, and federal)
- ► A copy of each monthly service contract (cell phone, cable, etc.)
- ► Monthly loan payments (student loans, car loans, etc.)
- ► Medical prescriptions
- ► Medical / Dental Records
- ► Warranties and/or receipts for big ticket purchases
- ► Diplomas, Degrees, or Certificates
- ► Any important signed contracts, agreements or proposals

Along with those scans, there are some files you'll need to include that can be saved or copied right from your computer:

- ► Names and License Keys/Serial Numbers of software you've purchased (see "Protecting your Investment - The Happy Audit", page 313)
- ► An exported copy of your Contacts List (e.g. - from Outlook, Address Book, etc.)
- ► A copy of your Password Locker file (see "Password Management", page 348)

- ► Recent ID-style photo(s) of yourself and anyone that lives with you
- ► Digital photos of inventory in each room (for insurance purposes)
- ► A current copy of your Resume, including any letters of recommendation (even after a disaster you'll need to apply for a job again someday)
- ► Any important documents that are impossible to replace

NOTE: The following steps are very general, meant for PC and Mac users. If you're not familiar with how to scan and save files, ask around. Young adults can be especially helpful with this.

1. Create a folder named "ImportantPapers" where you'll save all of your scanned documents.
2. Set your scanner program to use full color (at least 24-bit) and a resolution of at least 150dpi (I prefer 300dpi).
3. Scan the front and back of each page of each document.
4. Save each scan as JPEG, PNG, or PDF. Be sure you can tell what each scan is by its filename (e.g. - CarRegistration-front.JPG, etc.) before saving it in the ImportantPapers folder.
5. Once you've scanned in all your documents, copy that ImportantPapers folder to your thumb drive.
6. Put the thumb drive in a cool, dry, safe place.

The process of compiling these documents and scanning them into the computer can take a few hours. It might be worth it to break the task up into a few scanning sessions on over the course of a weekend. If you lack the time (or patience) and don't mind spending the money, copy shops like FedEx Kinkos can do the scanning for you.

Traditionally, disaster preparation had people compiling photocopies of all their information and put it in a waterproof bag or container. By scanning the documents and putting them on a flash drive, in the aftermath of a catastrophic event you can plug the stick into any computer with a USB port and print copies of documents as necessary.

Before putting away your thumb drive for safe keeping, an extra option is to make hard copies. Put the stack in one or more Ziplock bags, place them in a Fire-Safe Waterproof Document and Media Chest. The Sentry Safe F2300 is a good choice because it's fireproof up to one hour (UL classified) and ETL verified waterproof. It's also about the size of a ladies cosmetic travel case, making it easy to hide or carry during an emergency evacuation.

After sharing this advice with clients, some have asked about storing the ImportantPapers folder to disc media like CDs or DVDs. Although burned discs are much cheaper and could just as easily hold the data, they are nowhere near as reliable as thumb drives. The discs are easily scratched up or broken. They can't fit in your pocket. Extreme environmental conditions such as heat, water, or cracks from being damaged during the disaster event can make them unreadable. Worst of all, even time and the Earth's natural radiation can cause burned discs to go bad (see "Dirty Secret #3: Your Burned CDs and DVDs are not Permanent, page 331").

A single flash drive can hold the equivalent of a stack of DVDs, depending on its capacity. Most good quality thumb drives are rated for at least a decade of data retention, longer if you only use it just for your kit. They're also far more durable than discs and much easier to carry (or conceal). Lastly, even the cheap thumb drives tend to be water and heat resistant (see "The Pros and Cons of USB Flash Drives, page 374").

For my own purposes I put together three kits, each on a DataTraveler Locker+ G2. Although any flash drive with adequate space would suffice, I chose the DataTraveler Locker+ G2 because it is hardware-encrypted, password-protected, and comes in a metal casing with a key loop. Also, as of this writing, the 8GB model of this line sells online for less than $30 dollars (with shipping), which makes it an economical choice, too. By putting together three kits it allowed me to put one thumb drive on a lanyard and keep it with my disaster emergency kit, put the second in a safety deposit box, and mail the third to a family member in another state for safe keeping.

What about using The Cloud?

While I can already hear plenty of my peers recommending the use of sites like Dropbox or iCloud to stash your ImportantPapers folder, I'm not going to do that. I can't. Quite candidly, I personally wouldn't put that much faith in keeping a snapshot of my entire life in someone else's cloud so I can't recommend that anyone else do that either.

A few key reasons that come to mind:

► Not all cloud solutions are created equal.

► Most of the cheap (or free) cloud services are high-profile magnets for zombie attacks, plus their Terms & Conditions agreements also make sure that they can't be held liable for anything bad that happens. Every day I see alerts about new security vulnerabilities and major corporations getting hacked in ways that result in thousands of accounts being captured and leaked out into the wild.

► In the event of a natural disaster like Hurricane Sandy, Internet access is likely to be down indefinitely. Unless you are one of those Doomsday Prepper fanatics with a ruggedized laptop, gas-powered generator, and a satellite Internet subscription, you'll be offline like everyone else in your region. Depending on The Cloud to store your ImportantPapers may add unexpected days of delay to your getting started with rebuilding your identity (and your life).

Do yourself a favor—keep your Apocalyptic Emergency Identity Recovery Kit with you. It means one less thing to worry about, especially after a disaster. There's no chance of some cybercriminal stealing your ImportantPapers if they're in a little digital container on a lanyard hanging around your neck.

Small Office/Home Office (SOHO) environment safes

For most SOHO environments, Sentry brand safes are a great choice to check out, both for the quality and the price. Whatever safe you choose to purchase, I would recommend something that is at least ETL verified 1/2-hour fire protection for CDs, DVDs, USB drives and memory sticks up to 1550°F and verified waterproof for submersion. It should have enough space to house however many external hard drives you're using to hold your images.

ZOMBIE
F A C T O I D S

Characteristics Common to Most Known Species of Living Dead (cont'd):

Skin: The recently reanimated may look slightly pale whereas Berserkers that have been on the prowl range in color from bluish-grey to ashen-burnt sienna. Like normal homicide victims, they may have open wounds that have bled out. Their clothes are disheveled and commonly stained with coagulated blood and pieces of flesh, including their own, depending on what physical trauma they've experienced. NOTE: The longer a ghoul has been stalking the living, the more its flesh will take on the stained consistency of rancid meat.

Intent: To date, there's no scientific data to confirm if zombies have any thoughts or cognitive brain activity. If not standing idle (usually stuck in an enclosed space), they can either be found wandering aimlessly in search of prey, chasing prey, or feeding on a fresh victim. They don't seem to care about anything unless it moves and smells like dinner. In cyberspace, zombies only stop if commanded to do so—or they are deactivated and destroyed.

Dirty Secrets about your Computer

When you bought your computer there were a number of things "they" never told you. They, being the manufacturers, the sales rep, your local geeks and even your computer-savvy friends. Don't feel bad because they never told me, either. When I discovered each of these secrets it was like learning the truth about Santa Claus all over again.

Dirty Secret #1:
Your Computer is a Rat

No matter how secret you are with your online activities, a computer that has fallen into the right hands will rat you out every time. Whether it's a PC, Mac or something in between, the average person's computer is basically a high-powered evidence vacuum cleaner. Imagine taking a piece of duct tape, placing it sticky-side exposed on the sole of your shoe and leaving it there for a week as you go about your daily routine. At the end of those 7 days that piece of tape would be covered with dirt, dust, fibers, food particles, and all kinds of other microscopic debris. All of it would be evidence of where you had been that week. The same kind of thing happens anytime we visit websites using a standard web browser (e.g. - Internet Explorer, Mozilla Firefox, Safari, Chrome, etc.). Every web page we visit leaves trace footprints; IP addresses of these websites stored in the DNS cache, separate from the web browser cache. Bits of information and scripts and images in the form of numerous tiny files that are stored deep inside the computer in hidden temporary folders. Thousands of these files can accumulate in an afternoon of regular web browsing. And like the particles on the sticky-side of the tape, all of it can be retrieved, analyzed and identified—some of which is recognizable with the untrained eye.

As of this writing, most web browsers come with some sort of privacy mode. And while these settings do make a difference, they don't completely erase your tracks or make you invisible online. Quite candidly, they're about as effective as trying to make your phone line untraceable by paying extra to have it unlisted. The minute you find yourself under investigation (or your computer is infected with malware), throw that false sense of security out the window.

CCleaner:
http://www.piriform.com/ccleaner
CCleaner protects your privacy online and makes your computer faster and more secure. Available for both PC and Mac.

WIPE:
http://privacyroot.com/programs/info/english/wipe.html
WIPE is another free, easy to use and powerful security tool for clearing out the various temporary Internet files. Currently only available for the PC.

Dirty Secret #2:
Your Computer Storage has a Lifespan

...and it will die. It's not a matter of if but when.

As of this writing, most computer hard drives are prone to fail after 5 or 6 years, causing them to stop working. This is because the disc-based hard drives (IDE, SATA, and SCSI) found in most PCs and Macs these days are hermetically sealed shut with moving parts inside the case. The internal components bear a resemblance to an old fashioned record player. And just like the motor, belts, and stylus of a turntable can eventually fail and the vinyl records themselves can get scratched up, similar failings happen to hard drives.

Hard drives die in one of two ways: Slow or Quick.

The Slow Death—comes in the form of predictable failures. These are the result of gradual processes like mechanical wear and tear or degradation of the magnetic platters where your data is stored. Fortunately, hard drives made after 2003 come with S.M.A.R.T. (Self-Monitoring, Analysis and Reporting Technology). SMART makes it possible to spot possible hard drive failure long before it happens, giving you the opportunity to plan ahead for when to replace your current hard drive with a new one. Plenty of SMART utilities for Windows, Mac OS X, and Linux can be found here: **http://en.wikipedia.org/wiki/Comparison_of_S.M.A.R.T._tools**

The Quick Death—comes in the form of a failure that happens instantly and without warning. These failures include mechanical failure, electronic components burn out, sudden shock (e.g. - a hard knock or being dropped on the floor), and etc. Although mechanical reasons account for more than half of all hard drive failures, in many cases there may be indicators that this is about to happen. Sometimes the hard drives get noisier. Other times they start having problems reading and writing data. The downside is that hard drives are built with such precision that if any mechanical part fails the entire hard drive fails. The upside is that if a mechanical failure hasn't done any physical damage to the platters, all the data on the hard drive should be undamaged and retrievable.

The most common sign of imminent mechanical failure is known as the "Click of Death" (CoD). It's a rhythmic clicking noise made by a failing hard drive when the reading arms cannot reach the reading position on the magnetic platters. When your computer suddenly takes forever to load or save files and it sounds like the unit is whispering 'tsk tsk tsk' over and over again, there's trouble. Immediately go get an external hard drive, plug it into the computer and start copying your files over. Although you could go buy a replacement hard drive and begin copying files, in most cases this process requires turning the computer off in order to open up the machine and install the replacement. Once the CoD starts so does the final countdown. From that point, every time you reboot that computer there's a chance the hard drive may finally lock up, leaving you without access to your files.

Eventually the Click of Death stops… and the hard drive becomes unreadable. Many people misread this as the death knell of their computer because when they press the power button it "won't start at all". Too often people immediately lose all hope and throw away the hard drive; in some cases the whole computer. DO NOT make this tragic mistake. In most situations the right person with the right skills and tools would have been able to recover some (or all) of the data. Speaking from my own experiences, my data recovery success rate is better than 95%—and I don't have anywhere near the capability of the dedicated data recovery services. In any case, since the process is time consuming it is rarely ever cheap.

And while computer manufacturers are gradually changing over to solid-state drives (SSD), this form of storage is still far more expensive than comparable hard drives with the same amount of storage space. As of this writing, desktops, laptops and servers are still being shipped with hard drives while the SSDs and flash storage are primarily being dedicated to mobile devices.

NOTE for Mac owners: As of 2010(?), Apple started using Flash drives in their MacBook Airs and Solid State Drives (SSD) with the MacBook Pros, iMacs, Mac minis, and Mac Pros. Although Apple still sells SATA drives, it appears they intend to eventually discontinue supporting them.

Dirty Secret #3:
Your Burned CDs and DVDs are Not Permanent

There is no gentle way to share this dirty secret. You know those CDs and DVDs that we've been burning on our computers since the early 90s? They are <u>not</u> permanent. Matter of fact, they're nowhere near permanent.

For years, retailers and computer manufacturers have been selling people on preserving their memories forever on burned CDs and DVDs. Photos and videos. Tons of downloaded music. Through Lies of Omission, people were misled into assuming that these burned discs will last a lifetime like their professionally-made counterparts. This represents a huge problem for anyone that wants to keep this data as a legacy. The phenomenon is known as **Disc Rot**.

Yes, Disc Rot. Even in a book referencing the Zombie Apocalypse I can't make this stuff up.

Disc Rot, as defined by Wikipedia, is "a phrase describing the tendency of CD or DVD or other optical discs to become unreadable due to physical or chemical deterioration".

There are a variety of reasons why this happens: scratches, oxidation on the reflective layer, corrosion of the adhesives used to put the disc together and ultra-violet light. And when it comes to burned discs, even natural [cosmic] radiation causes the data to decay and eventually become unreadable.

According to the Optical Storage Technology Association (http://www.osta.org), the shelf life of unused discs is roughly 5 to 10 years whereas burned discs can supposedly last 25 years or more. The problem is that these numbers are subject to so many variables it is like trying to calculate how long it will take the walking dead to decompose to a point where they fall apart and no longer pose a threat to the living. In my own experiences, I've had some discs become unreadable after 2 years while others lasted more than a decade. Even if you regularly test a disc there is no dependable way to know when it is going to fail.

Is there a way I can check to see if my discs are OK?

The simplest way to check your discs is with the naked eye. Hold the disc up to a light and study the other side. If you see pinholes of light coming through, discoloration around the edges, or signs that the layers are starting to come apart, they are all are indicators of Disc Rot. You can also use a program like CDCheck (**http://www.kvipu.com/CDCheck/**) to check the integrity of any discs in question.

Now that you've handled the bad news, the good news is that there are many ways you can increase the likelihood that your discs will last you a long time. Here are some key pointers:

- ► Choose top quality discs from a good brand (see conclusion of this chapter).
- ► The discs with the maximum longevity have gold as a reflective layer for CDs, silver for DVDs.
- ► Write to your rewritable discs as little as possible.
- ► Use slow writing speeds to reduce errors and increase quality.
- ► Use only non-solvent based felt-tip permanent markers to write on your disc labels.

- Treat your discs like they are delicate treasures (e.g. - never touch them on the surface; always hold them by the outer edges or the hole in the center, keep them clean, etc.).
- Store them in a dry, dark, and cool place. Humidity, sunlight, high temperatures, and pollutants can damage the different layers.
- Store the discs themselves in jewel cases.
- If there are any paper-based disc labels inside the jewel case, tape them on the outside of the case. In a humid environment, improperly processed paper can hold moisture.
- Every 5 years or so, copy your current discs to new discs (or examine mass storage options that are available).

What to do when your disc won't read?

If you can't read a disc in your drive or it has errors, don't give up hope.

Here area few tips for what you can do to:

- Make sure you didn't accidentally insert the optical disc upside down.
- Carefully clean the bottom layer with alcohol to remove grease from fingerprints and dust.
- Try to read the disc in a different player. If the laser in your optical disc drive is old it may be failing; a different player can still read your disc.

There are also tools out there on the net that can be downloaded and used to retrieve as much of your data as possible.

CD Recovery Toolbox:
http://www.oemailrecovery.com/cd_recovery.html

CDCheck:
http://www.kvipu.com/CDCheck/download.php

Unstoppable Copier:
http://www.roadkil.net/listing.php/C1/Data%20Recovery

Dvdisaster:
http://dvdisaster.net/en/index.html

CDRoller:
http://www.cdroller.com/

PhotoRec:
http://www.cgsecurity.org/wiki/PhotoRec

Disk Utility for MacOS X:
http://support.apple.com/kb/HT1782

Conclusion

Always have a backup of your data and check all our backups regularly to make sure none of the copies have broken in the meantime, regardless of whether you store your data on a CD, DVD, or hard drive. When buying CDs, make sure their Life Expectancy meets or exceeds ISO 18927, ISO/IEC 16963. And for DVDs, it should meet or exceed ISO/IEC 10995, ISO/IEC 16963.

High quality discs can be purchased at the following sites:
http://www.memkeeper.com/

The National Institute of Standards and Technology (Information Technology Laboratory)
http://www.itl.nist.gov/iad/894.05/docs/CDandDVDCareandHandlingGuide.pdf

Council on Library and Information Resources:
http://www.clir.org/pubs/reports/pub121/sec4.html/contents.html

Dirty Secret #4:
Solid State Drives are NOT the Wave of the Future

They're fast. They're quiet. And best of all, they don't have any moving parts. After spending most of the past decade maintaining small business computer networks—along with a kind of nagging paranoia that only comes from rescuing data from countless failed hard drives—I thought that switching over to Solid State Drives sounded like the answer to all our prayers. And like with all other technologies, that's not quite the case.

As of this writing, a big part of the problems we face with SSDs are the very traits that make them attractive. When a mechanical hard drive crashes and stops working, usually it's the dead (or dying) motor inside that has locked up. The platters that hold the data are often fine, unaffected by the crash. If the dead hard drive has not been physically damaged (e.g. - slammed on the floor, drop kicked, etc.), it is possible to open it up and use some unorthodox tactics to get it operational long enough to recover the data by copying it onto a new hard drive. If we compare the data to people, think of the recovery process like rescuing them from a sinking ship.

SSDs, however, present a whole different set of problems. They are solid state chips and electronic components on circuit boards—with no moving parts. There's no industrious MacGuyver moment where you can swap out mechanical parts to get the device working long enough to pull yourself out of a jam. Unlike mechanical hard drives, when electronic components die, they don't make funny little noises. They just die.

While there are some technophiles out there who swear that SSDs will make HDDs a thing of the past, current industry trends point to the contrary. There is a synergy between HDDs and SSDs that won't be waning anytime in the near future. Typically your thinner devices such as tablets and ultrathin laptops will be using SSDs. Desktops and laptops have the ability to make use of both HDDs and SSDs. Wise IT geeks know how to take advantage of making the two work together.

NIGHT OF THE LIVING DEAD (1968)

General Defense Tactics
Against Zombies

The Joys of Bulletproof Passwords

When faced with zombies, whether one-on-one or in the midst of an outbreak, the first and last lines of defense work hand in hand: don't let them get into your space and don't get bit. The same thing applies to the zombies of cyberspace—and this is primarily done through the use of secure passwords.

Many industry analysts and rogue security samurai claim that secure passwords are as much a fallacy as an unhackable computer. Due to the ever-increasing processing speeds and how often yet another security hash or cipher getting cracked, I'm reluctantly prone to agree. Before we get into the meat of this chapter, two points about passwords should be made clear:

First, every hacker and cybercriminal with half an ounce of skill is a lifelong student of human behavior. Being creatures of habit and horrible about keeping secrets, people are the weakest link in any security schema. When it comes to passwords, most people aren't careful about guarding this information unless it involves something they personally deem valuable (e.g. - online banking account, etc.). Anything outside of that is often treated with little discretion. Ask 10 of your friends how often they'll leave their wallet sitting on their desk at work and they'll probably tell you "Never". Then ask those same people if they've ever written down a password on a scrap piece of paper or Post-It Note and stuck it somewhere near their computer or inside a desk drawer. More than half of them have forgotten how many times they've done that. It'd be like asking the average man how often he thinks about sex.

The second point is that there's no such thing as an unbreakable password. Given enough time, dedication, and resources, any password can be cracked. Every hacker will have at least one story about cracking someone's password that was a proper name (e.g. - a family member, friend, or pet), a birth date, a phone number, a favorite pastime, a word that can be found in a dictionary, or a combination of the above. Why? Because when it comes to coming up with passwords, most people don't know any better or they don't take it that seriously. Every cybercriminal knows this, too, and they take advantage of this while constructing their zombies to use this as part of their attack. This is the most evident in the findings of various reports about insecure passwords. One of the best "worst password" collections I've ever seen was compiled by Mark Burnett, IT Security Consultant and renowned password fanatic. Here are the top 50:

1. password
2. 123456
3. 12345678
4. 1234
5. qwerty
6. 12345
7. dragon
8. pussy
9. baseball
10. football
11. letmein
12. monkey
13. 696969
14. abc123
15. mustang
16. michael
17. shadow
18. master
19. jennifer
20. 111111
21. 2000
22. jordan
23. superman
24. harley
25. 1234567
26. fuckme
27. hunter
28. fuckyou
29. trustno1
30. ranger
31. buster
32. thomas
33. tigger
34. robert
35. soccer
36. fuck
37. batman
38. test
39. pass
40. killer
41. hockey
42. george
43. charlie
44. andrew
45. michelle
46. love
47. sunshine
48. jessica
49. asshole
50. 6969

Mark's entire list contains 10,000 of the most common passwords. It's freely available for download from his website and many others. While checking the security on a few client networks using a brute force program, I added Mark's list to the attack... and it turns out his estimates were pretty accurate. Roughly 7 out of every 10 user accounts that were cracked within a three hour period turned out to be on that passwords list. Every Security Professional and Malicious Hacker has this list (or many others like it).

The following should be taken into consideration with regards to coming up with secure passwords:

► NEVER use the word "password" in any part of your password. For decades, "password" has ranked at the top of the most commonly used passwords on the planet. It has since become neck and neck with "Password1" since the latter conforms to most minimum password requirements.
► NEVER use your username OR your real name.
► NEVER use birth dates—period.
► NEVER use any word you can find in the dictionary (e.g. - monkey, etc.). Any word in the dictionary that is used for a password can be cracked with ease, often in seconds.
► NEVER use any word in the dictionary with a character before or after it (e.g. - monkey1).
► NEVER use popular hacker jargon (e.g. - kluge, foobar, choad, etc.).
► NEVER use pet names or proper names, especially of close relatives, favorite celebrities, or cartoon characters. They're often too easy to guess.
► Avoid using the names of religious figures (e.g. - Christ, Mohammed, Buddah, etc.)
► NEVER use profanity or slang related to sex or drugs. For whatever reason, naughty passwords are incredibly common.
► NEVER use old military slang acronyms (e.g. - BOHICA, FUBAR, SNAFU, TARFU, etc.).
► NEVER use strings of characters that are beside each other on the keyboard (e.g. - qwertyu, asdfghj, 12345678, etc.)
► NEVER use simple letter/number combinations (e.g. - abc123, etc.)
► NEVER use any popular magic words (e.g. - abracadabra, opensesame, xyzzy, etc.)

- ► NEVER use your favorite sport or sports teams (e.g. - golf, baseball, Cowboys, Knicks, etc.)
- ► NEVER use the brand name of your favorite products (e.g. - Porsche, LouisVuitton, etc.)
- ► NEVER use cliché phrases, especially if they are sports-related (e.g. - letmein, getthere, makemoney, etc.)

The reason why passwords need all these stipulations? Math.

To put the math behind the safety factor into perspective, let's say a cybercriminal is trying to guess the password to your online bank account. Your password is "BR3adL1n3!" ("Bread" and "Line" put together with an explanation point "!" and numbers substituted for the vowels). Because you've got an 10-character long password (with upper/lower case letters, numbers and a special character) his password cracker program will have to go through roughly 60 Quintillion (60,000,000,000,000,000,000) possible character combinations to guess your password. If he was running an offline cracker program on a computer that can try 100,000,000,000 Passwords/sec, it could take just under 20 years to crack. As of this writing, the typical desktop computer would take almost 60 years. And using a typical online password attack method that averages a few hundred tries per second could take over 200,000 years—enough to see the Roman Empire rise and fall over 400 times. Fortunately most security-conscious websites suspend an account after the first few failed login attempts.

The validity of these statistics degrades over time. As computers get more powerful, cybercriminals will be able run crack programs that can process more password attacks per second. Encryption and other authentication methods will also get more powerful, too, making protection schemes harder to crack. It's all part of the never-ending arms race between security professionals and cybercriminals.

Whether we're thinking about today or the future, the key to good password protection is <u>discouragement</u>. That's it. Any password that is easy enough for you to remember, 11 or more characters long, AND obscure enough to thwart current cracking methods (such as brute force, cryptanalysis, or dictionary) will eventually drive a cybercriminal to give up and move onto trying to crack into some other system or account, leaving your account untouched.

There are plenty of ways to come up with secure passwords. For most people, I've found it best to come up with a simple formula they won't forget. When people ask me for advice on coming up with passwords, I often mumble the word "Rosebud". Most will respond with a strange look… unless they are avid movie buffs. In the classic film CITIZEN KANE (1941), leading man Orson Welles immortalized this single word in Kane's death scene. The rest of the plot revolved around a reporter interviewing a series of people that knew Charles Kane best, all part of writing a feature story that uncovers the mystery of what Rosebud meant. At the end of the movie we finally discover what Rosebud is (and if this piques your curiosity, go watch the film). The meaning behind Rosebud was something he'd never forget because it was so personal. Rosebud was also so obscure that even the people closest to him could only speculate as to its meaning. The lesson here is that the root of any password you choose can be just as familiar to you, enigmatic to everyone else, and still be just as secure.

For example, back in the early Dot Com days I went through a phase where I used "Yv3tt3#D1ll0n!" as one of my main network passwords. "Yv3tt3" was a variation of the name Yvette, the name of the first girl I ever had a crush on back in the 2nd grade. Her school bus used to go down Dillon Drive, hence the choice of "D1ll0n". Beyond some ancient school records on microfiche and maybe a handful of copies of our 2nd grade class photo, there is absolutely nothing out there that would ever connect the two of us. I haven't seen her since my last day in 2nd grade; her family moved away later that summer. I couldn't look her up using Google or Facebook if I wanted to—I don't remember her last name. And neither of us lived on Dillon drive. Although I knew that password as clearly as my own name, none of my closest friends and family members would ever been able to make the connection. Even the most industrious NSA agent with an inch-thick dossier on my life would have no chance of guessing the password or making the connection.

The trick to generating passwords that can be memorized is to come up with simple formulas that are easy to remember and apply. For example, aside from using the Rodent Speak (substituting letters for numbers that closely resemble them in shape), another tactic is to assign a numeric value to vowels in the order they appear in the alphabet.

A:1
E:2
I:3
O:4
U:5
(and sometimes Y:6)

Let's say I had to come up with a quick Facebook page password on the spot. Let's say I incorporated my first name "Max" and the name of the website "Facebook". After coming up with the password "MaxFacebook" I pass it through the formula where it becomes "M1xF1c2b44k". Just to top it off I add a special character, #, making the final password is "M1xF1c2b44k#". It's easy enough for me to remember the password "MaxFacebook" and then if necessary I can figure out how it's encoded by counting down the order of the vowels. It's also nearly impossible to guess using brute force methods and would require a supercomputer to crack.

Here's one last password formula; it's a bit of a process but it also works well and the end result is also easy memorize:

1. **Start with a phrase and make an acronym.** Choose a memorable quote, movie title, music group/album title, a lyric from a favorite song, or some other phrase and take the first letter from each word. Here are three examples:

   Star Wars Episode V: The Empire Strikes Back (swevtesb)
   One Flew Over the Cuckoo's Nest (ofotcn)
   Steely Dan: The Royal Scam (sdtrs)

2. **Add to the acronym.** Mathematically speaking, once a password gets longer than 8 characters it gets stronger. They might be a little irritating to type but they're worth it. One trick is to lengthen your password by adding the website name to the acronym. For example:

   swevtesb + gmail
   ofotcn + twitter
   sdtrs + facebook

3. **Mix it up.** By mixing it up, I'm referring to swapping out vowels for either numbers or punctuation and capitalizing the first letter of each phrase. After that I'll add an exclamation point either at the end of the first acronym or at the end of the whole password. For example:

   Swevtesb!Gma1l
   OfotcnTw1tt3r!
   Sdtrs!F@c3b00k

4. **(Optional) Pad the Password.** This one is for those that are either incredibly security conscious or terminally insane. Padding a password is simply the act of adding a pattern of characters on one or both sides of your password. As shown in the three examples below, I took the password "Swevtesb!Gma1l" and padded it with the character pattern "###!!!###" :

   ###!!!###Swevtesb!Gma1l
   (front padded)

   Swevtesb!Gma1l###!!!###
   (back padded)

   ###!!!###Swevtesb!Gma1l###!!!###
   (both sides padded)

Steps 1, 2 and 3 in this bulletproof password process will already produce a password that may take centuries to crack using current technology. By padding a password you're making it even more exponentially difficult (e.g.—for the "###!!!###Swevtesb!Gma1l" password, an attack program working at one hundred trillion guesses per second would take at least 9.88 billion trillion centuries to crack it). Extremely lengthy padded passwords are best suited for super important passwords that only get typed in occasionally, such as banking website logins, wireless router passkeys, website database passwords, etc.

Baron Samedi says

"Regardless of how you come up with your passwords, always remember to rotate and/or change them regularly."

and

"If you're using Microsoft Windows and want super strong protection, use a password that is at least 15 characters long. Windows will not store such passwords, meaning they can't be retrieved from system files and descrambled."

NOTE: Some of my IT comrades and security experts may have a difference of opinion about the password creation methods previously presented in this chapter. After all, there are plenty of free password generators out there that can create randomized passwords that are 12 or more characters long and virtually uncrackable by most standards. The main reason I shared the formulas is because (1) they work and (2) most people can't (or won't) memorize generated passwords, making them very inconvenient for most people outside of being used from within a password manager. When passwords go beyond the convenience of memory people resort to shortcuts. Randomized passwords often end up written down in notebooks, Post-it notes on the monitor, or not used at all.

Most people will read this chapter and may or may not use one of these methods to come up with a secure password. Unfortunately, many people are likely to make the mistake of using that new "secure" password for everything. While it may seem like there's no harm in that, the problem is that these passwords are stored in databases on webservers that are constantly under attack from zombie botnets. All it takes is for some cybercriminal to crack into a website, steal its user database and crack all the passwords in it. If they find your full name or username on some other website like Amazon, Facebook, or Paypal and you've used the same password then they will have complete control over whatever you have associated with that account.

Keep it Movin'—Routine Password Changes

In many business environments, IT people and/or policy requires the staff to change their passwords every few months. At home, you should rotate your passwords as a matter of good computer practice. If you are using different passwords for different websites, you can do yourself a favor by rotating portions of your passwords every few weeks. Keep in mind that something as simple as changing even a single character of a password will make it a completely different password. If a cybercriminal was running a password cracker on that password, changing that one character would mean the program would have to be started over in order to have a chance at figuring out the password.

A few parting tips for safeguarding your password(s):

To err on the side of caution, conventional IT wisdom will advise you to never give out your password over the phone/email to anyone—period. Not to your co-workers, friends, relatives, not even your IT administrator. Most would ask "Why not the IT administrator?" but the thinking is that a legitimate system administrator (or whoever handles your IT needs) doesn't need to know your password since their role grants them the ability to change or reset your password if necessary. Although this is good advice, I've found it rarely works in most small business environments. Business owners and managers like to have their own passwords plus ready access to the accounts of all their employees. Employee passwords are either non-existent, very generic, or passed around like the collection plate at church. Demands for routine password changes often met with either aggravated resistance or not taken seriously until their network has been hacked. From an IT perspective it is easier to take an approach comparable to the Old West Cowboys on a cattle drive: keep the cattle content, the chuck wagon safe, and focus on fending off cattle rustlers, wolves and coyotes.

Baron Samedi says

"Don't ever change your password following an email request sent from your system administrator. In cyberspace, even though this scam is about as old as the Three-card Monte it still happens—and people still fall for it. Anyone with legitimate access to your account won't need you to change your password; they can change it on their end. If someone claims they need you to change your password to can gain access to your account, contact your system administrator immediately."

Last but not least, if you'd like to test the strength of your passwords (or just curious about what works well), check out the following sites…

Password strength testers:

- ► **http://rumkin.com/tools/password/passchk.php**
- ► **https://howsecureismypassword.net/**
- ► **http://www.microsoft.com/security/online-privacy/passwords-create.aspx**

Brute force attack tester:
https://www.grc.com/haystack.htm

NOTE: Due to the constant upgrades in computing technology, neither the author nor publisher can be held responsible for the accuracy of the numbers or the claims on these websites. These links have been provided more for educational purposes and should be used with discretion and at your own risk.

Password Management

To make it easier to avoid using the same password for everything, I recommend using a password manager. A password manager (sometimes also referred to as a password locker, safe, or vault), is a program that helps a user keep track of usernames, passwords, PIN codes, credit card numbers, sensitive account information and the various programs or websites they are associated with. These programs are typically protected by encryption, making it so all you have to do is memorize a single master password or select the key file to unlock the files and get access to everything inside. There are numerous password managers available, ranging in price from free to roughly $50 dollars USD.

The following links are to four (4) free, very secure password manager recommendations:

KeePass:
http://www.keepass.info/ - KeePass is a free open source password manager. The databases are encrypted using one of the best and most secure encryption algorithms currently known (AES and Twofish). The professional version can be installed on PC, Mac and Linux computers. I found this to be an ideal solution for a number of reasons, including the ability to synchronize my password locker file between the different operating systems, including my Android phone.

KeePassX:
http://www.keepassx.org/ - KeePassX is essentially the half-sister of KeePass raised by different parents. This package shares many of the same features while incorporating many of its own.

Password Gorilla:
https://github.com/zdia/gorilla/wiki/ - The Password Gorilla is another password manager that is compatible with PC, Mac and Linux. Like the others, it stores all your user names and passwords, along with login information and other notes, in a securely encrypted file. The biggest difference is that if you want to log into a service or Web site, the Password Gorilla copies your user name and password to the clipboard, so that you can easily paste it into your Web browser or other application. Because the password does not appear on the screen, Password Gorilla is safe to use in the presence of others.

Clipperz:
http://www.clipperz.com/ - Clipperz is a free and anonymous online password manager. Local encryption within the browser guarantees that no one except you can read your data. Since it is web-based it is compatible with any computer or mobile device with Internet access.

More password managers can be found here:
http://en.wikipedia.org/wiki/List_of_password_managers

After you've chosen a password manager program and installed it, consider picking out a different password manager and installing it along with the first. In the event someone starts snooping around on your computer, if that person finds your password manager file they'll have no idea which program will open it—and there's a 50/50 chance they'll pick the decoy. In either case, their failed attempts to open your password file will leave trace evidence of their snooping (e.g. - the password locker filename will pop up in "Recent Documents" list, etc.). This trick is especially handy if you suspect a roommate has been nosing around on your machine when you're not there.

Zombies Don't Play—Gaming Console Security

NOTE: For the sake of simplicity and sheer laziness, the term "Gaming Console" will be used as a catch-all phrase for video gaming systems in general, including games on PC and Mac.

It never ceases to amaze me just how far gaming systems have come. The games are practically interactive movies, but what most people forget is that the consoles themselves are basically dedicated computers with high end graphics cards. As a result, many parents forget to treat consoles the same security concerns as with a computer, especially when it comes to their children. The consoles are online and with most multiplayer games, text and voice chat are very much a part of game play. Anytime there's a chat option to a game, there will be predators looking to exploit naïve players. This can be something as simple as another player pretending to be some kind of administrator asking for a password; other times there could be more nefarious intentions. Since game consoles and computers are both online, the methods for safer gaming and safer online computing are essentially the same.

Any children using your network that are old enough to play console games while online should be taught to practice the following:

► Never give out their passwords to ANYONE online. Never.
► Never give out real names, addresses, or phone numbers online.
► Never download and install any game hacks from unfamiliar sources. More and more incidences are popping up where cybercriminals are using these hack patches to infect systems/computers with malware.
► Know what games your child is playing. While this isn't necessarily a security risk, games that are rated for Mature Audiences are liable to expose the child to adults who will expose them to mature subject matter.
► On some of the Live sites (e.g. - Xbox Live), the language can get pretty foul. Again, not a security risk per se but it's better to keep that kind of audio muted.

- ► Avoid giving out the main WiFi password to your wireless router. If a visitor absolutely must bring over another console to plug into the network, use a direct connection through an Ethernet cable instead. Most wireless routers made after 2010 have a built-in "guest network" feature, allowing you to provide guests access to your Internet without access to other computers and devices on your network.
- ► Use strong passwords (see "The Joys of Bulletproof Passwords", page 338).
- ► Use different usernames and passwords for different sites, especially for sites that bill regularly (e.g. - Gamefly.com, etc.).
- ► Every game console has its fair share of 'hack' websites. These are sites generally geared toward gamers who are also hardcore tech geeks that are coming up with ways to make the console do things it wasn't originally designed to do. Sometimes this is with hardware mods, other times with homebrew (homemade) software. Before you try any of the hacks or mods, take time to get to know the sites and read the comments before trying any of them.
- ► Game consoles, like family computers, should be kept in community areas in the home (e.g. - family room, den, game room, etc.). This will help reduce some activities that may lead to risky behavior.

I think my [game console] has a virus!

As of this writing, there are only a handful of known vulnerabilities that can be used to exploit one or two of the game consoles currently on the market. To the best of my knowledge, none of those contagions have been able to successfully traverse the Internet or turn another console into a zombie. If you've got a game that is flaking out, more than likely that is due to Disc Rot or the optical reader laser inside your console is going bad. If your console seems to be malfunctioning, check with the customer support website to be sure. In any case, a contagion probably isn't the culprit.

If there's at least one other computer on your network that is currently engaged in a lot of heavy downloading (e.g. - streaming YouTube videos, downloading torrents, etc.) it may cause lags that will adversely affect game play. And this especially applies if that computer has been zombified.

My webmail got hacked— how come my anti-virus didn't catch it?

So you're going about your business one day and then a bunch of friends either call, text or email you asking about some message you supposedly sent. After you've assured the third or fourth person that it wasn't you, panic begins to swell. You discover that your Yahoo email account has been hacked and someone has sent a message out to everyone in your address book.

Short answer = your anti-virus software cannot disinfect what is not stored on your computer.

When I give this answer, people often come back with some sort of "Huh? But it IS on my computer" response. They see the webmail on the screen just like anything else, thus it is "on the computer". Well, this isn't the case. For the purpose of this chapter, let's classify email handling in one of two main modes: Store-until-Pickup and Remote.

> ▶ **Store-until-Pickup**—this is a more traditional email account, the kind we get when we subscribe to an Internet Service like Cable modem or DSL. Companies like Verizon.net, Cox.net, Comcast.net, and Roadrunner.net that provide Internet access also provide email accounts. Typically such an account is used like a P.O. Box in that it's available 24 hours a day but it has limited storage space. Since it's not designed to keep your mail there for long periods of time, most people use their email readers (such as Outlook, Thunderbird, etc.) to access the account where all the

awaiting messages are download to your computer, leaving the account's inbox empty. The upside to this mode is that we can keep the emails on our computers indefinitely and we don't have to be online to read them. This is very handy for travelers with laptops who may go for long stretches without Internet access.

▶ **Remote**—this is where your emails are not downloaded to your computer. Instead, they remain on a web server somewhere on the Internet and we use a web browser to read them just like we would any other web page. Often we sign up for free webmail accounts such as @yahoo.com, @gmail.com, or @hotmail.com to use them in Remote mode. Since these messages stay in the cloud we can read them from home, work, at a café, or on a mobile device. The downside is that when Internet access isn't available, we won't be able to read those messages, either.

Between the two modes, Remote is the lesser secure since these accounts logins are always available on the web and exposed to attacks in cyberspace or infected spam emails. With Store-until-Pickup, most anti-virus programs are designed to scan and clean emails as they are downloaded to your computer. As a result, even though the webmail services do their best to provide protection, if you click on the wrong email you can unleash a kind of worm that can't be detected by your anti-virus. In many cases this is how your webmail got spoofed or cracked.

Spoofed Email

When your email address is spoofed it simply means some tech-savvy person (usually a cybercriminal or a program they wrote) has forged an email header to make it appear that you sent it. Think of this tactic as the 21st century equivalent of stealing someone's official company letterhead and/or forging their signature and then sending out messages as that person. Although the spoofing is always intended to disguise an illicit email's true source, often it uses the name of whoever was spoofed to send the forged emails to everyone in their address book (and then some).

For example, Jane Doe's laptop was hit with a virus. Among the personal information it stole from her machine the malware then sends everyone in her address book an email. Within seconds, everyone she has corresponded with using that email account receives a message asking them to "check out this really cool website" with a link. For the recipients who know Jane well, any one of them is likely to open that email and click on the link without hesitation. Sometimes that link is to a spammer's website or phishing website. Sometimes it has an infected attachment. In any case it delivers a payload that infects the recipient's computer and repeats the vicious process just like it did on Jane's machine.

Baron Samedi says

"If you ever receive an email from a bank you don't deal with or from Western Union regarding a package you didn't order, delete it. And even if you get an email from your bank and have the slightest reservation about it then don't click on anything—call the bank or go to its website."

Cracked Email

Having your webmail account cracked is an entirely different scenario because it poses a much greater threat. Whether your account is with Gmail, Yahoo, or any other free webmail out there, it should be considered about as private and secure as a cheap hotel room. At the top of the reasons is the fact that someone with ill intent, a little know-how, and/or a gift for gab can often get access to your webmail without your permission. It doesn't take much to maintain access to these accounts, either, where someone can monitor your emails for other ways to exploit you identity. Most webmail accounts get cracked by Botnets because people set up those accounts using weak passwords. Once hacked, they are commonly used to send out spam—starting with everyone in your address book. The rationale is pretty simple: recipients are more prone to open messages and click on links when it's from the name of someone they know personally.

When a webmail account is manually cracked (i.e. – not through a Botnet automated attack) it is a sign of an entirely different problem. If you find yourself in this situation, more often than not someone you know is responsible for the breach. The purpose behind this kind of hack is usually spying or sabotage. Even though people are always quick to blame hackers, it's probably one form of hacking that many computer hackers don't bother to commit. There's no real skill involved, no benefit or thrill of bragging rights. Cracking into individual webmail accounts isn't profitable, either, since most people aren't willing to pay for the effort.

The culprit often knows the account holder well enough to use that intimate knowledge to guess the password, answer the secret questions, or call customer service and ferociously browbeat a support person into resetting the password. At the risk of sounding sexist, more often than not the culprit is a woman scorned. For whatever reason, women seem to excel at this tactic, especially those who have experience with being in relationships with unfaithful partners. I've lost count of how many men (and women) have called upon me regarding their hacked webmail only to find out that it was a female relative (wife/girlfriend/ex) who was responsible for the breach. Infidelity was almost always the rationale behind the breach with stalker-style jealousy a close second and everything else a distant third. In some cases the account holder changed passwords several times and each time the woman was able to regain access within a few days. Whether this ability is genetic or secretly taught between women is anyone's guess.

As of this writing, there's almost nothing that can be done to prevent spoofed emails from happening. When you receive them, just click delete. If your name is used in a spoofed email, try to let your people know as soon as possible not to click on anything it has to offer. And lastly, if your webmail has been spoofed or hacked, change the password (see "The Joys of Bulletproof Passwords" page 338 for tips on coming up with strong passwords) and change the secret questions to something more obscure.

Safer Web Browsing Habits

Contrary to the general tone of this book, your adventures on the web don't have to be a harrowing experience.

Many people tend to be a bit confused about what the Internet actually is. They tend to believe that the web is the Internet. The best way to put the Internet into perspective is subscribing to cable TV: Your web browser is the equivalent of a flatscreen TV. The different web browsers (Chrome, Internet Explorer, Mozilla Firefox, Safari, etc.) can be compared to the different brands of TVs (Samsung, Sharp, Sony, etc.). The cable bringing the signal into your home is your actual Internet connection. Each TV connected to cable brings the same channels regardless of the brand and they all generally look the same.

Baron Samedi says

"Your web browser should be treated as your first line of defense against anything that might infect your computer. Keep your web browser up to date."

Like Microsoft Windows, Mac OS X, and Linux, every web browser requires regular updates, too. Your web browser (e.g. - Internet Explorer, Mozilla, Safari, Chrome, etc.) is often your first point of entry for most viruses and other malicious code. The older the web browser version, the more vulnerable it is, giving that computer a much higher risk of infection. This is especially a big problem with most PCs that came off the assembly line before 2006 or running older versions of Windows XP. Here's why:

To start, the web browser that came with most pre-2006 PCs was Internet Explorer 6 (IE6)… a version that will forever be regarded as THE single most vulnerable piece of crap web browser in Internet history. Unfortunately, it came pre-installed with Microsoft Windows XP, one of the most popular versions of Windows throughout the first decade of the 21st century. And with the release of Windows Vista, another big piece of crap, many PC users decided to stick with XP. Even though Microsoft replaced IE6 with IE7 in late 2006, as of this writing roughly 2% of the PCs in the world—over a million computers—are still using IE6. (Source: Statowl.com)

The IE6 problem with Microsoft XP, coupled with the fact that most computer users don't do regular system software updates, makes for many older PCs that are either zombies or zombie bait. Using those machines to browse the web is about as risky as having unprotected sex with strangers and going for months without washing your hands.

I heard that Mozilla Firefox is safer than Internet Explorer? Is this true?

The answer is "Yes and No—it depends."

The saga starts back about 150 Internet years ago (1995) when Microsoft released the early versions of Internet Explorer. In those days, the IT world was in brilliant chaos, and the Internet was changing by the hour. For whatever reason, Microsoft tasked their engineers to do something that had never been done before—deeply integrate their web browser as part of their operating system. Since IE was so interwoven into Windows it opened up a source of all kinds of problems. Malicious code writers found countless ways to use this to exploit PCs, mainly by tricking IE to download contagions. This did for PC-based computer viruses what Prohibition did for bootlegging and organized crime. For IE, things got progressively worse over the years, peaking with the release of version 6.

Meanwhile, the Browser Wars raged on. Other browsers came and went; Mozilla Firefox was one of the few that rose to prominence. Firefox gained popularity as a secure alternative to Internet Explorer. At one point, even the execs at Microsoft had advised their staff to use Firefox over their own IE web browser. Finally, after some years of hard work, Microsoft engineers managed to get Internet Explorer back up to industry standard. Many of the security flaws during the mid-00s that gave IE a wide reputation as a slow and highly insecure web browser were resolved by IE9. As of this writing, the latest versions of Internet Explorer have risen up to be comparable with the latest versions of Chrome, Firefox, Opera and Safari.

Since it wouldn't be fair to give a professional recommendation endorsing one web browser over another, I'll share a personal one: I have Chrome, Firefox, Internet Explorer, and Safari installed on my main production computer. They all have their pluses and minuses along with some really cool plug-ins. And while I keep them all updated to the latest, I use IE primarily for any online services that require Active X or any other business-related websites that are specifically designed for IE. For all other websites I use browsers like Chrome or Firefox. My biggest concern is that IE still makes use of certain Microsoft-specific modules that have traditionally been a source of vulnerabilities that virus coders have used to infect PCs. Even though the modules are more secure than before, they are still there and being exploited to some degree. This is why I'll only use IE on secure websites that I really trust, particularly those that are dedicated to their own content with no offsite advertisements.

NOTE: this chapter wasn't intended to perpetuate the stigma towards Internet Explorer or any other web browser. I included it in this book because of the mixed reputation IE has gained over the years. The truth is, every browser has had (and will eventually have) its own vulnerabilities discovered and exploited until it gets patched.

What is Java? And should I let it update?

Java is a secure, highly portable programming language. Not to be confused with its distant cousin *Javascript*, Java was designed for developers to create programs that can be sent to your web browser and run on your computer or mobile device. Many feature-rich websites such as **www.apple.com, www.dell.com, and www.weather.com** use Java for their functionality. If you've got an Android phone or tablet, the apps and games are usually written in Java, as with most of the apps written for Blackberry, too. Generally speaking, if you're using an Internet-capable computer or device produced in the 21st century, it uses Java. And while the people that developed Java did a good job of making sure the language was complete, occasionally they still discover a bug or make some improvements. This is why every now and then Java needs to download updates—a process usually takes less than five minutes and won't cost you a penny. Not allowing Java to update is to make your computer vulnerable to malware and other threats.

Baron Samedi says

"When your computer asks to do an update, whether it's your operating system, web browser or even Java, if time permits you should let it. The longer you go between updates, the more your computer is vulnerable to online threats."

Evading Zombies at the Mall:
Steps to Safer Online Shopping

If there is a lesson to be learned from the DAWN OF THE DEAD tales, it is that Zombies and Malls are drawn together like ants and picnics. This also applies in cyberspace. Cybercriminals are at work 24 hours a day trying to find ways to get their hands on anything they can monetize. Their goals include cracking into online stores to steal credit card databases, ordering merchandise using stolen card numbers to resell, or finding new ways to steal data directly from you. Even worse, there are some legitimate shopping websites that seem to be run by the living dead, booby-trapped with bad products and services and poor customer support after they've got your money. Either way, once you encounter those zombies they are as much of a threat to your wallet as they are to your overall peace of mind.

The following tips will drastically reduce your chances of falling prey to those zombies and their criminal masters:

1. The #1 rule of shopping: If it's too good to be true, it probably is.

2. NEVER shop from websites by clicking on links sent to you in unsolicited (spam) emails. I'm referring to real spam here, not the promotional emails that many of us inadvertently agree to when we register an account or make an online purchase. Links in spam emails are commonly booby-trapped with Trojans that can often get around your anti-virus software and infect your computer in less than a second. This includes turning it into a zombie. NOTE: Spammers are constantly getting more sophisticated, occasionally sending spam disguised as coming from a real online retailer (e.g. - Amazon, eBay, etc.). When in doubt, go directly to the retailer's website instead of clicking on an email link.

3. NEVER select the checkbox "Remember my password" option when registering any website accounts. As of this writing, most web browsers store that info in plaintext, meaning that anyone who knows where it's stored inside your computer could open that file, steal your username and password, and use it to log into that website as you. Malicious Hackers know this and often program their zombies to take advantage of this convenience by grabbing anything stored in your browser. It's the digital equivalent of leaving your house key under the welcome mat by your front door.

4. Always have a personal firewall (e.g. – Comodo, ZoneAlarm, TCPBlock, etc.) running on your computer if you're not already on a network that has a separate, dedicated

firewall. This doesn't include the firewall that come stock with Microsoft Windows and Mac OS X. Although I haven't tested the built-in OS X firewall, the built-in Windows firewall is about as dependable as birth control at a frat party. NOTE: Most wireless routers provide basic firewall protection.

5. Keep your Operating System (OS) up to date. Regardless of whether you're running Microsoft Windows or Mac OS X, this is easy to do. If you're lazy, it's also possible to set your system to update automatically. The more current you keep your OS, the less likely many forms of malicious code are going to be able to infect your computer and steal your data. This should also include keeping your anti-virus and anti-malware/spyware products current, too.

6. Whenever you're shopping online, always look for the signs that you're using a secure connection. This includes (but not limited to) the address of the website begins with "https:" instead of "http:", the green Verisign display bar or the little padlock icon in the bottom right corner (for Internet Explorer), the lock beside https web address (for Chrome), the blue colored tab next to the web address (for Mozilla Firefox), or the grey lock icon in the upper right corner of the web browser (for Safari).

7. DO NOT USE a debit card for online purchases. Stick to using a credit card only. Most banks and credit unions have security measures and guarantees in place for credit cards that they don't provide for debit cards.

8. Caveat to #7 - Consider getting a pre-paid credit card that is used solely for online purchases. That way, even if the card number falls into a cybercriminal's hands they won't be able to steal any more than what's left on the card at the time. Examples of these cards include GreenDot, Visa Prepaid, Rushcard, PayPal, etc. Also, skimmers love tourists from out of town. Using a prepaid card when traveling will greatly reduce the chance of high losses if your card gets skimmed (or stolen).

9. Check your bank statements regularly. The instant you see any charges that look out of place, report it.

10. Be sure that your credit cards are registered with your card provider's security services like "MasterCard SecureCode" or "Verified by Visa".

11. Check the privacy policy on any website that requires you to register for an account—especially shopping websites (e.g. - Amazon.com, yourfavoritestore.com, etc.), social media websites (e.g. - Facebook, Twitter, Instagram, etc.), and cloud services (e.g. - Dropbox, iCloud, etc.). This is to let you know how your personal information will (and won't) be used, sold and/or traded to other companies. The basic rule of thumb is that if you're getting something for free on a website and you have to register to get it, you can bet money that your information is being used and/or sold somehow. Try to check it at least once or twice a year because these policies are subject to change without notice.

12. Read ALL customer testimonials (not just the most recent). Read them on both the purchasing site and from third party sites like Google. Look for confirmation of things like speedy shipping, any problems with returns, etc. If you see page after page of "glowing" reviews that cover the same compliments, take them with a grain of salt. Marketers have been known to pay people to write comments and testimonials for their products on various retail websites. As of this writing, fake reviews are still a legal tactic for vendors to increase sales and search engine visibility.

13. If you've never dealt with an online vendor before, check out a few third-party reviewer websites. A few good sites to refer to are **www.ripoffreport.com**, **www.sitejabber.com**, and the granddaddy of them all, **www.bbb.org**. Specifically look for recent complaints about return policies, poor customer support, and all the typical tell-tale signs of a troubled customer experience. NOTE: Although these might be isolated experiences, its better to know what you're potentially getting into versus learning the hard way.

14. Most major retailers like Amazon, B&N, Toys R Us, have begun adhering to much stricter credit card processing standards such as the Payment Card Industry Data Security Standard (PCI DSS). The problem is that these standards haven't been universally accepted to the fullest yet. This is why every other month there's news of some network or web server gets compromised, resulting in cyber-heists, digital vandalism, or tens of thousands of cases of identity theft. Between October and December of 2012, the list of [known] security compromises grew to include companies such as Adobe (150,000 user accounts), Barnes & Nobles (credit card data skimmed at 63 locations), Northwest Florida State College (300,000 confidential records stolen), Pizza Hut (reportedly over 240,000 credit card numbers stolen), and Citibank ($1 million in cash advances stolen from casino kiosks in Southern California). Things are likely to get worse long before they get better.

15. The second #1 rule of shopping: Caveat Emptor - Let the Buyer Beware.

Live CDs: The Secret to Worry-Free Web Browsing

If you need to

- ► safely do online banking or pay bills,
- ► safely rescue files from an infected computer,
- ► safely have a worry-free web experience on a shared computer,
- ► safely browse questionable websites without possibly compromising your computer

...then a Live CD will be your best friend.

Simply put, a Live CD is a version of an operating system (often Linux or FreeBSD) that can be run completely on removable media (CD, DVD, or USB Flash Drive) without installing anything to that computer's hard drive. It runs entirely independent of any operating system currently installed on that computer. Most Live CDs come with all the basics that the average person needs to use: Office suite (word processor, spreadsheet, maybe a Powerpoint clone), Internet access tools, media players, photo viewers and maybe a game or two. Many of them are also tailored for specific purposes (e.g. – anonymous web browsing, system diagnostics/repair, gaming, etc.). Because a Live CD is self-contained on the removable media, nothing gets written to that computer's hard drive unless you want it to be.

A few benefits of using a Live CD to browse the web include:

▶ **Security**—with most Live CDs you'll leave no traces on that computer about where you've been or what you've been doing. This is great for logging into security-sensitive websites from a computer you don't own (e.g. – Internet café, library computers, etc.) or visiting "questionable" websites that you'd rather not leave any residual evidence (e.g. - porn, downloading pirated files, etc.).

▶ **Virtually Virus-Proof**—if you happen to visit any infected websites there's less than 1% chance of infecting that computer. The only reason I avoid saying "no chance" is because someone just might figure out a way someday. For starters, most contagions are written to infect Microsoft Windows with Mac OS X a very distant second, and the typical Live CD is based on some version of Linux or FreeBSD. Along with that, Live CDs are generally designed to run in memory; if there was actually an infection caught while browsing a website you could simply reboot the computer and the virus would disappear once the Live CD reloaded fresh. The only way to possibly infect that computer would be to download an infected program, install it on that computer, and later run it.

▶ **Basic data recovery**—in the event that you're using a PC or Linux machine that won't boot, a Live CD can be used to allow you to see if you can access and retrieve your files. This may be problematic with encrypted file systems.

I would recommend using this approach on a machine that is connected to the Internet by Ethernet cable. While most Live CDs have the ability to use wireless, each time you boot up that disc you'll have to take a few minutes to configure the settings since it can't save them. If you're using a computer that is plugged into the LAN (instead of wireless) it will usually configure itself and connect to the Internet automatically.

http://www.livecdlist.com/

This site has an extensive list of Live CDs along with its size, main purposes, most recently released version and links to download them. Most of these sites will also have instructions available for how to burn to CD, DVD or USB Flash Drive.

http://www.ultimatebootcd.com/

From the website: Ultimate Boot CD (UBCD) is a bootable recovery CD that contains software used for repairing, restoring, or diagnosing almost any computer problem. Our goal is to be the most complete and easy to use free computer diagnostic tool. Almost all software included in UBCD is freeware utilities for Microsoft Windows. Some of the tools included are "free for personal use" copies so users need to respect these licenses. A few of the tools included in UBCD are paid for and licensed software owned by UBCD.

http://www.ubuntu.com/

Although I've been using Linux since the mid-90s, I fell in love with variations of Debian Linux such as Ubuntu and Mint. Thanks to the ease of use, in early 2005 I decided to experiment with switching most of the computers on my network over to Ubuntu... and I haven't looked back. The only reason I haven't completely disassociated from Microsoft Windows or Mac OS X is because I need to stay in tune with what people are using. Since the switch, I've been blessed with a clean, secure network with no viral outbreaks.

Travel Tips:
Smarter, Safer Computing while on the go

As an IT Road Warrior I've traveled from coast to coast. Hustling up a solid Internet connection has been second nature to me since college. When traveling, whether on an extended trip or just up the street to the nearest Starbucks, always keep in mind that you're not on your home network. As overdramatic as it sounds, effectively you're on hostile network.

Pointers to remember:

1) **Not all hotel Internet access is created equal.**

Hotels in locations that cater primarily to business travelers tend to have much better quality Internet access to their rooms. Since these guests may be staying days or weeks at a time, the Internet is often complimentary, too.

When staying in hotels that cater mostly to tourists (especially casinos), consider finding a local public Wi-Fi to visit instead of depending the Internet connection to your room. There are a number of reasons for this.

► To start, these hotels usually provide the minimum bandwidth possible to handle traffic from all their rooms. Management knows that most of their guests are vacationers, thus not prone to bring their work with them. The potential for bottlenecks can be compared to how the old fashioned boarding houses would have all the tenants share a single bathroom.
► These places often charge higher than normal fees for Internet access (possibly as a deterrent to prevent excessive use).
► In places where the guest network is wireless, the signal is often weak everywhere outside of the main lobby.
► Wired or wireless, the connection speeds are usually so slow they are only good for checking email and maybe browsing local nightlife websites.
► Aside from running on old hardware, these networks typically block access to certain types of traffic, making it impossible for guests to access websites like Dropbox, Netflix or

HBO Go. Since guests can't download or stream their own movies they are more likely to use the hotel's antiquated pay-per-view system.

► Last but not least, these networks are often crawling with contagions. For every 10 guest laptops on the network at least one will be zombie infested.

All of these issues bring the Internet access in the room to an overpriced crawl.

2) Not all Internet access is charged the same.

If you're traveling to an unfamiliar place and you need to maintain some kind of Internet access, it pays to always research any associated costs ahead of time.

Here in the continental United States, getting in-room Internet access is free in some hotels. In other hotels it may cost anywhere from $10 to $30 dollars USD per 24-hour period—and that fee is often per computer. When traveling abroad, some hotels charge as much as $22 Euros per 24-hour period (about $30 dollars USD). And if that wasn't steep enough, some hotels also charge rates on top of those rates, too.

The first time I experienced this was at casino hotel in Atlantic City. To get basic Internet access in my room they wanted to charge $100 dollars to my credit card plus $11 dollars per 24-hour period, and then after I checked out they would charge back the $100 dollars within a week. Because I had recently taken over as network administrator for a new client back home, I needed to have access at a moment's notice. I begrudgingly gave in and let them whack me for the $111+ dollars. Once Internet was turned on, the connection was okay for about 20 minutes before it flaked out. Since my laptop was outfitted with a bunch of hacker tools and network diagnostic programs, it didn't take long to determine the connection was horrible; smoke signals would have been more dependable. A call to the front desk prompted them to send up their tech: a mature attractive woman dressed like a mechanic with a Philips-head screwdriver in hand. After checking *the power outlet and the same cable I'd already checked twice, she pointed out a support number, claimed she had to check something downstairs, and said she would be back shortly. A call to that number turned into two hours on the phone before they finally conceded that they were clueless and their Internet just wasn't going to work. It took another half hour to get the hotel to immediately reverse the charges. The tech never returned.*

On cruise ships, like with remote areas, Internet access is handled by satellite. Connections on cruise ships are much slower than the high speed DSL and cable services, more expensive and notoriously unreliable. As of this writing, they charge anywhere from $0.35 cents to $1 dollar per minute with the typical per minute fee being around $0.75 cents. If you absolutely have to use Internet under those conditions, here are a few tips:

- ▶ For smart phones, tablets and any other mobile devices with data plans, check with your provider before you leave town. Roaming charges can be outrageous.
- ▶ Avoid uploading a bunch of photos. Depending on the upload speed and size of your photos, you may find yourself spending a few dollars per image.
- ▶ Pre-write any emails you plan to send so once you log in you can just cut and paste it into the email message and click send. This way you can send out a bunch of emails in less than the amount of time it would take to write and send just one.
- ▶ If your email service allows it, download your incoming messages and read them offline.
- ▶ Stick to using the Internet late at night.
- ▶ When the ship is docked and you've got time to go ashore, find an Internet café or restaurant with public WiFi (if you brought a laptop).
- ▶ Before leaving home, check with your cell phone service provider to see if there are any packages available for tethering your laptop to your phone's data plan. Also check with them to make sure you won't inadvertently rack up a bunch of unexpected international roaming charges.

3) A wired Internet connection is just as vulnerable as a wireless.

Contrary to popular belief, a wired Internet connection provides virtually no additional protection beyond the limits that come from a lack of physical access to the cable or the machine. Wireless or wired, it doesn't matter—a computer faces the same threats once it's on a network. Always make sure your anti-virus is up to date before you leave home. If you're not sure if it's current, contact customer support and they will be able to find out for you.

4) Turn off any shared folders on your laptop, netbook or tablet.

If you're not familiar with how to share folders, chances are you haven't changed that setting on your laptop. Shared folders continuously "announce" themselves over a network—and they don't care what network it is. On a public network of some kind, anyone scanning the network traffic can spot a shared folder like runway lights at an airport.

5) Do not use public computers to access sensitive websites (e.g. - online banking, company intranets, etc.).

NOTE: Some advice in this section may sound paranoid. It is, but with good reason.

This kind of public computer is usually a desktop PC that can be found in a library, cybercafé or in hotel rooms that cater to business travelers. The good news is that generally the upper range hotels that provide desktop PCs are so exclusive that they can afford to provide complimentary Wi-Fi access. The not-so-good news is that these computers are prime targets for cybercriminals.

But isn't "https" secure enough? Yes and no.

Although the https connection insures that the information sent from your computer is only readable by the intended recipient, it doesn't protect against local eavesdropping. Think of it like having phones that can scramble outgoing calls and unscramble those calls on the other end. Even though anyone that may intercept the call won't be able to understand the message, it is still possible for anyone standing next to the caller to hear what is being said before it gets scrambled.

One way this can be achieved is for a cybercriminal to plug in a hardware keystroke logger on the computer itself. Also called "keyloggers", these devices record everything that is typed on the keyboard (including backspaced characters and invisible passwords). Unlike software keyloggers that can be easily detected and removed with anti-spyware, hardware keyloggers are more dangerous because they can be virtually undetectable except for by someone (usually an IT person) who is savvy enough to notice them. Many of these devices are designed to blend in, looking like just another cable or some kind of USB plugin adapter that is part of the computer. Upon being identified they have to be removed by hand.

Baron Samedi says

"When you're traveling, stay off any sensitive websites—your bank, favorite online store, or your office intranet—unless you're using your own laptop or mobile device and it's using a secure connection (e.g. - https, VPN, etc.)."

6) Turn off your Bluetooth when you're not using it.

When it comes to our mobile devices, we love our hands-free headsets, wireless mice, in-car connectivity, iPod and etc. These all connect to each other with Bluetooth, a type of short range radio frequency used to create a personal area network. And while Bluetooth has been great for getting rid of all those extra cables between devices, most of them use the default PIN number of 1234, 0000, or 1111—and people make the mistake of never changing them. The problem is that (1) most smartphones these days are basically mini-computers, (2) they are constantly broadcasting out for anything within a few meters that will recognize them, and (3) the simple PINs leave our mobile devices open to various forms of Bluetooth attacks (Bluesnarfing, Bluebugging, etc.).

With 4-digit PINs there are 10,000 possible combinations. People are predictably bad at picking PIN numbers. Based on personal experience and security research papers I've read over the years, here are a few general observations:

- For every five Bluetooth devices protected with a 4-digit PIN, at least one of them could be cracked quickly by using either 1234, 1111, 0000, 6969, 4321, 2580 (straight down the middle on the phone keypad), numeric couplets (e.g.—1212, 1313, 3434, 5656, etc.) or repeating four digits (e.g. - 2222, 3333, etc.).
- Birth years are also very common (e.g. - 1950, 1951, etc.). Anytime I've cracked a 4-digit PIN that turned out to be a birth year I did so by guessing the age of the owner of the device (+/- 10 years) followed by trying more recent years in the event that person used a child's birth year. This applies to business startups, too.
- Statistically, one-third of the 4-digit PINs can be cracked by trying just 61 combinations (source: DataGenetics.com). A lazy hacker working by hand can go through that many codes in about 15 minutes.

Preventing such attacks is best done by remembering to turn off your Bluetooth when it's not in use. That's it. And for those who think putting their Bluetooth in private mode is the same as turning it off, think again. Freely available programs like Bluelog and Bluescanner can detect hidden Bluetooth devices just as easily as all the others in range.

The first time I dabbled in the power of Bluetooth hacking was back in 2010. I was grabbing a late lunch at a popular café, tinkering with my laptop when a loud voice broke the peace. With the thunder of self-importance, a guy in a nearby booth spoke into his wireless headset to place a call. Everyone in the dining area that wasn't fortunate enough to have earbuds was at the mercy of his conversation. That's when I remembered I had recently installed a suite of wireless hacking tools on the laptop, some of them Bluetooth related. Mr. Loud Talker's obnoxious conversation seemed like the perfect reason to test them out.

I followed a somewhat cryptic set of instructions that came with the tools: picked up the addresses of all the Bluetooth devices around me, determined which one was Mr. Loud Talker's phone, and made a few tweaks on my end. Within a couple of minutes (and some nonchalant typing) I was able to pair with his phone and issue a command to disconnect his call. Instantly his chatter dropped into "Hello? Hello?" followed by awkward silence. Several times he redialed the number, each time I disconnected it again. A wave of quiet relief passed over the dining area as he finally left the building.

Keep in mind I pulled that stunt as a complete novice at Bluetooth hacking. All I did was possess the right tools and adapters on my laptop and simply followed some instructions. I could have downloaded Mr. Loud Talker's phonebook, sent SMS text messages using his phone, turned on his camera, and even record a conversation from his headset. While my prank may have seemed more like a brief source of amusement (and it was), the stunt represents the tip of the iceberg of possibilities. More and more cell phone owners constantly leave their Bluetooth turned on to accommodate their hands-free headsets, streaming music to the stereo, and the in-car speakerphones that come standard with the newer cars.

Fast forward to the fall of 2012; I was on my annual trip to Atlantic City. Aside from all night stretches on the Poker tables, whiskey, slots, and sleeping it off the next day, I took the liberty of using my laptop to scan the area's wireless cyberspace to see what was exploitable. After spending so many months working on this book, it was easy to see that the AC boardwalk is an open-door orgy of cybercrime waiting to happen. While sitting in a crowded casino restaurant I did the Bluetooth scan. Roughly a dozen cell phones came up in close proximity. On three of them I was able to grab their phonebooks, steal access to their Internet, browse miscellaneous data, and probably take complete control over the phone if I had known the right commands to send. Five phones didn't connect properly (not sure if that was due to better security or my own errors) and I wasn't able to get to the rest of the phones on the list...

I could go on with the tale but my point is simple: although Bluetooth security is steadily improving it still has a long way to go.

7) Check for tether rates before you hit the road.

The ability to tether your laptop or tablet to your cell phone to use its Internet can be a lifesaver in a pinch. While it's true that some providers have started charging extra for the tethering service, others will still let you use a third party tether program. Unlike phones and tablets, laptops are prone to use a lot more Internet bandwidth in the background—software updates are automatically downloaded (and often much bigger), weather reports, news crawlers, etc. It quietly adds up. And depending on your data plan, when those overages hit they can come with a big whack on your next bill.

8) When possible, set up a VPN connection before traveling.

By having a VPN connection established between your mobile device and your home/office network, you'll have a secure tunnel through any network you go through, regardless of the quality connection. Anyone or anything spying on the data passing through that network won't be able to view what you're transmitting. If you've never set one up, you may need to consult with an IT professional.

Characteristics Common to Most Known Species of Living Dead (cont'd):

Physical Threat Level: All zombies that haven't been properly dispatched are equally as contagious. The most dangerous ones are physically intact and mobile. Before turning, they were victims who were attacked, bitten, and managed to escape being eaten. Eventually those escapees succumbed to the contagion, died, and reanimated.

The Pros and Cons of USB Flash Drives

While writing this book, I saw first hand how dependable USB Flash Drives can be. I accidentally left a nearly full 8GB SanDisk Flash Drive in the watch pocket of my jeans. Since it was in that goofy little pocket just inside the right pocket, I didn't notice it was there when I checked my pockets. I threw the jeans in with a full load of clothes in the washer. A cup of liquid laundry detergent, full cycle, and a run through the dryer later, I discovered the thumb drive sitting in the dryer as I pulled out the last of the clothes. Horrified, I quickly plugged it into the nearest computer and the drive came right up. All 7.31GB of data were totally intact.

The biggest problem you'll face with using USB flash drives for long-term archival purposes is the unanswerable question of whether or not computers 10 or 20 years from now will come with USB ports.

Kingston's DataTraveler flash drives are a good all-round balance of security and durability.

http://www.kingston.com/us/usb/encrypted_security

For anyone that prefers a more ruggedized flash drive, the Corsair Flash Survivor line is for you. They are waterproof up to 200 meters, heat resistant and shock resistant. If a person had this thumb drive in his pocket and he got hit by a car, you can bet money that his data will survive.

http://www.corsair.com/en/usb-drive/flash-survivor-usb-drives.html

Mobile Devices:
The New Trend in Organic Dining for Zombies

The biggest new targets for cybercrime are mobile devices. Virus writers have already been busy at work coming up all kinds of code specifically to crack and attack smart devices.

According to a report published by F-secure Labs, a Finland-based security firm, they received more than 5000 malicious Android applications in Q2 of 2012. This was a 64% increase compared to Q1 of 2012, comprised of 19 new contagions and 21 new variants of existing contagions. Although these viruses shared many similarities, each new find seemed to do a better job of defeating the anti-virus than its predecessor. Simply put, if we thought that we had witnessed the height of the zombie outbreak, think again. Reports like this only confirm that the battle has just begun.

SMiShing

One of new attack forms gaining popularity is called SMiShing (pronounced "Smishing"). It's essentially Phishing done by way of sending out dangerous text messages. Many times these will come as texts with a link sent either with the claim that it's a giveaway or a "check this out" from someone who supposedly knows you. The link is often booby-trapped with a link to turn your phone into a zombie. Other variants include links that will automatically bill your cell phone or data plan for something you didn't ask for, solely because your click on the link was considered authorization to do so. These fees are usually very nominal, like $2 or $5 dollars a hit. With such a low amount, victims often either don't notice or they don't think it's worth the headache to report it to the authorities.

With over 419 million mobile devices sold in Q2 of 2012 (Gartner), anyone who successfully scammed 1% of those phones at a meager $2 dollars per click would have just under $8.4 million dollars practically handed over to their bank account. The Lufthansa heist, the infamous 1978 robbery made famous by films like GOODFELLAS (1990), required six men and scored a little less than $6 million in cash and jewels.

A simple SMiShing scam could be done by a team of one. And scariest of all, witness accounts would be useless; there aren't any. CSI investigators might as well stay home that day; there would no crime scene to comb for fibers and DNA. Unless the financial institution handling the receiving account was to tip off the authorities, a single scam like this could probably continue for days before attracting any attention. And if such stunts became as common as spam the results could be devastating.

Baron Samedi says:

"Don't click on links without explanations. And install a reputable anti-virus on your smartphones and tablets. Not doing so is only inviting disaster to happen. Whether you've got an iPhone, iPad, Android, Blackberry or anything else still on the market after 2010, it's only a matter of when."

The Frankenstein Lie: "Fix-My-PC-for-Cheap" websites

As a child of the 70s, I was a huge fan of all things Frankenstein. Mary Shelley's book was the first novel I ever read. To this day I still believe Boris Karloff was the perfect Frankenstein's Monster. I even took issue with THE MUNSTERS because they took Frankenstein and made him a likeable bufoon. It was during this phase I eventually experienced The Frankenstein Lie.

One afternoon while checking the TV Guide, I spotted a listing that looked promising: FRANKENSTEIN MEETS THE SPACE MONSTER. Even better, it was the featured film on DR. MADBLOOD'S MOVIE, one of my favorite shows. For those readers who aren't old enough to remember, most people back then didn't have a way to record a show for later playback. You generally had two chances to watch a TV show—when it first aired and if you caught it during rerun season. Madblood's show came on at 1am, following SATURDAY NIGHT LIVE. Good movies or bad, I stayed up late and tuned in religiously. That night was no different.

Forget about the plot; there wasn't one. The Princess was a Playboy Playmate with a lamp shade on her head. Her assistant was an amphibian elf wearing a sparkling, studded leather outfit that spoke to a flamboyantly alternative lifestyle. Their minions had pointed Papier-mâché ears and ran around kidnapping bikini-clad women. The Monster was a hodge-podge of leftover costume parts held together with electrical tape. There wasn't anything resembling Frankenstein in the movie. No lumbering flat-headed giant. No neck bolts. Not even a mad scientist lab. There was only "Frank", a deranged homicidal astronaut with half of a fruitcake for a face, staggering from scene to scene as if he was trying to find his way out of the movie.

When the credits rolled I felt cheated. How could they use Frankenstein in the title yet have no Frankenstein in the movie? Convinced that a crime had been committed somewhere, I asked my father how they could get away with this. "TV is full of lies," he said. "Hollywood sells stories… they don't have to sell the truth."

Decades later my father's remark rings true with many of those "Too Good to be True" offers I see floating around cyberspace. I call them Frankenstein Lies because they're constructed from various half-truths and technology components. They become monstrous deceptions that take on a life of their own, often doing more harm than good. Some prime examples come in the form of those TV commercials promoting those online Fix-My-PC-for-Cheap services. I regularly get inquiries from residential clients about whether or not they are real. Are they scams? Most of them, no, technically not. Are they traps? Typically, yes.

► These services have been known to find "errors" with a PC even if it was brand new out of the box.

► Anywhere from 10% to 70% of the initial PC maintenance calls will require the technician to be sitting at the computer and cannot be done over the Internet. This is because some types of diagnostics, cleanup or repair can't be done when the PC has booted from its hard drive. Technicians can also look around where the PC is set up and visually spot out other potential sources of problems (e.g. – bad cables, router issues, pet hair, etc.). Without the technician being able to complete those tasks in person, by default it means that some types of problems would never be addressed.

► Many forms of malware and rootkits cannot be adequately cleaned from a system unless the removal software is run on an unmounted hard drive; this cannot be done during normal startup. In most cases, attempting to perform this kind of task from remote would require the technician to walk the customer through the process of manually setting up their Internet connection again (not to mention installing the remote access software). For an inexperienced PC owner, this process would be about as nerve-wracking as using text messages to walk someone through the process of changing a car tire.

► Most of these services target consumers that are (1) basic computer users, (2) buying a new computer is a low priority and (3) their current computer is over three years old with an expired warranty.

► These services end up billing their customers for more than $200 dollars, regardless of whether or not they truly fix any problems.

► Most of these services provide the cleaning processes that can be done by the average computer user with software that costs less than $50 dollars.

ZOMBIE TRIVIA

Q: How many actors starred in both the 1978 and 2004 versions of DAWN OF THE DEAD.

(answer on page 384)

There are no single magic bullets to protect your computer from the threats out in cyberspace. To illustrate the ease and inexpensive nature of cleaning your PC or Mac, here are the following:

http://www.pendriveapps.com/software/portable-disk-defragmenters/

http://www.pendriveapps.com/software/portable-registry-tools/

And for Mac OS X, the following site:
http://www.easemac.com/products/maccleaning-free.htm

Contrary to how the TV commercials make it seem, it's not their responsibility to clean up your PC for little or nothing with the trial version.

The Big Question: Is there any Hope?

There are always unspoken questions in the middle of every zombie outbreak. They especially come to mind when the battle grows quiet, those times where you've got time to stare up at the ceiling and think: is there an end to this? Is there any hope?

Those questions also haunted me as I wrote this book. Information Security is a constantly evolving convergence of crime, replete with shocking stories, some of which would cause panic with Mr. and Mrs. Citizen if they received adequate coverage on CNN and BBC. That's why this book skimmed the surface of the digital mayhem going on in cyberspace. I had no choice because if I didn't set limits and cutoffs this book would have perpetually stayed in production.

So is there any hope? I believe so, yes.

There are two key changes that would be an excellent defense against most viruses floating around out in cyberspace today: (1) Eliminating Sloppy Programming practices, (2) the adoption of better network and security protocols and (3) Virtualization.

Eliminating Sloppy Programming Practices… yeah, right. Condoms have been around since before the 15th century and other forms of birth control that reach back to the ancient Egyptians. Even with all that the U.S. couples experience more than 3 million unplanned pregnancies every year. Until such a time where people can consistently handle a simple concept like "wrap it up", it's safe to say that eliminating sloppy programming is a lost cause.

Okay, so what about adopting better security protocols and Virtualization? There's a glimmer of hope with both.

With the network and security protocols there are always plenty of new and exciting innovations, such as IPv6 or Multi-Factor Authentication. The problem is that when it comes to Information Technology the best solutions aren't always the ones that are adopted. For example, the Internet as we know it today has been based on something called IPv4. The next generation of this protocol is IPv6. Originally introduced in the late 90s, it is more efficient and takes care of many flaws that have been long exploited with IPv4. As of May of 2014, more than 95% of the Internet was still based on IPv4. The reasons (and excuses) why companies are slow to switch over to IPv6 are worthy of their own book.

And with security protocols, often the chosen solutions are a compromise between convenience and cost-to-implement. For example, with Multi-Factor Authentication it would be possible for banks to give its customers little devices about the size of a USB flash drive that can generate special numeric tokens on demand. Banking websites could be set up to require the numeric token (in your hand) and your username and password in order to access your account. Far more secure? Definitely. The problem? The cost of these little devices would add up into the millions for any given bank, not to mention all the resources required to maintain them or replace lost units. As crazy as it sounds, from a Risk Management standpoint it is almost better for the bank to risk a customer's password being compromised than to spend the money to implement this extra layer of security. Although it would benefit the customers in the long run, ultimately it would have to be financed through additional banking fees that many people would prefer not to pay.

Virtualization is a slightly different story. Short for Hardware Virtualization, this technique refers to creating a virtual machine (VM): a self-contained computing environment, complete with the operating system (e.g. - Microsoft Windows, Mac OS X, Linux, etc.) and installed software. It is literally the ability to run multiple computing environments inside a single physical computer. A VM operates inside its own window just like any other program. Thanks to the vast amounts of storage space available on most hard drives and solid state drives, you can have multiple VMs.

For example, let's say you have an iMac that is set up as a virtualization host and there are several virtual machines installed on it: a Windows 8 VM, a Windows 7 VM, an Ubuntu Linux VM and a Redhat Linux VM. Including the iMac itself, there are effectively five (5) different computers running inside that one computer. Each VM can have its own software installed and running. All of them use the hardware resources available on that host computer (e.g. - input/output devices, memory, processor speed, storage, optical disc drives, USB ports, etc.). Each VM is more or less unaware that it is running inside the host and all the virtual machines are isolated from each other. And if the host computer has the capacity to handle it, all the VMs can efficiently operate at the same time.

This approach comes with many advantages, the biggest of which is functional isolation. Since each virtual machine operates in its own space, any kind of system damage that happens within a VM it shouldn't damage the host OS or the other VMs. This is why malware research and development uses virtual machines as containment laboratories to study viruses because, as of this writing, a malware outbreak on a VM cannot damage the host OS or other VMs.

The isolated environment for each virtual machine not only makes them easier to deploy (and re-deploy if damaged by some kind of corruption), traditionally VMs haven't been aware that they exist within another computer. Unfortunately, malicious hackers have been working to make their malware resistant to analysis. Smart malware is a reality. Along with the ability to detect when they are being analyzed in much the same way many of us can detect when we're being watched or followed, newer malwares are able to determine whether or not they are running within a virtual machine. Known as "Red Pills" (an homage to the 'Red Pill or Blue Pill' scene in THE MATRIX), any malware with red pills will act differently if it determines that it's running inside of virtual machine, making it much more difficult for researchers to study and come up with an antidote. Unlike the stone stupid zombies we have grown accustomed to battling, these would be considered Revenants—creatures that are frighteningly indistinguishable from zombies except they retained whatever intelligence and memories they had at the time of their death. Such computer viruses are not self-aware yet... but this is a scary start.

Aside from preventing the spread of most simple contagions, this new paradigm is a game changer as far as malware is concerned. Many of the traditional methods of spreading malware will become as outdated as floppy disks. A whole new set of rules apply. Unfortunately, before this book went to press many of the hints of this New Day were already upon us. Newer strains of malware are able to detect when they are being analyzed in much the same way most people can tell when they are being followed. They can also tell when they have been unleashed within a Virtual Machine, similar to how a pilot can feel the difference between flying in a real airplane versus being in a flight simulator. Where this unveils scary possibilities is that point where malware becomes smart enough to detect if an infected computer is hosting multiple VMs, too, simply because such attacks would be virtually undetectable from within the VMs. Imagine discovering that the planet Earth is merely a biosphere inside a box within another dimension and you've been tasked to figure out how to protect Earth against attacks from that outer dimension. If this sounds like a nightmare to you, welcome to the world of IT security.

And if all that wasn't enough to fry your brain, the Internet of Things is going to open up all new dimensions to privacy and security issues. It starts with the fact that companies have discovered that it's fashionable to come up with new ways to make an old product "smart". Take a television, add an internal computer and some software to it, and it becomes a whole new product. Same with a refrigerator or the lights in your home. The problem is that companies are constantly scrambling to be the first to market with these innovations, so much that security issues are often neglected until they're widely known in the cybercriminal underground. They don't give much though to the reality that it's difficult enough to keep computers and devices clean and secure. Imagine the mayhem when John Doe's thermostat catches a virus, Jane Doe's car gets hacked, or some worm interrupts every broadcast in the country with a message from the Emergency Alert System. The sick thing is that each of those examples will probably come to pass someday and eventually be considered quaint pranks in comparison to the possibilities to come. The bottom line is that we'll have to see how it all plays out. The only thing I'm fairly certain of is that this book will have sequels.

The zombies are out there... and they aren't going away anytime soon.

ZOMBIE TRIVIA ANSWERS:

Page 64: Bill "Chilly Billy" Cardille, starring as the Field Reporter. He was the host of CHILLER THEATRE, a show that featured horror and sci-fi movies. It was a staple of Saturday late-night television in Pittsburgh from the 1960s to the early 80s.

Page 75: Barbara. Although Shaun refers to her most of the time as "Mum", it is through Ed and Philip that we learn her name.

Page 80: Everett and Fort Pastor. Although these places are supposed to be near Milwaukee, Wisconsin, both are fictitious.

Page 100: 28 DAYS LATER. Unlike with the others, the outbreak in 28 DAYS is driven by "Rage". a man-made virus, and the infected killers are not undead cannibals.

Page 132: Plantation owner 'Murder' Legendre (Lugosi) drugged people, transforming them into mindless minions at his command.

Page 145: THE ISLAND OF DOCTOR MOREAU by H.G. Wells. Even though there are no walking dead in the story, some would consider this classic an early literary influence to the Modern Zombie genre.

Page 245: The Old Priest in the original DAWN OF THE DEAD. The priest says this to Roger and Peter in the basement. Played by Jese del Gre, Romero is said to have cast this real-life priest for the role because he only had one leg.

Page 378: The answer is three: Ken Foree (Peter / The Televangelist), Scott Reiniger (Roger / The General) and Tom Savini (Motorcycle Raider / The County Sheriff).

Acknowledgements

Before I get to the thank-yous, I have to pay homage to the memory of a few special people who, in retrospect, were instrumental in making this book happen:

To my Grandparents—without you I wouldn't be here; at least not in the skin I'm in today. Thanks to you I've come to learn about a different kind of destiny: We become who we are through nature and nurture yet some things are passed in the blood through the generations. The stories of how you persevered through hard times shined a light on the strengths you passed on to me. I can only hope that somewhere out there you're proud of what you see.

Ford & Essie

Judge & Jesse

To Eastwind—my friend and comrade in digital mischief, all of us in the old crew still miss you. Wherever you are, rest assured that even though we've all grown up we're still adventurous geeks at heart. Since those rogue days, our vices have become virtues and we've all gone on to do great things. You were an integral part of those times... and we can't thank you enough.

"Eastwind"
Feb 12, 1970 - Jan 30, 1994

To Libby—your endeavors touch a lot more lives than you realized, including my own. And at a time where I was figuring out how to shift my business focus in a new direction, our phone conversations inspired me to reboot the hacker inside and use those talents for good. Thank you for helping me redefine my mission.

"Libby"
May 16, 1959 - Jan 30, 2012

By the time I started writing this section my workspace had become an academic disaster area—a snowpocalypse of books, boxes of computer parts, CDs and DVDs, unidentified flash drives, and paper. Lots of paper. Printouts everywhere; tiny scraps, marked up chunks of notes, research materials, mail (mostly unopened), and manuscript parts that were saved for reasons that I've long since forgotten. Writing this book has been a quest that was far harder than I would have ever imagined. At times the research was all-consuming. Day after day for more than two and a half years I typed notes into an old HP iPAQ or alone in front of a laptop, knowing that every manuscript isn't necessarily meant to survive long enough to make it into print. Stillborns happen at all the time. And for that reason I couldn't have accomplished the task without help and inspiration from many sources. This section is an attempt to acknowledge everyone that provided assistance, showed support, or had an influence or direct connection to the events this book. I had to dedicate several pages to the task. Faced with a deadline, if I forgot to mention you please forgive me.

As always, my eternal thanks to God, King of Kings, Lord of Lords—thank you for listening to my rambling thoughts and prayers during those long stretches of solitude. Thanks for getting me to this point in spite of myself.

To my mother Shirley—because you always inspired us to strive to be the best at whatever we do. You taught us how to go forward with compassion and courage, even in the face of possible failure. Thank you for everything. Without your loving guidance I could have easily become a lost criminal statistic.

To my father Johnny—for being tough on us, teaching my brothers and I how to think logically and not to be afraid to stand up for ourselves. Thank you for seeing far enough ahead of the curve to bring the first computer into the house when I was 10. It taught me how to hunt in cyberspace, long before cyberspace had a name.

To my brothers Jason and Jarvis—Gentlemen, we've come a long way, from Steak-umms to Steaks. I couldn't have been blessed with better brothers. It feels good to know that you've always been in my corner and enjoy taking pride in my creative achivements just as much as I take pride in yours. Here's to you, your families, and many more years making great things happen along the path less traveled.

To all my aunts, uncles, cousins, in-laws and extended family—what can I say? We're a beautifully eclectic clan of clans, spread out all over the country. Surnames change but the love remains the same.

I have to give special thanks to Arun, Nekki, and Jazzy. Each of you has brought sunshine into my life. Even from across the country you constantly remind me to smile, enjoy exploring life, and admire everything I see with fresh eyes.

...And everyone else (listed in no particular order):

My corporate clients (past and present, always a pleasure working with you), Sheryl and Lady C, Robin (love your cookies), Rev. Allen and the Family at First Lynnhaven Baptist Church (still miss you Rev. Lewis and Rev. Haynes). APND (looking forward to my jar of 'shine), Betty and Bill G, Lord Egg and EUO, Dease and 4Core (Black cowboys will ride again), Houseflower Sha, The Rainey family (shout out to Li'l Teddy, Haptae and Zion), T Drum and the Bobo family (shout out to Morgan and Sloan), Juliette (stay deadly, JuJu), The Education Association families (EAN, VBEA, VEA – never give up the fight), Basil Rouland, Kelvin and Larry (ETE Inc.), Dr. Madblood and cast, Major D, Stan, Phelix, Snarf, Ironwolf, Roadkill, Duncan, Jason, Ella, Ken, Par, Sir Huggybear and the Atomic Wasteland, the 757s, the 804s, the 202s, the 414s, the 212s, the MOD crew (NYC), Phrack magazine, QSD, 2600 magazine, IP2 (the rest of the original Fab Five – Keith, Mark, Anil, and Jason), iTRiBE, 9x, THC, NSU (good lookin out Mr. Clemmons), Urban L, Peter G and the ever-rising Atlantis, George K and the Greek Mafia, Doctor P and family, SCOPE security, the Turners, the Millers, Edna and Willie, the Khannas (welcome baby Andrew), the Montgomerys, Verbal Threat Posse (we miss you Big D), Wikipedia, the Intells, IRC, The Black Futurists, STIR, Allison, TMW, the Portsmouth Epicureans (and Deputy Derek – thanks for the safe trips to AC), Coursera, Canonical Ltd. (Ubuntu Community), and too many Sci-Fi conventions and computer conferences to name.

On the nights away from the solitude of the desk I spent hanging out at Lynnhaven, people-watching while enjoying a few drinks and revising parts of this manuscript. Since my social circles run wide and deep, I've spent many random nights talking with people from all walks of life. They've all sparked thoughtful perspectives that helped shape this book in some way. The following is just a brief snapshot of a few who were in that scene as the summer of 2014: TGIFridays—Emily, Geoff, Jason, Ling Ling, Heather, John, Scott, Amber, Michelle, Kristin, Poopie, Chris,

Brandon, Joe and all the others that have moved on into the four winds. And among the managers and servers there were so many I had to draw a few from a hat: Lisa M, Rob, Jennifer, Dave, Christine, Courtney, Gerald, Danny, Rachel, Will, and Freddy. Almost forgot Gus and Maxine. The conversations and being entertained by the late-night weirdness was worth the outrageous bar tabs. Much love and best wishes as you all catch flight with your destinies. And among the regulars I have to give a shout out to The Silent Partners (Big Will, Virgil, JB, Mark, Matt, Dwayne, Sam, Daryl, Babs, Professor X, Tone, Jenn, Blunt, and all the others that have come and gone). Nicole and the Pharmacy Crew (Ashley, Sherwin, Sherwood), Dave and Donna, Phil, Brad, Daniel, Gene, Nora, Tony, Tracy, Kevin, Cervantes, Drew, ateddy and Ken—I have to stop here because the full list would go on for pages.

The Poker Night Jokers: Bill, Kevin, Pete, Rich (along with the past allstars like John, Ken, Kevin D, and Len). In between the spirits and shenanigans each of you has shared a wealth of insight. Thanks again and, remember, don't hate on the Mojo!

Special note of appreciation to a few whose achievements taught me strategies from their playbooks: Melvin Van Peebles, Pete Masterson, George A. Romero, Hunter S. Thompson, Max Brooks, Oprah, Jay Conrad Levinson, Jim Rohn, Gordon Parks, Nicholas Pileggi, Dr. Lorenzo Cavallaro (University of London), Assoc. Prof. Charles Severance (University of Michigan), Assoc. Prof. Barbara Endicott-Popovsky (University of Washington), Judge Greg Mathis, and Linus Torvalds.

Last but not least I have to thank the computer underground, past and present—anarchists, allies and agents alike. Over the years I've had the honor of dealing with some of the most respectable, talented (and devious) minds in Cyberspace. No need for a list because most of the time we never exchanged names.

Bibliography

One of the problems with a book of this nature is that most of the information and tips comes from years of learning the hard way, getting advice from interviews during business case studies, real-world application, rifling through countless tech books, and trawling the Internet like a fishing boat. Unfortunately it is also far from complete—learning on the fly doesn't always mean keeping up with the sources of the knowledge. Eventually I will probably compile an update to this bibliography and post it on the website.

Gragg, David. A Multi-Level Defense Against Social Engineering. SANS Institute, 2003.

Kshetri, Nir. The Global Cybercrime Industry: Economic, Instutional and Strategic Perspectives. Springer Heidelberg Dordrecht. New York, 2010.

Lilley, Peter. Dirty Dealing: The Untold Truth about Global Money Laundering, International Crime and Terrorism (Fully Revised and Updated Third Edition). Philadelphia: Kogan Page, 2006.

McQuade, Samuel C. Encyclopedia of Cybercrime. Connecticut: Greenwood Press, 2009.

Sullivan, Dan. The Definitive Guide to Controlling Malware, Spyware, Phishing and Spam. Realtimepublishing.com

Wells, Joseph T. Fraud Casebook: Lessons from the Bad Side of Business. John Wiley & Sons Inc. New Jersey, 2007.

Kay, Glenn. Zombie Movies : The Ultimate Guide. Chicago Review Press. Chicago, 2008.

Brooks, Max. The Zombie Survival Guide. Three Rivers Press. New York, 2003.

Wiles, Jack et al. Low-Tech Hacking-Street Smarts for Security Professionals. Syngress. Massachusetts, 2012.

Brooks, Max. World War Z: An Oral History of the Zombie War. Crown. New York, 2006.

Mattheson, Richard. I Am Legend. Tor Books (reissue). New York, 1954.

Shinder, Debra Littlejohn. Scene of the Cybercrime: Computer Forensics Handbook. Syngress. 2002.

Goncharov, Max (2012), Russian Underground 101: Research Paper, Cupertino, Trend Micro Inc.
http://www.trendmicro.co.in/in/security-intelligence/research-and-analysis/#research-papers

NIST Computer Security Resource Center
http://csrc.nist.gov/publications/PubsDrafts.html

Publishers of books that I've read or referred to too many to list here:

O'Reilly Media, Microsoft Press, SAMS Publishing, John Wiley & Sons, Manning Publications, APress.

The following is a sampling of URLs from my notes and bookmarks:

www.techrepublic.com

https://www.nicb.org/theft_and_fraud_awareness/fact_sheets

http://www.nist.gov/computer-security-portal.cfm

http://www.nij.gov/nij/topics/crime/id-theft/welcome.htm

http://www.scamdex.com/

http://www.ftc.gov/bcp/edu/microsites/idtheft2012/

https://www.botnets.fr/index.php/Accueil

password crack speeds:
http://www.lockdown.co.uk/?pg=combi

password tester:
https://www.grc.com/haystack.htm

Microsoft study of web passwords:
http://research.microsoft.com/pubs/74164/www2007.pdf

Life expectancy of Information Media:
http://comminfo.rutgers.edu/~lesk/spring06/lis556/life-expect.pdf

http://www.osta.org/technology/cdqa13.htm

PCI SSC Data Security Standards Overview
https://www.pcisecuritystandards.org/security_standards/documents.php

iPhone revenues higher than all of Microsoft's revenues:
http://www.businessinsider.com/apple-is-quietly-working-to-destroy-the-iphone-2012-12

http://www.forbes.com/sites/timworstall/2012/08/19/
apples-iphone-is-now-worth-more-than-all-of-microsoft/

Cloud Study stats
http://www.citrix.com/lang/English/lp/lp_2328330.asp

http://www.scientificamerican.com/article.
cfm?id=fungus-makes-zombie-ants

Deep Web:
http://anonymousnews.blogs.ru/2012/10/15/the-deep-web-part-1-intro-duction-to-the-deep-web-and-how-to-wear-clothes-online/

Dark Internet
http://www.guardian.co.uk/technology/2009/nov/26/
dark-side-internet-freenet

Spammer income:
http://blogs.msdn.com/b/tzink/archive/2008/08/28/how-much-do-spammers-
actually-make.aspx

Russian organized crime:
http://www.fas.org/irp/world/para/docs/rusorg1.htm#tc

Money Laundering:
http://www.dirtydealing.org/pages/money_laundering_statistics.htm

Exclusive: New Malware Targeting POS Systems, ATMs Hits Major US Banks
http://www.securityweek.com/exclusive-new-malware-targeting-pos-systems-
atms-hits-major-us-banks

Porn stats:
https://wsr.byu.edu/pornographystats

How Bitcoin works:
http://gizmodo.com/how-a-bitcoin-transaction-actually-works-504922955

PIN numbers
http://www.datagenetics.com/blog/september32012/index.html

Botnet
http://www.cs.ucsb.edu/~chris/research/doc/oakland12_evilseed.pdf

http://www.itmanagerdaily.com/how-malware-bypasses-antivirus-software/

http://www.statisticbrain.com/credit-card-fraud-statistics/

Parasitic mind control
http://www.youtube.com/watch?v=lGSUU3E9ZoM

World Military Spending stats:
http://www.sipri.org/yearbook/2013/03

Throughout this book, screen captures were used from the following films. These timeless classics are an important "must see" for any fan of the Modern Zombie genre. They have been used here with great appreciation—and without expressed permission—since they are either in the Public Domain (via www.archive.org) or permission is pending.

Night of the Living Dead. Dir. George A. Romero. Perf. Duane Jones, Judith O'Dea and Karl Hardman. Image Ten, 1968. Video (Internet).

White Zombie. Dir. Victor Halperin. Perf. Béla Lugosi, Murder Legendre, Madge Bellamy, Robert W. Frazer, John Harron and Joseph Cawthorn. United Artists, 1932. Video (Internet).

Island of Lost Souls. Perf. Charles Laughton, Richard Arlen, Leila Hyams, Béla Lugosi, and Kathleen Burke. Paramount Pictures, 1932. Video (Internet).

The Plague of the Zombies. Dir. John Gilling. Perf. André Morell, John Carson, Jacqueline Pearce, Brook Williams and Michael Ripper. Hammer Film Productions, 1966. Internet.

The Last Man on Earth. Dir. Ubaldo Ragona, Sidney Salkow. Perf. Vincent Price, Franca Bettoia, Emma Danieli, and Giacomo Rossi-Stuart. American International Pictures, 1964. Video (Internet).

Index

CPSIA information can be obtained at www.ICGtesting.com
Printed in the USA
BVOW09s1944081214

378492BV00020B/865/P

9 780971 544291